DEATH BY PRESCRIPTION

William A. Siler

MICHAEL R. SAWDEY

BARBARA C. MEIHOEFER

SHERBOURNE PRESS
Nashville, Tennessee

Library of Congress Cataloging in Publication Data

Siler, William A.
Death by prescription.

1. Pharmacy—United States. 2. Medication errors—United States. 3. Drug trade—United States. I. Sawdey, Michael R., joint author. II. Meihoefer, Barbara C., joint author. III. Title.
RS67.U6S57 615'.4'0973 77-9454

Manufactured in the United States of America.

ISBN 0-8202-0137-5

to

the Health

of the

American Consumer

Contents

Preface

Death by Prescription had to be written and it could only have been penned by an experienced community pharmacy practitioner. He alone stands at pharmaceutical ground zero between the physician and the patient. He alone is in a position to see the failure of the American health care system in the area of drug marketing, choice, delivery and monitoring. Intuitively, I have known this for more years than I have been a practitioner, and the great majority of my pharmacist colleagues have known it as well. The problem always has been: how to express this sense of a system gone wrong, how to make clear to all involved—consumers and professionals alike—the urgent need for improved control and more careful use of prescription drugs? Over the years I have come to the conclusion that it is probably not possible to achieve this sort of awareness by working solely from within the health care professions. It is essential that the health care consumer also be as fully informed of the shortcomings of the health care system as possible. Hence the reason for this book.

The theme of *Death by Prescription* is one of collaboration among professionals and between professionals and consumers. Fittingly enough, the book itself was produced by a collaborative effort. I am a pharmacist; Michael and Barbara Sawdey are humanists and historians of ideas. Working together, we have sought to present a vertical as well as a horizontal view of the American health care system. So far as the horizontal view is concerned, the facts are not hard to come by if you are a health care professional—and I have practiced pharmacy for some twenty-five years. On the other hand, the facts of drug misuse are often meaningless *even to the professionals involved* unless they are viewed and weighed in the light of the historical and social context of the practice of medicine. Thus, although *Death by Prescription* is written in the first person singular—my own—it is in fact the product of an extensive literary and intellectual collaboration with the Sawdeys. Given our very different backgrounds and orientations, we have not always agreed on the implications of the material, but this heterogeneity of approach has also saved us, on many occasions, from being satisfied with traditional, simplistic answers to the hard questions which consumers are now beginning to ask about the health care establishment. Together we present a picture not merely of *what* is happening to the American health care consumer, but also *why* it is happening (and is certain to continue to happen unless the existing system is changed). We also present several possible blueprints for change, some of them mild and procedural, others radical and structural.

It is a cruel paradox that the pharmacist who, at least theoretically, should be in a position to protect the consumer from irrational drug therapy is, with astounding frequency, systematically prevented from doing so. Nearly forty years ago, Dr. C.O. Lee, giving an introductory lecture to new pharmacy students at Purdue University, would explain that the words pharmacy and pharmaceutical are derived from the Greek word for poison. "Never," he would charge, "not even for a moment, dare you forget! Every prescription you dispense is potentially lethal!" He would follow this with a carefully cadenced explanation that a prescription, in the strictest sense, is a physician's written order to a pharmacist for drugs to be delivered to the patient, who would consume them in trust. Then, in a clearly audible voice, but so paced that I tend to recall it more as a conspiratorial whisper, he would close with something like, "You, as pharmacists, stand between the physician and the consumer of these drugs. It will be *your* duty to protect the patient."

It is a fact that the pharmacist occupies a unique position, but in actual practice he cannot properly protect the drug consumer—generally, he has the ability but not the leverage. This is a critical, vexing mortification to a great many professionals and may well have inspired Dr. C.W. Blissett, Dean of the University of Oklahoma College of Pharmacy, to say of the American health care delivery system, "The only area in which the U.S. can boast of being first is the cost of health care."

The costs of health care *are* monstrous, in more ways than one, yet this is merely a highly visible symptom of the underlying ailment. It is the combination of contemporary health care education, the contemporary practice environment, and the oligarchic power relationships in existing consumer-medical-nursing-pharmaceutical interactions—a hopelessly intermingled triad of problems—which are fundamental. The failure to solve these problems helps explain such statistics as the one indicating that the longevity of the American male has dropped from eleventh to fortieth place in world health standings over the last twenty years. American consumers spent over $80 billion in 1972 and nearly $120 billion in 1975 in an effort to stay alive and well. Yet with all this expenditure the quality of health care they receive is actually declining.

Death by Prescription essays the agony of the able practitioner as he undertakes his hopeless charge to deliver safe and rational care. The reader sits *in camera* reviewing the painstakingly assembled circumstantial evidence which places him at the point of disaster; he is presented with information which has previously been known only to professionals. Step by step, he witnesses deaths and injuries as they actually happened—as they will continue to happen on an increasingly grand scale unless he is moved to action. In essence, this book is a call of distress—a mayday—to consumers and conscientious professionals in an effort to save what could easily become the best health care delivery system in the world. To a degree, it is also a plea for the professionals involved, since it is clear that in far too many cases "they know not what they do."

WILLIAM A. SILER

Prologue

On October 18, 1975, Esther Sudell of Milwaukee, Wisconsin, awoke with a stuffy nose and a blinding headache. The weather had become stormy overnight and she assumed that this had triggered an attack of sinusitis. Mrs. Sudell, age fifty-seven, had been mildly afflicted with sinus congestion for several years, but it had always responded to acetominaphen and rest, so she had never consulted her physician about it. Today, however, the pain not only persisted but worsened, so that by 10 o'clock she knew that medical attention would be necessary.

Since the Sudells' family physician does not keep Saturday office hours, Mr. Sudell drove his wife to the outpatient clinic of the nearest hospital. There the intern on duty examined her and concurred in her self-diagnosis of sinusitis. Since the condition appeared to be mild and seemed to require only routine treatment, the intern did not take a detailed medical history; he recommended the prescription of cephalosporin, a synthetic cousin of penicillin often used to treat infections of the upper respiratory tract. A resident physician wrote the prescription, it was filled by the hospital's pharmacy, and the couple returned home.

Mrs. Sudell was a diabetic with a history of "sensitivity" to such drugs as aspirin and penicillin as well as to certain foods, animal hair, some pollens, dust and molds. After taking the first antibiotic capsule, she lay down to rest, but soon was alarmed when she found it difficult to breathe. A call to the outpatient clinic brought her an assurance that nothing was amiss: she was probably developing a respiratory congestion that is commonly associated with "draining sinuses." In other words, she was coming down with a cold.

By noon Mrs. Sudell's breathing had become more labored and Mr. Sudell called their family physician, who had treated her for sixteen years. He assured the concerned husband that the condition was only temporary and that if she took the medication and stayed in bed, the respiratory distress would cease. At 1:05 P.M. it did: Mrs. Sudell stopped breathing. After brief attempts at mouth-to-mouth resuscitation, Mr. Sudell summoned the emergency squad, whose heroic efforts to restore breathing were also unsuccessful. At 1:55 P.M. Esther Sudell was, as a legal formality, pronounced "dead on arrival" at the same hospital where she had been treated less than four hours earlier.

This was death by prescription.

1 *Distress Signals* FROM THE HEALTH CARE ESTABLISHMENT—WHY THIS BOOK HAD TO BE WRITTEN

This is probably not the first book you have seen which deals with the shortcomings of the American medical establishment, nor is it likely to be the last. Such standard works as Edward Kennedy's *In Failing Health,* Abraham Ribicoff's *The American Medical Machine* and Daniel Schorr's *Don't Get Sick in America* all focus on the soaring cost of medical care. Up to the present, however, the basic theme of all such investigations has been this: American health care is enormously expensive and the present system of private medical insurance is incapable of softening the economic blow to the patient. Consequently, many who need care do not get it and those who do often face economic ruin. But economic problems are not as important as the life or death of the patient, and this book will focus not on the economic wastefulness but on the professional inadequacies of the American medical system, inadequacies which prevent the safe use of existing medical knowledge.

This probably *is* the first time that you have seen the workings of the American health care system from the viewpoint of a pharmacist. I have been a community pharmacist for some twenty-five years and I have seen how the system works. I have seen the ignorance of physicians with respect to potentially lethal prescription drugs. I have seen the failure of hospitals and medical boards to control the prescription practices of physicians. I have seen patients hospitalized and even killed for lack of a few simple instructions and precautions about their prescriptions. I have seen conscientious pharmacists lose their jobs—and I have lost a few myself—for daring to question a physician's unsound drug therapy. My theme is not money, although billions of dollars are wasted every year on useless drug prescriptions. My theme is life and death by prescription.

In part, then, this book is an act of exposure—I am going to take you through the dirty back alleys and smoke-filled rooms of the American medical establishment, areas that you never see in the glossy TV medical shows. But the act of exposure is merely a part of my larger purpose, which is to force major reforms in the structure of American medicine. Our medical professions have failed almost completely at ensuring adequate pharmacological education for our physicians, let alone at achieving a working professional relationship between physicians and pharmacists. The result is a fragmented system which wastes the training of some professionals (primarily pharmacists) and forces others (primarily physicians) to work in areas beyond their professional competence.

In turn, this willy-nilly system denies the consumer—that is, *you,* the patient—both the safety and the effectiveness he has a right to expect from modern medicine. Some of the incidents of the failure of the medical system described in this book may appear so bizarre as to be unbelievable; others may be coldly alarming or simply pathetic. What they all have in common is that they are all based on reliable eyewitness information from pharmacists, physicians and patients, or from my own experience in the profession of pharmacy. In all cases (except, of course, those in which I am quoting published authorities) I have taken care to disguise names, dates, and places; beyond the obsurities of the libel law, no purpose would be served by identifying individual malefactors in a pattern of failure which pervades the entire medical establishment.

As the title of the book indicates, my examination of American health care centers on prescription drugs—how they are developed, promoted, distributed, used, and misused. The plain fact is that in just about 90 out of 100 cases in which a physician does anything substantive about a patient's malady, he prescribes one or more drugs. Thus the hundreds of millions of patient/physician contacts each year generate almost as many hundreds of millions of prescriptions annually. This sheer volume of prescriptions is bound to lead to a large number of errors, even given the very best rate of success that can be expected in a field as complex as medicine. In fact, however, the rate of failure is far in excess of this expected, irreducible minimum. For some categories of drugs the level of irrational therapy (that is, prescribing drugs that could not be expected to cure or relieve any condition indicated by the patient's symptoms) has been documented to run in excess of 80 percent. Furthermore, over half of all drugs prescribed in America today are prescribed for sociological reasons, often with little consideration of the medical consequences. We live in a society that can send men to the moon and back safely; why can we not manage to successfully and consistently pair up known drug effects with the symptoms which indicate the status of the patient's body?

Why is it that with 25,000 pharmaceutical items on the American market (representing about 1,200 distinct drugs), the average physician does nearly all of his prescribing from a selection of between 100 and 500 pharmaceutical items?

How can this be squared with the results of one study which showed that this average physician is only capable of keeping about 60 of these items straight in his head?

Why, in the course of his medical education, does the physician spend only about ten semester hours learning about drugs, the major weapon he will use against disease?

What about the other professionals involved in the health care picture? The nurse has far more contact time in which to observe the patient. The pharmacist has had a minimum of *five times* as much drug education as the physician. When was the last time you heard a nurse or a pharmacist advise, let alone contradict, a physician? Better yet, when was the last time you heard a physician *ask* for advice from one of these fellow professionals?

Indeed, the answers to most of these questions proceed from the sad fact that, in the midst of a vast confused maelstrom of information and choices, the physician stands alone. And this aloneness, despite his being one of the most highly trained and highly rewarded members of our technocratic civilization, makes him almost impossibly vulnerable. During 1975, malpractice insurance for a general practitioner in New York cost as much as the total income of an average American family. For an anesthesiologist practicing in California, such protection cost as much as the salary of one of the professors who educated him in medical school. Since 1970, not only has the incidence of malpractice suits against physicians increased at least fivefold, but the likelihood of the suit being settled in the patient's favor has increased appreciably, and the average amount awarded in damages has just about tripled. Not only have malpractice insurance rates climbed astronomically, but several major insurance companies have simply discontinued such coverage as economically unfeasible. Physicians have retaliated with strikes and work slowdowns, and in several instances state governments have had to intervene to the extent of underwriting the insurance losses and/or limiting the amounts of malpractice awards, in order to restore essential medical services.

Even the most superficial examination of the situation is instantly thwarted by emotional charges and countercharges—lawyers blame the arrogance of physicians, physicians blame the paranoia of the patients, the insurance companies claim that juries overreact to painful cases, and everybody attacks the percentage basis on which lawyers handle damage suits. No matter what position one takes, the imagination is in a continual state of bogglement over the staggering sums of money being hurled back and forth over the battlefield. In one celebrated case, a physician's misplacement of a decimal point (.01 gram of morphine came through as 1.0 gram, causing cardiac arrest and brain damage to the patient) resulted in a settlement which would take the average American wage-earner *twelve* lifetimes to work off.

All this malpractice furor, however, is only the visible—and distracting—tip of the iceberg. The great mass of the problem does not lie in the hard economic facts of insurance income and outgo; likewise, no real solution will be afforded by government intervention at the level of premiums and awards. (Haven't the physicians themselves given us fair warning of the complications of socialized medicine?) Rather, the problem lies in our society's basic conception of the physician as a superhuman Promethean figure who, like the gods and heroes of classical antiquity, is subject to rewards and punishments of titanic proportions, as befits the magnitude of his successes and failures. A $3 million malpractice suit, or a $300,000 annual income, would be inconceivable in a situation where, as in the Soviet Union, physicians were regarded as middle-level technicians, two cuts above TV servicemen and a cut below high school teachers.

In this book, however, I will not advocate a social realignment of the medical profession into a subservient technical role. To do so—to thereby sacrifice all pretenses to Promethean striving—might lead to an improvement in the malpractice situation, but would also make it impossible for us to expect in the future the soaring medical achievements of a Lister or a Fleming, a Salk or a Sabin, a Cooper or a DeBakey. Indeed, the need for what Sir Francis Bacon called "the amelioration of a man's estate" is so pressing that we must have every daring accomplishment of which the medical imagination is capable.

In any case, it is not the Coopers and the DeBakeys, the leaders of the profession, who are being sued; it is the average physician to whom you or I would be likely to turn in the year-in, year-out course of sickness and health. It is this man—the "average physician"—who is likely, through ignorance of pharmacology, to prescribe drugs which are, at the very least, a waste of your health care dollar, and at the most a serious threat to your life. In most cases you will not know that you have been falsely served, because you will not know how to distinguish the side effects of the drug from the effects of the disease it is supposed to cure. In fact, your physician would probably be unable to clearly express this distinction. If his prescription makes you ill enough to require further medical attention, he will probably not inform you of the cause of your worsened condition. This may arise in part from an understandable desire to save face, but it may also merely indicate that the physician himself does not know that the problem has arisen from his earlier treatment; to most physicians, for instance, convulsions indicate a need for an anticonvulsant drug, not a need to investigate the possibility of side effects from the other drugs.

The means to combat the chaos of drug prescribing are readily at hand, but, unlike most reformers in our modern age, I am not going to advocate a primarily technical solution to the problem. I will advocate the more efficient and whole-hearted use of certain technical resources which exist, fully developed, at the present day, but in the main I am presenting a *human* solution to a technological problem. A logical approach, I think, since the problem has arisen in the first place through the misuse of human resources.

When asked how he managed to cope with the problems of the presidency, Abraham Lincoln replied, "I use all the brains I have, and all the brains I can borrow." Most physicians are reasonably intelligent people; they have to be to survive medical school, to make their way through the intensive years of internship and residency. But they are in a position of having to cope with a technological field that has proliferated beyond any individual brain's capacity to grasp, decide, and apply. In this complex situation the physician must cease to see himself as a virtuoso performer and see himself instead as a part of an interlocking professional team which includes the pharmacist and the drug industry. Such a solution is, as I will show, entirely possible, but is at present further complicated by the failure of the other players to fully prepare themselves for their vital functions on the team. The drug industry has largely reduced itself to a packaging and marketing machine, and the pharmacist has most often become an amoral automaton. But unless the potential of these players is tapped and exploited by the physician, he will shortly find himself completely crushed between the opposing forces of technical proliferation and a heightened public awareness of the shortcomings of existing health care. If the situation is resolved by government intervention, the results may well exceed the medical profession's worst nightmares of socialization. Therefore, in the final chapters of this book I have attempted to portray American health care as it might be, given new and more humane attitudes toward existing technology and a new team spirit of cooperation which our medical professions now sadly lack.

2 *The System* OF HEALTH CARE PROFESSIONS AND HOW IT GOT THAT WAY

The delivery process of modern medicine seems to roll along like a hypothetical frictionless cart down some hypothetical inclined plane: physician examines patient, physician prescribes drug, patient takes prescription to pharmacist, pharmacist fills prescription, patient takes drug as directed. . . . There's the rub. In a world which really did run on perfect wheels and perfect planes, we would simply finish the litany with "the patient recovers," and that would be the end of it. As you the reader have surely concluded by now, I the author do not see it that way. In reality, our health care road is full of potholes and switchbacks, and our medical cart suffers from occasional blowouts and steering failure, aggravated by constant dirt in the bearings.

These imperfections arise partly from the complexity of the human body—it is not always amenable to quick and foolproof diagnosis. But further, there is something wrong with our division of labor between the physician and the pharmacist. This division is placed at some hypothetical point between the decision on what drug to use (if one is called for) and the onset of the logistical problem of supplying and regulating the use of the drug. As we will see in this chapter, the division of labor as it stands today has very little rational basis. It is a hodgepodge of ancient tradition, legal restrictions, inter- and intra-professional rivalries, economic considerations and abdication of professional responsibility.

The following case illustrates one way in which the smooth progression of medical treatment goes awry:

> Allen Harper, age twenty-two, was admitted to a military field hospital during World War II with shrapnel wounds in the left arm and second- and third-degree burns over 60 percent of his

body. For the first two weeks of treatment the usual procedure of petroleum jelly compression dressings was followed. Progress was satisfactory, considering the extent of the burns, but the patient was in constant pain as the healing tissues tightened, and consequently required heavy doses of pain relievers. To abate some of the pain and speed healing, the medical officer decided to substitute sulfathiazole ointment and loose gauze dressings for the petroleum jelly compression dressings.

The pharmacist mate on duty pointed out that there was a possibility that the sulfathiazole would be absorbed through the denuded areas of the skin. Since the patient was already taking a heavy dose of the drug orally, this could lead to serious complications: excessive doses of the not-very-soluble sulfa drugs can result in the formation of crystals of the drug in the kidneys, especially in burn victims, who are in a delicate state of hydration. The medical officer suggested that the pharmacist mate go to medical school before attempting to advise a physician, and ordered the treatment started.

The patient's pain was reduced by the new regimen, but after six days of treatment his kidneys failed and he died. The autopsy revealed that the kidneys were clogged with crystals. The medical officer noted on the report that there was "some possibility of excessive sulfa prophylaxis as a result of unforeseen absorption of sulfathiazole by the burned tissues."

That was thirty years ago. It couldn't happen today, right? Sulfathiazole was a relatively new drug then, right? Conditions were pretty primitive out there in the New Guinea jungle, right? It couldn't happen here in America, in a well-equipped, modern hospital, right? Wrong. Read on.

George Billings, sixty-six years old, was admitted to the community hospital in a midwestern city of about 100,000 population. Diagnosis: double pneumonia. As the disease progressed, Mr. Billings's breathing capacity fell to about 15 percent of normal and he was put on a respirator to keep him alive. This caused problems because, although he was unconscious, the patient's breathing reflex continued to operate. As a result, his body would try to "fight" the respirator, attempting at times to inhale when the machine was on the exhale cycle and vice versa. This was causing Mr. Billings to rapidly expend his remaining strength. To suppress the breathing reflex and thus stop the "fighting," the physician had instructed the nurses to administer morphine as needed. Between 3 P.M. and 3 A.M. some 200 mg of

> morphine was administered—a heavy dose, but it did control the "fighting." At 2:30 the nurse on duty observed a restless twitching in Mr. Billings's extremities, a possible sign of the onset of convulsions. She immediately called the physician at his home; he ordered an intravenous dose of chlorpromazine, a sedative drug which controls restlessness, to be administered while he was on his way to the hospital.
>
> When the hospital pharmacist received the prescription, he became suspicious because he was aware of the large amount of morphine which the patient had been given. As a result he refused to dispense the chlorpromazine until he could confer with the physician involved. His reasoning: first, high doses of morphine tend to cause convulsions; chlorpromazine actually *lowers* the convulsive threshold. Thus, if Mr. Billings was moving toward having convulsions, the chlorpromazine might trigger them. Second, both morphine and chlorpromazine lower the blood pressure. Mr. Billings's blood pressure was already depressed from the morphine; injecting the chlorpromazine directly into his veins (as opposed to injecting it into muscle tissue where it would be absorbed more slowly) would almost certainly cause a disastrous drop in blood pressure which would kill him instantly.
>
> The pharmacist went personally to the intensive care unit where he attempted to persuade the physician to confer privately on the problem. When the physician refused, the pharmacist gave his explanation of the danger to the patient in the presence of the nursing staff. The physician concurred in the pharmacist's judgment and ordered alternate treatment. The patient's restlessness was controlled and he eventually recovered from the pneumonia.

Ah well, most of us will be content to say, at least the patient recovered. The point is that not one pharmacist in a thousand would have (1) questioned the prescription presented to him, let alone (2) made an effort to dissuade the physician from his chosen course of treatment. And with good reason: about two weeks after the above incident, the pharmacist involved was "terminated," allegedly because the hospital could not accommodate his request for a change in working hours. "But the message from the grapevine was a bit different," reported the pharmacist. "They didn't want me around because I wasn't 'cooperative' toward the medical staff." In the other 999 instances the pharmacist would simply have filled the physician's prescription, and the patient would have died quickly and quietly from lack of sufficient blood pressure. The death would have been ascribed to pneumonia and, considering that the patient *was* in pretty bad shape from the disease, nobody would have questioned it.

Doctors, Physicians and Apothecaries

Why are there prescription drugs at all? Where did we get this system which, despite certain rigidly observed formalities, is almost a total failure when it comes to preventing the underuse, overuse and misuse of powerful drugs by consumers? I could give a pat answer by citing laws and dates, but the real picture is much more complicated. Finding the full answer will require us to take a look at the history of medicine in our civilization, with special reference to the mindset which still dominates our thinking in the matters of the use of drugs and health care delivery. This "look" will of necessity be somewhat extended because it is difficult to achieve a "whole systems" view of modern medicine.

Triggered by the key word "drugs," the average person's reactions will range from "physician," "pharmacist," and "drug company" to "dangerous," "sick," and "addict." All of these responses merge into an image of the health care system, although the actual structure and interrelations remain confused and vague. This is not surprising when we consider that our present health care system is actually a jerry-built institution that has "just growed" for most of the 3,000 years that we in the West have been calling ourselves civilized. Present-day health care is actually an uneasy alliance of some four or five historically separate professions. The relations between these professions are often defined by law, but the real relationships are sociological and hence the situation is really one of de facto, rather than de jure interaction. It is primarily the historically developed attitudes of our culture that determine the kind of medicine we currently receive.

One of the most basic of these attitudes, the idea of "taking something" to cure disease, is not only very old—there is no reason to doubt that it extends well back beyond all written history—but it has almost continuously remained an accepted and respected process in Western medical practice. By contrast, surgery has often been (and by some people still is) regarded as something of a black art. The Oath of Hippocrates, for instance, contains a clause (usually omitted from the fancy parchments that hang on physicians' office walls) which forbids doctors of medicine to "cut for the stone," that is, to operate for the relief of bladder stones. Such things are to be left to "practitioners of that trade." Historically, surgery was delegated to persons of the mechanic class, often barbers, who were outside the official ranks of medicine.

The official practice of medicine, on the other hand, tended to remain, until quite recent times, an almost totally intellectual discipline. The physician was a man of learning—"doctor" means, after all, "teacher"—concerned primarily with the transfer of information. When confronted with a diseased person, his job was to correlate the symptoms displayed by the patient with the cures recorded in the voluminous literature of medicine. By the late Middle Ages this literature was cluttered with literally hundreds of treatises, all derived from one another, on the use of drugs, mostly of herbal origin. The practice of medicine was primarily a task of information retrieval tinged with literary criticism and sometimes obscured beneath sweeping philosophical assumptions. Then in the fifteenth century the picture was further confused by the addition of hundreds of mineral drugs advocated by the Swiss practitioner Paracelsus and his followers.

In all this welter of information, empirical observation of cause and effect seems to have been a rarity. The physician, being concerned with ideas rather than patients, apparently found it beneath his dignity to stay in attendance through the course of disease and therapy. This could be left to underlings while the "doctor" returned to his writing desk to record what "cure" he had prescribed for what symptoms, without any reference to the reality of the patient's condition. Such instances of empirical observation as one can find are often grotesque. In one gruesome case the French king Francis I and his court physician Ambroise Paré (one of the first barber-surgeons to gain notice and position) induced a condemned man to drink a quart of sulfuric acid in order to test the reputed anti-toxin effects of a "philosopher's stone" which the king had purchased from an alchemist. The results might have been predicted even by a book-bound doctor of the period. It is not recorded whether the stone was recovered from what was left of the test subject's stomach.

What continues to amaze modern researchers is that some truly effective therapeutic agents did emerge from the mass of early *materia medica.* Digitalis (from the foxglove) for the treatment of dropsy, quinine for malaria (a South American Indian cure) and sulfur for skin diseases are just three examples that come to mind.

Other early remedies have only been supplanted with the advent of the modern "wonder drugs." In the main, however, the early medicines were either not demonstrably effective, or at times definitely harmful; as late as 1865 one popular herbal manual recommended extract of poison oak as a diuretic! Clearly medicine could never make more than a glacially slow advance until it ceased to be a purely intellectual discipline and made contact with the real world of pathology, anatomy and physiology.

The magnitude of the gap between empirical reality and theoretical constructs in early medicine can be demonstrated by the fact that the Roman physician Galen, on whose work almost all premodern medical writing is based, had never personally dissected a human body. Instead, he had contented himself with studying the Barbary ape. The situation was compounded during the Middle Ages because the Church frowned on the use of human cadavers. The intellectual aloofness of the physician was a further complication: when a medical professor conducted an anatomy class, he himself would lecture from his books while the actual dissection was performed by an assistant—again, often a barber-surgeon. The body and the book often disagreed, but this was accepted as part of the mythology of the discipline.

It was not until 1636 that the first clinically oriented medical school was opened, at Leyden in the Netherlands. And even there, clinical methods of research and teaching were not established until the work of Herman Boerhaave, beginning in 1701. Boerhaave's students in turn founded the school of medicine at Edinburgh, Scotland. Throughout most of the eighteenth century these two schools, Leyden and Edinburgh, were the only ones requiring clinical experience for the M.D. degree; most others continued to grant it, as in the Middle Ages, entirely on the basis of disputation.

The medieval M.D. was essentially an intellectual surrounded by a trio of mechanics who gave tangible form to his ideas. Assistants or apprentices were the physician's eyes, ears, and hands, caring for the patient and reporting complaints and symptoms. When the physician had thought out his course of treatment, he then either wrote a prescription for drugs to be prepared (and possibly administered) by the apothecary, or he supervised a surgical procedure performed by a barber-surgeon. Eventually, of course, the barber-surgeons joined the ranks of formal medicine and the functions of physicians and surgeons were often combined in a single person.

The assistants who took care of the patients were replaced about a century ago with women known as nurses. This leaves the apothecary (or druggist, or pharmacist, depending on local usage) alone in a position approximating that of his medieval counterpart to the medieval physician. The early apothecary, who generally was not a man of learning but a technician who had learned his trade by apprenticeship, must have led a scrambling existence. Not only did he have to personally collect, identify and store hundreds of natural substances, but he also had to trade for those not locally available and perform a certain amount of chemistry upon others. Then he must deal with each physician's idiosyncratic combination of drugs, compound the mixture and put it in the correct form: tincture, unguent, powder, pill, bolus, plaster, etc. Finally, he actually supervised the patient's use of the medicine, since the physician was too busy to be concerned with such mundane matters.

Much of the apothecary's dispensing of drugs took place with no input from the physician at all. Nowadays you can still, of course, ask your community pharmacist to recommend "something for a cough" or other minor ailment. After some murmuring and consideration of profit margins, he will probably reach down some proprietary medicine or other, accompanied by the suggestion that "you might try some of this." In premodern times, on the other hand, the apothecary might well hand out to his customers any drug that might have been prescribed by a physician. Hence the apothecaries, with the physicians and barber-surgeons, represented a third distinct group of medical practitioners. In England, from 1532 to 1830, the apothecaries were legally recognized, licensed and regulated in the practice of medicine, the original legislation having been instituted to protect them from the jealous attacks of the physicians and barber-surgeons. Until the late nineteenth century even such dangerous substances as opium and morphine were routinely sold over the counter at the corner drugstore.

Gradually, such practices were brought under control in the United States by the implementation of food and drug laws in the early part of this century. It is interesting to note, however, that it was not until 1951 that drugs which are not narcotic but which do require supervised use were legally labeled with what pharmacists call "the legend" ("Caution: Federal Law prohibits dispensing without prescription"). With the advent of such legal controls, the pharmacist has been stripped of much of the medical autonomy which his counterparts have enjoyed in other historical periods and still enjoy in numerous other cultures. Later in this chapter, when we discuss the development of modern drugs, it will become clear that this loss of autonomy has important implications for the future of our health care delivery system.

THE "EXPECTANT ATTITUDE" V.S. "DO SOMETHING"

Years ago I heard a historian remark, "We Americans are like the Romans in that we tend to measure civilization in terms of plumbing." On reflection it is not difficult to pinpoint many areas in which our modern mindset coincides with that of the ancient Romans and, incidentally, is in opposition to that of the Greeks, to whom we generally give lip service as our intellectual forebears. (1) Our preoccupation with sanitation and the public works that necessarily accompany it; item: the Romans built fourteen aqueducts capable of supplying Rome with 300,000,000 gallons of water a day, and the Cloaca Maxima, the main sewer of Rome constructed long before the time of Christ, is still in use today. (2) A preference for action over contemplation: the Romans we remember today are primarily soldiers and statesmen, not philosophers, while the Roman taste in science runs primarily to engineering and mechanics, not physics or mathematics. (3) An acceptance of patriotism and military service even unto death; the Greeks were tormented by the philosophic ambiguities of dying for one's country, while the Romans found it *dulce et decorum*—sweet and appropriate. (4) A tendency to equate wealth with personal worth and with it a propensity for conspicuous consumption; it is literally inconceivable to think of Socrates sitting down to a Lucellan banquet of peacocks' tongues. (5) An obsession with leisure-time activities and "recreation" and "entertainment"; the Roman schizophrenic attitude toward work (it is distasteful, but necessary in order that one may earn the wherewithal to play) manages to bleed through the massive armor of our Germanic-Protestant work ethic.

In view of our general adoption of Roman culture, it is not too surprising that our attitudes toward medicine are predominantly those of Rome rather than Greece. Greek medicine revolved around a concept known as the "Hippocratic expectant attitude." The Greek physician Hippocrates had observed that the natural tendency is for sickness to pass and give way to renewed health. Therefore, he reasoned, the role of the physician is to "wait upon Nature," to care for the sick by diet and hygiene until time has healed them. To this end, Hippocrates and his followers kept careful clinical records of the courses of various diseases. Their observations are unflinchingly accurate, and the Greek physicians must have managed a good degree of ego detachment from their practice, since the vast majority of the clinical records end with the observation that the patient died. Drugs were used sparingly, if at all, and surgery was left to the barbers.

The Hippocratic view of medicine persisted for several hundred years, but did not take root in Rome. Instead, the Roman attitude is epitomized by the vituperations of the Romanized Greek physician, Asclepiades of Bithynia, who in the first century before Christ condemned the Hippocratic expectant attitude as a "mere meditation on death." Instead, the physician was to intervene actively in the course of the disease so that the cure would be "seemly, swift and sure." Just as a Roman engineer would generally cut away a hill that stood in the way of his road, rather than build around it, so the Roman physician would be likely to resort to surgery, bloodletting and purgative drugs in order to force some change in the patient's condition.

One hesitates to say that such intervention resulted in an increase in the number of patients cured, although some aspects of Roman medicine are strikingly "modern." (For instance, at Pompeii archaeologists have unearthed sets of surgical instruments which, except for the lack of chrome plating and stainless steel, are nearly identical to those in use today.) In fact, from the time of Hippocrates until the eighteenth century it is difficult to get any idea of the efficiency of the medical profession, because, after the Greeks, there is little systematic clinical record keeping. One suspects that physicians tired of having to record the regularity with which the course of treatment ended in the death of the patient. Statistical estimates produced from historical materials are notoriously inaccurate, but authorities have not come up with any striking differences in life expectancy in ancient Rome, compared to ancient Greece. Life expectancy (at birth) is in both cases put at about thirty years. By the late Middle Ages life expectancy in Northern Europe had increased some five years (estimated), but it would be very difficult to attribute the increase to the efforts of the medical profession.

On the other hand, it is not hard to see that this Roman pressure for results has led to a long and gradual shift in the emphasis of medicine from contemplative to active. Precious few Westerners, Roman or otherwise, have ever taken a stoic attitude toward pain, disease or death, and it is probably because of this attitude that we have exerted continual pressure on our medical establishment to "do something" about those aspects of the human condition which so many other cultures regard with nonchalant fatalism.

These then are the two conflicting elements which go together historically to form what one might call the personality of modern medicine: on the one hand, a certain aloofness and a sense of being involved in an abstract exercise of intellectual manipulation; and, on the other, a pressure to intervene actively in the processes of the body, either by means of surgery or drugs, in order to produce some visible change in the patient's condition. This means that although modern medicine has taken on the observational trappings of the hard sciences at the research level, at the everyday clinical level the average physician handles patients in very much the same way as his medieval forebears. The only difference is that the ponderous leather tomes full of crabbed Latin scribbling and drawings of herbs have given way to long sheets of thin paper covered with "fine print" and folded up as package inserts by drug manufacturers.

A Galaxy of Professionals

The package insert is, of course, a primary symptom of the separation of functions in our modern health care system: a piece of information from the drug manufacturer—whose main goal is to promote the sale of drugs—which ends up primarily in the hands of the pharmacist—whose goal is to fill prescriptions—bypassing entirely the physician whose business is to consider symptoms and plan therapy. The futile trajectory of the package insert will recur as we consider each component of the health care system. At this point it raises the question: how well prepared is today's physician to deal with the drugs available for therapy?

A physician currently practicing in the United States holds, more or less by definition, a degree of "Doctor of Medicine." (The usual abbreviation, M.D., follows the word order of the phrase in Latin.) This degree belongs to a group of degrees known in educational parlance as "professional degrees." Also included in this group are J.D. (Doctor of Law, the attorney's degree), Pharm.D. (Doctor of Pharmacy), Doctor of Arts (a college-level teaching degree) and D.O. (Doctor of Osteopathy). What all of these degrees have in common is that, like the undergraduate degrees (B.A. and B.S.), they are granted after completion of a fixed course of study. Once the student has successfully completed a series of courses and, in some cases, a period of on-the-job training, he is graduated. As a check on the quality of education, graduates in certain fields must then pass a government examination (such as the state medical board exam or the bar exam) before they are licensed to practice their professions.

On the other hand, most master's degrees and all Ph.D. (Doctor of Philosophy) degrees are classified as "research degrees." That is, formal classwork constitutes only a small part of the work for the degree. The student must also demonstrate competence on a wide range of written and oral examinations and prepare a dissertation demonstrating his ability to conduct original research and to defend his results in the circle of his peers. In general, the professional degrees are awarded after a three- or four-year course study (beyond the bachelor's degree). Ph.D. programs vary widely, but most candidates require a minimum of three years to complete the degree, and the average time is closer to six or seven years.

Perhaps the most important distinction is that, while professional degrees are intended to prepare the candidate to engage in a complicated and demanding trade, research degrees are intended to prepare thinkers who can make original contributions to a field of knowledge. If one were to look at the subsequent life histories of a class of M.D.'s, for instance, one would find that nearly every one of them entered the practice of medicine. A class of Ph.D.'s in, say, psychology would have a much more heterogeneous history: some would enter research and teaching at the college level; others would enter private clinical practice; some would join hospital or other institutional staffs; still others would enter advertising, media research or the business world. (Dr. Frank Stanton, former president of CBS, is, for instance, a Ph.D. in psychology.)

The distinction between professional and research degrees can be further dramatized by the fact that any medical student who plans to pursue a career primarily in basic research, rather than patient-oriented practice, will generally enter a graduate degree program, concurrent with or following his medical studies. After a very lengthy course of study (often ten to twelve years past the bachelor's degree), he or she will emerge with an M.S. (Master of Science) or Ph.D. as well as an M.D. degree. The graduate degree will commonly be in some field such as physiology, microbiology, or biochemistry, all of which are related to medicine. The implication is fairly clear: the M.D. degree prepares one as a skilled technician who uses the available fund of knowledge to perform diagnosis and then to manipulate the thing diagnosed. A crass comparison: medical researchers are akin to the electronics engineers who design a new TV set; M.D.'s correspond to the TV servicemen who keep the sets working—with the help of information supplied by the engineers.

Herein lies one of the major problems in the organization of our current medical system: the M.D. is not a *generator* of information, he is a *user* of information. This in itself would create no problem were it not for the fact that most M.D.'s regard themselves as the center of the galaxy of professional health care. In fact, if one regards this galaxy as a system for the generation and utilization of information, then the core of the system is really an unholy mixture of medical/pharmaceutical researchers coupled with the research and marketing departments of pharmaceutical manufacturers.

This core is then surrounded by a layer of decision-making technicians (primarily M.D.'s) who apply the previously generated knowledge to specific cases. Finally, the outer ring of the galaxy is made up of the paramedical professionals—the nurses, physician's assistants, opticians and therapists—who actualize the decisions of the decision-making technicians. Beyond the last layer of the galaxy we enter the nebula of patients.

And the pharmacists, where are they? At the present time it is very difficult to say. If M.D.'s are forever trying to imagine their way into the inner core, they are also simultaneously trying to imagine the pharmacists into the outermost ring of technicians. As we will see when we consider the pharmaceutical professions, the physicians are not solely to blame for this shift of the pharmacists to the outer layer: there is considerable pressure in the same direction from within the ranks of practicing pharmacists.

The question before us now, however, is simply this: for what position in the galaxy are pharmacists and physicians best suited by their *training?* In other words, where can they function most effectively in providing rational and cost/safety-effective health care to the patient—the consumer who requires their services and pays for them? The strengths and weaknesses of the physician's education do much to define the place of the pharmacist in a rational system of health care delivery.

"If This is Strep Throat, It Must be Penicillin"

Put very briefly, the medical school curriculum can be described thus: a concentrated course of study in the following disciplines (the list varies slightly from school to school): anatomy, physiology, biochemistry, pathology, histology, cytology, immunology, pharmacology, embryology, microbiology and genetics. All of these subjects are taught from the aspect of their impingement on the human body. In other words, these disciplines are pursued for what they have to say about the condition of the body in health and the deviations from the normal state which constitute disease. This emphasis is underscored by the organization of one innovative medical education program at a major midwestern university. After basic study of all the areas listed above, the student then accompanies practicing physicians on their rounds and studies actual patients representing nine general types of clinical problems. For each of the problems the students must then bring to bear his knowledge of the relevant aspects of the various medical disciplines.

The emphasis on the diagnosis of body states continues and is accentuated as the medical student passes on through the succeeding years of medical school. One educator has estimated that the average medical student memorizes no fewer than *40,000* terms and definitions before graduation. During the years of internship and residency the new physician works intensively with his senior colleagues to shape this knowledge into a reliable ability to observe patient symptoms and convert such external signs into a diagnosis of the internal condition of the patient's body.

Once diagnosis has been established, the physician must be capable of performing or directing treatment of the patient. Virtually all treatment can be contained in four categories: (1) drug therapy, (2) surgery, (3) "expectation" (that is, letting the body heal itself), and (4) therapy by external agency (x-ray, diathermy, physiotherapy, exercise). These categories do not contain equal percentages of cases, by any means. Official figures suggest that at least 55 percent of all office calls result in one or more drug prescriptions. These figures do not include hospital treatment (either inpatient or outpatient), where it is exceedingly rare that a patient/physician contact does *not* result in a prescription. Surgery takes place as a result of no more than 5 to 7 percent of diagnoses. In perhaps the same number of cases the patient is told simply to "wait it out." (One physician for instance, used to snort, "Cold takes two weeks with medicine; cold takes two weeks without medicine." Many of his colleagues, although they might *think* the same way, would probably write as many as three prescriptions for a patient with a head cold: antihistamine, antitussive/expectorant, and an antibiotic.) In a still smaller number of cases the patient may be referred for treatment by x-ray or diathermy, or for treatment or counseling by a physiotherapist. All these figures deal with situations where a definite physical condition exists. In the case of emotional/psychological problems (which most physicians are scantily equipped to diagnose) the usual treatment would be referral to a psychiatrist or clinical psychologist. Even in psychological cases, however, the average physician's first line of attack is to reach for the prescription pad and put the patient on tranquilizers: the tranquilizer Valium is reputed to be the most heavily prescribed drug in the U.S. today.

Given that the physician's primary response to diagnosis is to prescribe drug therapy, we come face to face with a basic shortcoming of the physician's education: with perhaps 80 to 90 percent of his therapy involving drugs (even if he decides against drug therapy, he needs a rational basis for doing so), the physician has only the least rigorous 10 percent of his education to fall back on.

For a good many years now, it has been almost standard practice for every nutritionist writing in the popular press to bemoan the M.D.'s ignorance of nutrition. Likewise, a seemingly endless line of psychologists has informed us of the medical profession's woeful lack of understanding of psychology, particularly in the area of human sexuality. I think it is now high time that the profession of pharmacy had some input on the most pressingly important area of physician ignorance—pharmacology.

Even the most rudimentary perusal of a medical school catalog reveals something disturbing: the medical student typically spends less than ten semester hours on all subjects dealing with drugs. Depending on the medical school, this represents between *one tenth* and *one twelfth* of the total classroom curriculum. Nor is the entire ten hours really relevant to the drug-related problems the physician will encounter in practice: one semester hour is generally spent on prescription writing, a necessary talent but not one which involves knowledge of drugs—it is a question of learning the shorthand.

In addition to the miniscule part of the curriculum which it occupies, pharmacology shares another characteristic with the medical school teaching of nutrition and psychology: all three are taught almost exclusively in the lecture room as theoretical subjects. Anatomy comes alive through the study of patients and the dissection of cadavers. Cytology and microbiology are taught with constant reference to the microscope and culture dish. Of the major medical disciplines, pharmacology alone remains almost totally in a theoretical context. Furthermore, it is a subject which only really comes alive to the student who has a thorough understanding of organic chemistry and mathematics. Contrary to popular belief, medical students as a group are not overly strong in the hard sciences. They have pursued a wide variety of majors as undergraduates, and those who do have strong backgrounds in the hard sciences are most likely to be those who will ultimately pursue careers in medical research, *not* in clinical practice.

The overall result is that the new M.D. leaves medical school with a sketchy knowledge of pharmacology and a dangerous tendency to use only a "surface" approach to the subject. That is, since he does not have an in-depth understanding of drug action, he will tend to prescribe by rule of thumb or according to the advertising of drug manufacturers that continually deluge him. His observation of symptoms will trigger patterns of diagnostic reasoning in a brain which has been exhaustively trained in anatomy and physiology. But the resulting diagnosis will then, like as not, be paired up with one of a limited list of drugs, based on certain surface characteristics of the drugs, not on an understanding of their action on the body: "If this is a strep throat, it must be penicillin."

Following graduation from medical school, all M.D.'s serve a one-year internship at a teaching hospital. At the end of this year they take state examinations and only after passing them are they licensed to practice medicine outside the hospital of which they are a part. At this point, those M.D.'s who wish to enter general practice may do so. Those who wish to become specialists must continue to work at a teaching hospital as "residents" for a period of one to six years, depending on the specialty. During this period, the resident works closely with a "preceptor," a senior physician in the specialty the resident wishes to enter.

Needless to say, internship and residency are ad hoc situations so far as teaching is concerned: they are not under the control of either the medical schools or the state licensing agencies. Consequently, the quality of instruction depends almost entirely on the new M.D.'s choice of a hospital and preceptor, and competition is fierce for a chance to work with the leading practitioners in any given area of specialization. As happens in any "free enterprise" educational system, the best students will generally end up with the best teachers, and the worst students with the worst teachers.

Consequently, even though everybody ends up with an M.D. degree after four years of medical school, by the end of residency the system has produced a vast disparity between the best practitioners and the worst.

What all practitioners, good, bad or indifferent, have in common is that a significant part of their medical education—internship and residency—has been conducted at the hands of teachers who are themselves mostly *users,* rather than *generators* of medical information. Consequently, the intern or resident is in most cases in a position only to learn what generally *is* done in the profession, not what *could* or *ought* to be done. Again, those who study with the elite are comparatively well off—their preceptors are often generators of information comparable to the institutional and industrial researchers. For most practitioners, however, the situation is one of careful perpetuation of the existing level of knowledge—or ignorance.

Once the physician enters practice, the situation may actually get worse rather than better. According to Department of Labor statistics, the average physician works a sixty-hour week, and it should be pointed out that this average is lowered by numerous semi-retired physicians who work only one or two days a week. The physician beginning in private practice will probably work seventy to eighty hours per week in order to build up his clientele, pay off his medical school debts, and generally "make a name for himself." There is, quite frankly, little time left for study, and what time there is will probably be used in skimming medical journals, which rarely display a strong pharmacological orientation except in their advertising pages. In this atmosphere, continuing education quickly gives way to daily survival.

The one other body of material which a physician commonly reads, besides his handful of medical journals, is the flood of drug advertising which pours across his desk at every mail call. The pharmaceutical manufacturers begin cultivating a buddy-buddy relationship with the future physician in the first years of medical school. One major manufacturer sends every medical student a black leather "doctor's bag." The outside is stamped with the student's name in gold; inside, where the student will see it every time he reaches for his stethoscope, is another stamp: "Compliments of J——F—— Pharmaceutical Co." Other manufacturers fly groups of medical students to major cities for "medical symposiums"—a euphemism for a round of wining and dining and friendly chit-chat with the company salesmen. The overall relationship built up between physician and drug company is warm, fraternal and pseudo-professional. In the context of this relationship, the physician's response is likely to be uncritical and tinged with well-nurtured favoritism. Furthermore, the flood of promotional material is almost the only source of current drug information that reaches the physician at all.

This is definitely *not* to say that other sources of information and guidance are not readily available, a point which brings us to a discussion of the profession of pharmacy.

"If Doctor Prescribed It, It Must Be Right"

True or false: "The pharmacist is by training and experience the health care professional best equipped to deal with problems of drug therapy." Answer: True *and* false. The profession of pharmacy, as it stands today, is no great help in straightening out our tangled American system of medicine. If anything, pharmacy as it is now practiced is an integral part of the problem of drug misuse. Properly evolved, developed and utilized, professional pharmacists could revolutionize drug therapy.

What is a pharmacist, anyway? Quite simply, he is the most overtrained and underutilized of our health care professionals. Unlike the physician, the pharmacist does not generally hold a degree beyond the bachelor's level, but his Bachelor of Science (Pharmacy) degree is acquired in a manner different from that which leads to other undergraduate degrees. While the physician may have majored in just about anything as an undergraduate, the pharmacist has majored exclusively in pharmacy from the time he enters a school of pharmacy. And the program takes five years, rather than the usual four.

When he graduates, the new pharmacist will have received some fifty semester hours of instruction dealing directly with drugs (five times what the physician receives). In addition, he will typically receive some twenty to thirty hours of chemistry, eight hours of mathematics, eight hours of physiology, eight hours of microbiology, and four hours of physics. Finally, he usually receives sixteen or more semester hours in public health and community health care. Several of the drug-related courses are taught with reference to anatomy and physiology. Following graduation, the pharmacist must serve a one-year apprenticeship and pass a state-administered examination before he is licensed to practice.

It is at this point, when he begins to practice, that the pharmacist discovers the true degree to which he is—or rather, is *not*—utilized by the medical establishment. Whether he is working in a hospital or a community pharmacy, the pharmacist is generally somebody's employee, and as such his efforts are of necessity directed toward fulfilling his employer's wishes. In the case of the community pharmacy, the employer's wish is that as many prescriptions be filled as possible. Turning away prescriptions that are dangerous, incorrect, illegible, redundant or unnecessary is frowned upon. In a hospital, a pharmacist who questions prescriptions is a potential source of disgruntlement to the medical staff and is thus likely to arouse the ire of the hospital administrator. After all, the business which the physicians bring in is the hospital's bread and butter, while the hospital pharmacist is a single, easily replaced cog in the machine. Furthermore, the hospital pharmacy generally turns a tidy profit which helps offset losses in other departments, so any restriction on prescribing is liable to have adverse effects on the budget.

I have already related the case of a pharmacist who was removed from his hospital job for challenging a physician's method of treatment. The following case may help to elucidate the situation in which a community employee pharmacist often finds himself if he attempts to utilize his knowledge of drugs:

> Charles Frost worked in a pharmacy belonging to a local chain of some ten stores. This particular store was located near a university campus and, in the liberated sixties, Frost found himself filling a large number of prescriptions for birth control pills. In his first few weeks on the job he noticed that many of the girls who came in for birth control pills complained of one or more eye problems, usually associated with wearing contact lenses. Since the manufacturer's literature had mentioned certain eye conditions as possible side effects of the pill, Frost alerted the physician who was doing most of the prescribing at the university health service. The physician shared Frost's concern and notified his patients to come in for an eye examination. Of twenty-five who responded, eight were found to have excessive intraocular pressure, the result of a glaucoma-like condition which could lead to eventual blindness. The physician cancelled the prescriptions of these patients and advised them to adopt a different method of contraception.
>
> When Frost refused to refill the cancelled prescriptions, the

girls had them refilled at another of the chain's stores and then complained to the manager of the chain. The manager, fearing the loss of student trade, fired Frost. Three years later Frost and the manager met at a regional pharmacy convention. The manager explained that he was having trouble staffing a new store and offered Frost a job. When Frost reminded the manager of what had happened between them, the manager replied: "It was no big deal anyway. We were only grossing forty cents per package on those pills."

The message to the employee pharmacist is clear: You are part of a profit-making arrangement whereby the physician writes prescriptions and you fill them and everybody gets a cut, *so don't make waves.*

Nor is the profit motive the only part of the medical system that prevents the pharmacist from utilizing his knowledge of drugs to protect the consumer: there is simply no mechanism to get this knowledge to the places where it is needed. A pharmacist who detects an apparent error in a prescription and calls the physician about it will probably get a very indignant response—if he can ever reach the physician at all. Usually he will not be able to penetrate the palace guard and will receive a saccharine assurance from the office nurse to the effect that "If Doctor prescribed it, then it must be the right thing."

On the other hand, if the pharmacist attempts to warn the patient that the prescription is of a dubious nature, then the physician can sue the pharmacist for damaging his professional reputation, an offense for which the courts are known to make uncommonly generous awards. So if you have ever wondered why the pharmacist never asks you any question but your address and never makes any comment about the drug except "That will be $14.55, please," be it known that there is good reason for his tight-lipped stance. He has nothing to gain and everything to lose by sharing his pharmaceutical knowledge with either physician or patient, and it takes a good deal of resignation to put up with his lot. To count tablets, type labels and operate the cash register, you don't *begin* to utilize five years of professional education.

A Prima Donna and an Automation

This much everybody seems to know about our health care system: physicians are imperious, pharmacists are automatons and the drug companies are making mega-money. Everybody senses that this is in some way wrong, that in some way the reality of American medicine is a sick parody of the selfless, heroic ideal which the TV medical serials constantly feed us. But you can't get too upset about deflated dreams; that, after all, is life. On the other hand, there are at least two points over which the health care consumer ought to get very upset indeed.

The first point is this: the system of interrelated professions which ought to result in the orderly generation, application and implementation of health care knowledge has clearly gone awry. Physicians have tried to assign themselves a central position in the system which, as technicians, they clearly do not merit. They have lost the necessary humility about the limits of knowledge which ordinarily leads professionals to borrow the brains of other professionals when the situation warrants. Then too, a combination of economic pressure, physician arrogance and pharmacist acquiescence has displaced the very group of professionals—the pharmacists—who by training and experience ought to be the technicians of drug-related information. The overall result is that in health care you aren't getting what you pay for: instead of two skilled technicians, you are getting one prima donna and one automaton.

The second point over which consumers should be irate is really a consequence of the first: because the health care system has failed to develop a meaningful partnership between professions, the patient often receives only the lowest common denominator of professional knowledge. You have no way of knowing whether your life depends on an available drug of which your physician is ignorant. Likewise, you have no way of knowing whether the next prescription he hands to you will be your death warrant—or, more likely, a ticket to a few extra days in bed from side effects—because he has failed to read the fine print about contraindications, or failed to check for the correct dosage. Nor do you have the guarantee that your pharmacist, for all his education in drug-related matters, will catch and correct the physician's errors. In similar conditions of ill-founded blind faith, most consumers would hesitate to buy a used pogo stick. It is not a reassuring picture, nor is it meant to be. In the next chapter I will detail actual cases of misuse. This misuse occurs in every category of drugs available today, and arises from the very nature of our health care system.

3 *Any Way You Turn:* SIX CLASSES OF DRUGS AND WHAT GETS DONE WITH THEM

If you add up all the items listed in all the pharmaceutical catalogs available to your community pharmacist, you will come up with a list of over 25,000 items, any of which could be prescribed for you by your physician. The question which immediately arises in the layman's mind is "Oh my heavens! How can the poor physician ever possibly keep them straight?" When we begin to scrutinize this list in terms of pharmacological action, however, this figure turns out to be misleading. Numerous drugs are produced under different trade names by different manufacturers, but this represents only a part of the proliferation; dosage forms, packaging variations and other less rational distinctions account for thousands of items.

A common example will serve to illustrate. Phenobarbital is a sedative and anticonvulsant which is considered by most experts to be indispensable in the treatment of epilepsy and has certain other uses of lesser importance. One manufacturer of phenobarbital (and there are many) lists the drug as follows:

Phenobarbital, compressed tablet, white	8 mg
Phenobarbital, compressed tablet, white	16 mg
Phenobarbital, compressed tablet, white	32 mg
Phenobarbital, compressed tablet, white	50 mg
Phenobarbital, compressed tablet, white	60 mg
Phenobarbital, compressed tablet, white	100 mg

This is a good span of doses and one could rationalize the need for all of these sizes, although slotted 16 mg, 60 mg and 100 mg tablets would cover most contingencies. But this is not the end of the list, because it then repeats itself for tablets colored blue, brown, green, orange, pink, purple, yellow and mottled. Nor is this the end: sugar-coated tablets are available in white, blue, green, yellow and pink. Then there is an ovoid pill in white, blue, green, yellow and pink and, finally, a chocolate-flavored tablet. Each type and color is available in two to six sizes, for a possible grand total of some 120 "different" phenobarbital tablets. Overall, I would estimate that there may be as many as 2,500 phenobarbital products on the market.

Obviously, not all drugs are available in such a multitude of forms, but the extent of duplication is far greater than most people—physicians included—generally realize. Exact figures are difficult to come by, but the best estimates are that the 25,000 available pharmaceutical products represent no more than about 1,200 distinct drugs. Furthermore, it is only in recent years that the Food and Drug Administration has begun to require proof of *effectiveness* as well as safety. Consequently the shelves are still cluttered with drugs of dubious value. Other drugs, although safe and effective, have such limited uses that there is little reason for them to be offered for general sale. The extent of this excessive proliferation is brought home by the following case:

> An experimental health clinic was established in a small town in rural Iowa. The town had previously had no physician and no pharmacy, hence the clinic was to include a pharmacist in addition to two physicians. Since funds for establishing the clinic were meager, the physicians and pharmacist conferred on the stock to be carried by the pharmacy. Among them they were able to arrive at a list of 140 drugs which would cover almost every contingency of the clinical practice. Even allowing for different dosage forms, the resulting inventory ran to less than 200 items. The entire inventory was purchased for $1,600. At that time (1973) the typical community pharmacy (nationwide) had a prescription drug inventory of $13,969. After six months in operation the inventory had risen to approximately $2,500, but the clinic was quick to point out that the increase was due to having increased quantities of drugs on hand; only "a few" new drugs had been added to the list. One research team studying the clinic observed that "the small size of the formulary [list of drugs] was possible because of the elimination of brand name duplication, irrational combinations, and 'me too' drug products."

How can a pharmacy carrying less than 200 items manage to render approximately the same service as one which carries the more usual average of 3,000 to 10,000 items? The answer is that, for all the apparent complexity of the drug market, the vast majority of the drugs themselves can be divided into a handful of categories: antimicrobials, analgesics, diuretics, sedatives (including tranquilizers), steroids (primarily birth control pills), and anorexiants (stimulants such as amphetamines). There are a few drugs which do not fall into these six groups, but they are used for special purposes and do not enter the normal course of prescribing.

Perhaps this simplified breakdown of the vast *materia medica* of modern medicine into a few general categories will help to explain how it may be possible in this chapter to explore with some thoroughness the general patterns of drug misuse in American health care. In fact, it is not necessary to study 25,000 drug entities, or 1,200 drug ingredients, to get a reasonable picture of what is going on. The average physician does all his prescribing from less than 300 drug items, virtually all of which fall neatly into the categories listed above. A look at each of these categories will provide a remarkably complete view of what happens when physician meets drug, physician prescribes drug, and patient takes drug.

Antimicrobials: The "Wonder Drugs"

To most people, antimicrobials (primarily antibiotics and sulfas) symbolize the new wave in drugs; they are the "wonder drugs" which actually cure diseases instead of simply altering symptoms or modifying body states. The word "antibiotic" means literally "against life," and these drugs do in fact help to destroy the tiny one-celled organisms that cause many diseases. As such, they have become the modern physician's front line weapon against disease and their very effectiveness—reputed and actual—has led to gross overuse and misuse.

The first "modern" antimicrobials were offshoots of the German chemical industry's research with coal tar dyes. It was found that certain of these dyes, a group generally called the "sulfonamides," were only mildly toxic to humans, but were powerfully toxic to disease-causing organisms. The sulfas work by blocking the synthesis of folic acid, an essential nutrient. Since higher animals, such as man, do not depend on folic acid synthesis (we get the vitamin in our food), the sulfas do not have this action on our body cells. These drugs do not kill the microbes outright, but do keep them from growing and multiplying, thus "buying time" until our normal body defense mechanisms can finish them off.

There are numerous problems associated with sulfa drug therapy, not all of which are satisfactorily resolved by current medical practice. One of the most serious matters is crystal precipitation in the kidneys, the effect responsible for Allen Harper's death in the case given in the previous chapter. The problem is that not only are some sulfa drugs only marginally soluble, but even some of those which are very soluble (mostly the newer varieties) can suddenly precipitate crystals if the pH of the solution (urine) changes from slightly alkaline to neutral or acid. To some extent this can be controlled by giving a mixed dose of several different sulfas and careful therapy to keep the patient's urine alkaline. This requires constant dietary supervision and constant testing; few physicians make provision for either. The situation has also been helped by the development of sulfas which are much more soluble and less prone to precipitation than the original drugs. Finally, all sulfas are to some extent toxic to the human body. This toxicity has been reduced over the years by developing new compounds, but is still a small yet definite risk to the patient.

Sulfa therapy is not as common in the U.S. as it used to be, because of the development of the "antibiotics." Nearly everyone has heard the story of Sir Alexander Fleming who, in 1928, observed what happened when one of his culture dishes was accidentally contaminated with penicillium, a common bread mold. In the dish he had been growing a flourishing colony of staphylococcus bacteria. In the area around the mold colony, however, bacterial growth was inhibited. Eventually it was found that the mold produced a substance, later named penicillin, which would inhibit the growth of many varieties of bacteria. The best thing was that this substance was virtually non-toxic to higher animals. At first penicillin was not available in sufficient concentrations to be useful as a medicine, but in 1939 a research team at Oxford University succeeded in isolating and purifying the substance. During World War II penicillin saw extensive use in military medicine, becoming one of the Allies' most important "secret weapons." After the war, penicillin was released on the civilian drug market, where it quickly proved its worth by producing rapid cures of previously incurable diseases.

One aspect of penicillin (and all subsequent antibiotics), however, was often not appreciated by physicians: antibiotics are fairly specific in their action, attacking some bacteria powerfully and leaving others completely untouched. This was brought home to me personally one day in 1947. Like countless other GIs, I had come home from the service with a little extra bonus: malaria. As often happens, the disease resolved itself after a few years in a temperate climate, but for a while I was subject to recurring attacks. One day while going from class to class on the campus where I was attending pharmacy school, I had a violent chill. I made my way to the university health service and collapsed in a shuddering heap.

"What on earth is the matter?" the elderly physician on duty wanted to know. I managed to get out that it was a malarial attack. "Molly!" he shouted triumphantly to the nurse, "bring on the penicillin!"

I was really in no shape to argue, but I tried to make the good man understand that malaria is not caused by a bacterium but by a plasmodium, which is not sensitive to penicillin.

"And just what the hell," he wanted to know, "is a plasmodium?"

"It's a one-celled animal, a protozoan," I replied.

"Well, it's an organism, isn't it? And penicillin kills organisms, doesn't it?"

I finally managed to put him off until I could see the other health service physician, who knew a bit more about modern therapy.

Today it is unlikely that a physician would attempt to treat malaria with penicillin, but antibiotics are still often used in shotgun fashion against unidentified disease organisms. Part of the problem arises from the large number of antibiotics now available. The original penicillin has now been joined by numerous other antibiotics, and each of these drugs has a range of organisms against which it is effective—and others against which it is useless. In cases where the disease organism is unknown, a specimen from the patient is cultured in a clinical laboratory and a variety of antibiotics are applied to the culture plate. The physician is then informed as to which antibiotics have an effect on the culture, and from this he can make his decision on which drug to use. This procedure is time-consuming, however, and many physicians prefer to simply start with one antibiotic and then, if there are no results, switch to another.

When physicians' prescriptions for antibiotics are scrutinized by qualified outside observers, the results are often embarrassing. In 1974 a research team from Ohio State University reported the following facts from a study of a large (500-bed) community hospital: During a one-month period, 1,035 patients were admitted. Of these, 340, or nearly one-third, were given "systemic" antimicrobials (given by mouth or injected to assure a level of drug in the blood). Of these, only 44 patients, or less than 13 percent, could have been expected, on the basis of their medical records, to benefit from such drugs. Another 21.5 percent of the therapies were judged to be questionable—the records contained insufficient evidence. The remaining 65.5 percent were labeled by the researchers as "irrational," a medical term indicating that the treatment did not fit the diagnosis. In 111 cases the therapy was judged to be both "unnecessary and unwarranted," and of these, 102 cases showed no clinical evidence of infection.

The implications of this sort of shotgun medicine are threefold. First is the unnecessary cost to the patient. In the study cited above, the total cost for drugs was $18,244.55; of this total, 76.8 percent ($13,989.28) was expended on irrational therapy, 14 percent ($2,577.89) for questionable therapy, and only 9.2 percent ($1,677.38) on rational therapy. If the month during which the study was conducted is typical, then over $160,000 is wasted annually on antimicrobial drugs in this one hospital. Extrapolated nationwide, the waste figure for antimicrobials probably exceeds $500 million annually.

Even such monumental waste might be tolerable (we Americans seem, after all, to have invented the cost overrun) were it not for the fact that unnecessary antimicrobial therapy exposes the patient to considerable medical risk. Those of us who are over thirty will recall the terrifying "penicillin reactions" of the forties and fifties. In the early days of penicillin as much as 2 percent of the population experienced allergic reactions to the drug, and numerous deaths resulted. Reactions are less frequent nowadays (.12 percent is a recent figure) because modern penicillin is, among other things, purer. This still means that about one person in 800 stands a chance of dying from casually administered penicillin.

Other antibiotics can also cause severe allergic reactions, and the picture is further complicated because a person who tolerates one drug may react to another—or, again, he may not. It was this sort of "cross-allergenicity" that killed Esther Sudell: her family doctor's records showed she was allergic to penicillin, but it apparently did not occur to him that her respiratory distress could be the sign of a reaction to another antibiotic, cephalosporin. Yet the drug manufacturer warns that up to 10 percent of those people who are allergic to penicillin must be considered to be allergic to cephalosporin as well. Clearly, the danger involved dictates more careful medical record keeping than is now generally practiced. In particular it would seem to demand taking a thorough drug history *before* the drug is administered, a practice that is by no means universal today. Finally, it means that these drugs should *never* be used indiscriminately: the odds of a reaction are admittedly slight, but the consequences, if one does occur, can be serious.

Yet another medical problem arises from the use of antimicrobials, and that is the production of disease resistant organisms as a result of an insufficient dose of the drug. What happens is this: in most cases antimicrobials do not kill bacteria outright; instead they hold the organism at bay, keeping it from growing or multiplying until our normal body defenses can kill it off. If, however, the concentration of antimicrobial drug in the tissues is too small, the organism will continue to grow and multiply. In so doing it will gradually give rise to offspring which are resistant to the action of the drug. To some extent this occurs in all antimicrobial therapy and consequently hospitals become reservoirs of resistant organisms. In particular, though, any patient receiving a subtherapeutic dose of an antimicrobial is a mutation generator producing resistant strains of organisms that may infect others in the environment. This effect is in addition to the obvious one: a patient receiving a subtherapeutic dose is simply not going to be cured by it. The dangers of subtherapeutic dosing have been recognized for over thirty years, but some physicians continue to practice it, usually for medically irrelevant reasons.

Hattie Miller, age seventy-six, was admitted to a community hospital with a condition diagnosed as bronchitis. In view of her age and previous history of respiratory conditions, her admission to a hospital was considered a routine safety precaution. When her condition showed no improvement after two weeks of hospitalization, however, Hattie's relatives prevailed upon her physician to "do something." In response, he prescribed a dose of 250 mg of the antibiotic ampicillin, to be administered intravenously twice a day in 250 ml of saline solution. This dose is *well* below the therapeutic level, but the method of administration was impressively visible: every time the relatives came to see Hattie, she was on the receiving end of a substantial IV bottle.

One week later, Hattie died. The autopsy revealed that she

had not been suffering from a respiratory infection at all; her "bronchitis" had merely been one of the classic symptoms of congestive heart failure.

When the hospital pharmacist reminded Hattie's physician of the dangers of underusing antibiotics, the physician registered some surprise. Since ampicillin was a new (to him) antibiotic, he had assumed that he need not worry about the development of resistant organisms. Any second-year pharmacy student could have told him that resistant organisms begin to appear within two to three bacterial generations after the administration of the antibiotic. Since some common disease organisms may divide every twenty to thirty minutes, they may be producing resistant organisms within a few hours after the first dose of the antibiotic is administered.

Clearly, from the dangers involved to both the patient and the environment, antimicrobial therapy should almost never be pursued in the manner now prevalent—as a happy-go-lucky shotgunning expedition. Not only are there certain dangers to the patient, who also happens to be underwriting the cost of the expedition, but there is real danger of educating the game—the bacteria—until it is virtually hunt-proof.

Anorexiants: "Uppers"

The current misuse of antibiotics seems to arise from a pair of factors in the physician's ego and education: (1) the desire to go for the cure that is "seemly, swift and sure," and (2) a failure to appreciate the complexities of biological interaction at the unicellular level. When we enter other categories of drug misuse, however, we find a different set of pressures at work on the physician. And neither his education nor the current structure of our health care system gives him much help when it comes to resisting misprescribing. An example from my own experience may help to illustrate:

> A middle-aged family man came storming into the pharmacy one day, demanding to know why his wife couldn't get her "diet pills." When I looked up the prescription I found that it had recently been cancelled by a telephone call from her physician. I also noted that the prescription was one of several for this woman in the previous year. The prescription was for a long-acting amphetamine capsule. When I tried to explain the physician's probable reasoning for cancelling the prescription, the

poor fellow became desperate. Finally he confided to me (man to man, as it were) that his wife either couldn't or wouldn't function as a wife ("you know what I mean") without her "pills." This confirmed my suspicions: I had met the woman and she was the original string bean—on the order of 110 pounds on a 5′ 11″ frame. There was no way in which she could require "dieting," let alone diet pills. Yet, to my surprise, this woman appeared two weeks later with a new prescription for the same drug—from the same physician.

The amphetamines are a good example of a drug whose uses are based almost solely on sociological motivation—coupled with the failure of most physicians to recognize the dangers involved. To the street drug addict, the amphetamines are known as "uppers" or "speed"; to the pharmacist they are anorexiants. They are, in effect, powerful stimulants which are thought to accelerate the body's physiological processes, thus giving the user extra "energy" and "stamina." It was because of the way in which these drugs appeared to increase energy output and metabolism that it was originally thought that they would be useful for weight control. After all, it was reasoned, weight control is a matter of balancing intake and output. If you can't get the patient to restrict his intake of food, perhaps you can make him increase his energy output with amphetamines. This proved not to be the case, since the obese person generally increased his caloric intake to meet the increased output. Amphetamines do have the initial effect of curbing appetite. Unfortunately, after a period of eight to fourteen days, this effect disappears and the patient stops losing weight. Thus, amphetamines should, by all rights, have fallen into disuse; that they did not, but remained a heavily prescribed drug for some years after their ineffectiveness became known, is a curious phenomenon of American medicine.

When I checked out the physician who had prescribed amphetamines for the string bean lady, I discovered that he was running an obesity clinic. His entire practice was conducted something like this: most of his patients (almost all women) were chronically overweight. On the first visit to his clinic, the patient would receive a cursory physical examination and then be given a diet (a preprinted sheet provided by a drug manufacturer, free of charge, to the physician) and a prescription for amphetamines. The prescription was for a week's supply and could be refilled once. Therefore the patient had to return every two weeks for another office visit (at $10 each time) in order to obtain another prescription. On these subsequent visits the patients were not seen by the physician. The nurse weighed the patient and then filled in the patient's name and address on a preprinted prescription blank already signed by the physician.

When one considers that the patients were paying something like $5 per minute for the services of an office nurse, it makes one think that they must have been getting something out of it besides the occasional slight weight loss that resulted. In most cases they were buying "energy"—the chemically-heightened energy to sweep through trying days of endless housework and impossible children and still be ready (like the string bean lady) to function as a vivacious bed partner.

Just to make sure they appreciated what they were getting, this physician regularly took each patient off the amphetamines for about one month out of five. Predictably, the patient would grow depressed at the resulting lack of energy, take to overeating for solace, and put on additional weight which would send her scurrying back to the obesity clinic to beg for more amphetamines. This is what had happened to the woman in the case related above: her physician had cancelled her prescription to make sure she would not take it for granted.

This particular physician no longer runs a wholesale obesity clinic: new government controls make it less convenient to prescribe amphetamines. He must now make out a new prescription each visit—no refills are permitted—and the prescription in his state is an elaborate three-part form requiring specific information. It is time-consuming to fill out and a copy goes to the narcotics agents (although they rarely bother a physician about his prescribing practices). The upshot is that this particular physician has found it less tedious and more lucrative to return to his original speciality—psychiatry.

Lest you jump to the conclusion, however, that government control is the key to regulating the aimless prescribing of physicians, consider the following case: For many years codeine-analgesic combinations were classified with the "hard" narcotics (such as morphine), and stringent government regulations required that they be prescribed differently than other drugs. As a result, codeine was never very heavily prescribed, even though it is a useful, inexpensive drug. Then a few years ago codeine was reclassified and the elaborate precautions were no longer required. One would have expected that there would have been a great upsurge in codeine prescribing, but none occurred. Most physicians had simply gotten used to prescribing substitutes for codeine and never went back to it.

This sort of phenomenon has intriguing implications for federal drug control: it seems to indicate that regulations which complicate the prescribing process *do* control physicians' prescribing patterns. But the problem is that the average physician simply crosses the controlled drug off of his mental list of commonly used drugs. The effect is not medical but time-motion efficient: a physician seeing forty to fifty patients a day does not wish to take time to stop and fill out a new prescription or a controlled-drug form. An ordinary prescription for an uncontrolled drug takes less time to write and doesn't arouse the patient's suspicion, as does the ominous-looking narcotics form. There are obviously limits to how thorough the average physician wants to make the thinking process that precedes the writing of a prescription. If they are forced by law to make very many decisions, most physicians will simply sidestep the issue by turning to a drug with fewer legal question marks about it. That the alternative drug may sometimes bear more *medical* question marks seems to bother no one.

All in all, the discouraging of amphetamine-dispensing obesity clinics is one of the few bright aspects of federal drug control. Still, you can't help feeling a little sorry for all the Mr. and Mrs. String Beans who built their version of the American Dream on a week's supply of "speed."

Diuretics: "Instant Slimness"

Most Americans are at least vaguely aware of the connection between the "uppers" and our universal dream of a sleek, high-powered world full of "all things bright and beautiful." On the other hand, few people are aware of the part played by the lowly diuretic in our scramble after the dream, or of the drug misuse that results. Put simply, diuretics are drugs that make you urinate more than you would otherwise. If you do not simultaneously increase your fluid intake, a diuretic can thus cause a decrease in the overall water content of your body. Diuretics are among the oldest drugs: together with laxatives and emetics (to cause vomiting) they were an important part of the medieval physician's practice. Legend even has it that gin (juniper berries infused in alcohol) was invented by a Dutch physician in search of a new diuretic.

Modern diuretics are mostly compounds related to the sulfa antimicrobials, and they have one very important use in medical practice. Certain of these diuretics (the group known as the thiazides) provide dramatic relief from certain types of high blood pressure ("hypertension" in medical language). At first it was thought that the diuretic action was responsible for the reduction in pressure, but it was found that sulfa diuretics other than the thiazides had no such effect. Consequently the effect of the thiazides on blood pressure is still ascribed to an "unknown mechanism." Nonetheless, the effect is very real and the thiazide diuretics are an important part of the standard treatment for high blood pressure. Unfortunately the fact that all of these diuretics, and numerous other drugs, are classified as "sulfas" caused problems for some physicians:

> Laura Steiner was fifty-one years old and carried nearly 170 pounds on her 5′ 3″ body. For some years she had shown signs of the onset of diabetes, so her family physician had undertaken a course of treatment involving diet and tolbutamide, a sulfa drug which reduces the level of blood sugar. After some time Laura's condition was stabilized with respect to blood sugar, but the diet was doing no good with respect to her weight. When she began having dizzy spells, she immediately concluded that she had high blood pressure and, fearing a stroke, went to a heart specialist. Her blood pressure was indeed perilously high and this second physician prescribed hydrochlorothiazide, a diuretic.
>
> When Mrs. Steiner took the new prescription to be filled, the pharmacist—one of the few who keep a drug profile of each customer—became alarmed. She was receiving tolbutamide, which is given for excessive blood sugar levels, and now here was a prescription for hydrochlorothiazide, which, as a side effect, interferes with the body's ability to metabolize carbohydrates. The drug is classified as a "diabetogenic" and could certainly complicate the treatment of her diabetes.
>
> When the pharmacist called Mrs. Steiner's family physician, he was not interested in listening. "Look," he replied, "I'm already giving her a sulfa [the tolbutamide], so what difference does it make if somebody else gives her one, too?" The heart specialist seemed more cooperative. He said he would "talk to Mrs. Steiner about it."
>
> "Apparently he did talk to her," the pharmacist adds, "because she never came in here again. She must have taken her prescriptions somewhere else."

Somewhere, one might add, where the pharmacist did not bother to keep a check on patients who visit several physicians clandestinely. Curiously, some of the other sulfonamide diuretics actually help in the control of certain types of diabetes at the same time that they help reduce blood pressure. Nonetheless, in dealing with an obese, middle-aged patient, the heart specialist should routinely have checked her for diabetes before prescribing hydrochlorothiazide.

So much for the essential uses of diuretics: these account for about one-half of the prescriptions issued for this class of drugs. A large part of the remaining 50 percent is prescribed in pursuit of one facet of the American dream, a mindset which requires that everyone be slender, lithe and youthful. To a detached observer the way to this ideal seems simple: get plenty of hard exercise, don't drink or smoke, and cut the food intake to the point where you are never really full and usually just a bit hungry. Unfortunately, another clause in the American dream dictates that we need never do things the hard and straight way: our supertechnocracy will provide us with a pill or a machine to do it for us. The amphetamine having fallen not really into disrepute but into disuse, the diuretic is now to many consumers the "instant slimness pill."

The reasoning is simple: water weighs a good deal; therefore, if you can increase your output of water, you will weigh less. There are three common conditions in which the body has excess water. First is obesity. An obese person usually does retain considerable water—but in general this is merely symptomatic of his improper eating habits. Almost any reasonable sort of reducing diet will quickly get rid of the water *and* the fat. No real need for a diuretic here. Second, many women retain considerable water at one point in their menstrual cycles. Usually a reduced-salt diet will handle this situation without recourse to a diuretic. Finally, I would estimate —based on experience in a number of community pharmacies— that upwards of 60 percent of those women who take birth control pills also take prescription diuretics. The reason? One of the discomforting side effects of the pill is that it causes excessive water retention. While the pros and cons of the pill will be discussed in the next section, suffice it to note here that there is something dubious about prescribing one powerful drug which is not essential to the patient's health (the pill) and then prescribing another powerful drug (a diuretic) to deal with the side effects of the first drug.

In view of the considerable nonessential usage of diuretics, does the situation have adverse implications for the patient's overall health? It is difficult to say, because the action of diuretics is really quite complicated. Some facts, however, are known. Diuretics do tend to deplete the body of dissolved sodium and potassium, especially the latter. This can have serious implications because our American diet is notoriously poor in potassium. Further, some nutritionists have voiced concern over the fact that diuresis leads to wholesale loss of the body's supply of the water-soluble vitamins (C and B complex).

Finally, diuretics have strange effects with regard to what are called "binding sites," the points in the body's molecules where drugs attach themselves. This interference can have adverse effects on some types of essential drug therapy. In some aspects of the treatment of heart disease, for instance, anticoagulant drugs are needed to prevent the formation of blood clots. The presence of certain diuretics can prevent the anticoagulant drug from "binding" in the normal manner. As a result, large amounts of the anticoagulant may remain free in the blood. This may in turn prevent the body from effectively sealing up the internal "leaks" that constantly occur in the circulatory system. The result: hemorrhaging.

To put it plainly, physicians today are prescribing too many diuretics for medically superfluous reasons. The potential health menace of these drugs, as well as the complications which they can cause with other—and possibly life-saving—drug therapy, indicates that they ought not to be prescribed routinely for reasons of vanity.

Steroids

The birth control pill (or BCP, for short) is at once one of the great success stories of modern pharmacology and an absurd test case by which we may experiment with the definition of the "human need" behind medical advancement. Introduced at the beginning of the sixties, the BCP is simply a small hormone dose used to temporarily "trick" a woman's reproductive system into thinking she is pregnant. During pregnancy no eggs are released from the ovaries, so the BCP creates a similar condition of temporary sterility, without pregnancy. Effective it is—probably more so than any other single method of contraception except total abstinence. Safety, as just about any literate American knows, is another matter. It has been belabored by the popular press to such an extent that I will avoid an extended discussion here. However, a few observations related to the purpose of this book are in order.

Considered in relation to the "medical need" for, say, penicillin, is the pill "necessary"? That is, does the pill perform the usual drug function of altering the state of the body in such a way as to relieve a state of disease? For the vast majority of uses to which the BCP is put, the answer has to be an emphatic no. (The BCP is used in very few instances to treat irregularities of the menstrual cycle.) The usual medical justification for the pill is that it is statistically a bit less potentially lethal than pregnancy. This has always seemed to me to be a bit of specious reasoning: it presumes that the alternative to taking the pill is getting pregnant. In reality, the alternative is to use one of the other—safer—forms of contraception. In those few cases where it can be established beforehand that pregnancy would be dangerous to the health of a particular woman, it seems clear that sterilization would be simpler, cheaper, more effective and safer than consuming BCPs for a twenty- to thirty-year period.

We only "need" the pill in the same way that we "need" Cadillacs, SSTs or color television sets, and the consumer attitude toward BCPs is very much like that toward such items of conspicuous consumption: if it's available and there is status attached to possessing it, then I have a *right* to have it. Charles Frost lost a job for refusing to refill cancelled BCP prescriptions and learned something about consumer attitudes in the process: "When I told the girls that Dr. —— had cancelled their prescriptions because the pill might cause them to go blind, they had a one word reply—'Bull!' They seemed convinced that I was taking away something that they had a guaranteed right to have. I'm convinced that if I had told them that their dermatologist's prescription for tetracycline had been cancelled because it might give them diarrhea, they would have thanked me." The pill, like the amphetamines and most diuretics, is primarily a social rather than a medical phenomenon.

This is not to say that there are not valid *social* reasons for mass prescription of the pill. Not only has it been a major element in the sexual "liberation" of the last decade, but the pill is probably largely responsible for America's near attainment of zero population growth. On the other hand, however pressing or valid these social needs may appear to be, they must not be confused, as is often the case at present, with actual *medical* needs.

In terms of the prescribing practices of the American physician, this means that a powerful drug is dispensed on a mass basis for what can only be termed a dubious medical "need." The physician is in fact a victim of massive pressure on two fronts—from the drug manufacturer and the drug consumer—to prescribe BCPs to meet a social condition of our society. And rarely does he have the sound pharmacological knowledge to resist this pressure on medical grounds.

SEDATIVES

At the beginning of this chapter I reviewed the many forms in which phenobarbital is available from one drug manufacturer. Although phenobarbital is a useful drug, it is by no means so useful that it would need to be available in such an array of different colors and shapes. In addition to being an antispasmodic used in the treatment of epilepsy, phenobarbital is also a good general purpose sedative, and it is in this latter capacity that it finds the majority of its use in American medicine. Do so many patients in fact require sedation? Not really. The process works something like this:

> George Cavelli, a fifty-two-year-old salesman, goes to his physician with a case of "nerves"—can't sleep soundly, heart seems to be pounding all the time. Yes, that's it, he's sure there's something wrong with his heart. The physician gives Mr. Cavelli a physical examination, finds nothing much amiss. Blood pressure is a little elevated, but nothing serious. All the while, the patient is keeping up a constant patter: "Is it the ticker, huh, doc? I know something's not right in there. . . ." When the physician is through, he realizes that what he has on his hands is a mild hypochrondriac in a reasonably good state of health. After a few moments, he reaches for the prescription pad and writes down a scrawl that few non-pharmacists would be likely to decipher. He is also careful not to check the box at the bottom of the blank where it says, "Label as such." "Here, Mr. Cavelli," he says, handing over the paper, "take this as directed and your heart will be just fine."

When George takes the prescription to a pharmacy he will receive a bottle of tablets or pills in any of several dozen shapes, sizes, colors and coatings. The label will say, "One tablet, twice daily," but it will not bear the name of the drug, nor will the pharmacist legitimately be free to tell George what it is.

Surely you have guessed by this time that George has been given a bottle of phenobarbital, not a "heart medicine" as he will describe it to his friends, but a simple sedative. And it will probably work, too, for a while. It will work until George's mind concocts more "heart pains" and he goes scurrying back to his physician. At this point the rainbow of colors comes in handy because the physician can simply prescribe blue, sugar-coated tablets instead of mottled, plain, compressed tablets, and the psychosomatic effect will be renewed.

This sort of treatment is known as "placebo therapy" (the Latin word means "I will please") and it is disturbingly common in American medicine. Many dentists, for instance, keep three varieties of aspirin on hand: you receive an envelope of white ones after a tooth extraction. If you still complain of pain, you will receive an envelope of green ones; further complaints are handled with pink aspirin tablets. By this time nature will generally have taken care of the pain. In fact, placebo therapy does "work." In one embarrassing study, a placebo capsule filled with milk sugar proved to be more effective than an impressive line-up of pain-relieving preparations. The problem is that such treatment amounts to shotgun therapy when the patient's real problem is psychological and may require professional help.

In addition to drawing attention away from real problems, placebo therapy can be medically dangerous when practiced with real drugs. Phenobarbital, for instance, causes the liver to overproduce certain enzymes. These enzymes may then, in turn, cause the body to rapidly break down other drugs given to the patient. Thus, important therapy may be defeated by a drug which the patient takes so routinely that he does not even regard it as a drug. Also, like the diuretics, phenobarbital may displace other drugs from their binding sites, leading to unplanned fluctuations in the blood level of the second drug. Phenobarbital is not particularly addicting, but some of the related barbituates, such as amobarbital, pentobarbital, and secobarbital, are extremely addicting. In the past these more dangerous compounds were sometimes dispensed interchangeably with phenobarbital, but they are now, fortunately, under federal control.

Twenty-five years ago as much as 30 percent of all prescriptions were for one form of phenobarbital or another. Today the percentage is much lower, although still well above the level that would be dictated by medically necessary use (such as relief of occasional insomnia or control of epilepsy). Instead, if George Cavelli were to walk into his physician's office today, he would most likely walk out with a prescription for a "minor" tranquilizer, such as Librium or Valium. These drugs are mild sedatives which are nevertheless addicting in many cases.

If George were less fortunate, he might even walk out with a prescription for one of the "major" tranquilizers, such as reserpine or phenothiazine derivative. Any pharmacology text would tell George's physician that the "major" tranquilizers are useless for treating simple anxiety states; they are used to modify the behavior of psychotic patients in mental hospitals. In fact, when administered to more or less normal humans, some of these drugs may cause bizarre, belligerent behavior—not exactly what George needs for his nerves. Yet pharmacy investigators suspect that this sort of prescribing represents the largest category of misuse for these drugs. About the only good thing that can be said for these drugs when they are misused in this way is that they are not addicting.

Although there are no nationwide figures available, my personal observation from behind the pharmacy counter suggests that the minor tranquilizers as a group account for a substantial share of all prescriptions. Among women, the percentage seems to be especially high indeed. My suspicions in this area are substantiated by a recent survey conducted in the Chicago area which revealed that some 28 percent of the women interviewed regularly take a minor tranquilizer on prescription. When sedatives, amphetamines, and pain relievers are added to the list, nearly 50 percent of the women were found to be taking one or more of these drugs on prescription. Furthermore, a major women's magazine recently estimated that as many as 75 percent of all housewives take at least one of these "mood-altering" drugs and that three of every four prescriptions written for women are for one of these drugs. On the other hand, apparently only one man in eight takes minor tranquilizers. (Others use the original sedative—alcohol—or resort to illegal drugs, or content themselves with over-the-counter preparations.)

What all the figures point to is a massive overuse—and with it, misuse—of the mood-altering drugs, especially the minor tranquilizers. If one might paraphrase Marx, this sort of "opiate" has virtually become the religion of the people; as one harried executive put it, "Valium has to rank with the invention of the wheel." As the drug of choice for middle-class anxiety, the minor tranquilizers, together with the other mood-altering drugs, have created some severe socio-medical problems. Many of the same people who take mood-altering drugs also engage in "social drinking" and generally regard both the drugs and the drinking as harmless. Individually, mood-altering drugs and alcohol are far from harmless, although most people survive them. Taken together they can be a lethal combination.

Recently a traffic accident occurred near a small midwestern city. Two cars collided head-on under ideal weather conditions, on a straight stretch of road. There were no survivors. Since the driver of one car was a man of local prominence, the city police were reluctant to test for blood alcohol levels. The Highway Patrol, however, was insistent and the tests were conducted. One driver had no blood alcohol level, but the local VIP showed a level of 88 milligrams percent. Since this level is well below the legal definition of drunkenness in this particular state, no further investigation was conducted.

An interview with one local pharmacist, however, produced some disturbing facts. The pharmacist had in his files three prescriptions filled for the VIP driver. Each had been written by a different physician for a different mood-altering drug: two different minor tranquilizers and an analgesic. Combined with alcohol, any one of these drugs could have rendered the driver "bombed out of his mind," as one witness described his condition a short while before the accident.

Drug manufacturers' literature is filled with warnings about such hazards. One states: "Patients should be cautioned against driving or operating machinery since this drug [a minor tranquilizer] may impair mental alertness." Likewise, manufacturers warn against mixing the mood-altering drugs and alcohol. Unfortunately, package inserts usually end up in pharmacists' wastebaskets, and physicians rarely convey adequate warnings to their patients. As a result, accidents such as that detailed above are becoming increasingly common, and comas resulting from the combined effect of these drugs and alcohol show up all too frequently in hospital emergency rooms.

But the minor tranquilizers have not remained the middle-class drugs they were ten years ago. Like almost everything else that can be swallowed, sniffed or injected, they have taken over the street. Not only is Valium an essential relief to drug addicts hard-pressed to keep up the necessary supply of heroin, but it has even penetrated skid-row: a couple of tablets a day serve to prolong the effect of alcohol, making it a wino's delight.

And who supplies the street? Aside from an occasional black market transaction, virtually every tablet sees the light of day through a prescription written by a duly licensed physician. The reasoning behind the speak-easy prescribing of minor tranquilizers seems to go something like this: (1) they are, after all "only" sedatives, (2) we've always prescribed sedatives for "what ails you" (remember the good old days of phenobarbital), so (3) why not just prescribe a minor tranquilizer and be done with it?

Why not indeed? First, because placebo therapy alone has never been a very sound approach to helping patients really overcome their psychological problems. Second, unlike phenobarbital, many of the minor tranquilizers are physically addictive. Third, the minor tranquilizers provide one more path to drug-induced dissociation from reality in a society that has too many such paths already. Millions of people who, for various reasons, would never think of consuming a quart of alcohol per day achieve similar effects from a few tablets prescribed to be "taken as needed."

American physicians desperately need to infuse some of their basic conservatism into their prescribing practices with respect to the mood-altering drugs.

Analgesics: Pain Relievers

In the final category in our survey of drug misprescription we have the analgesics, or pain relievers. The most widely used analgesic is, of course, aspirin. It is cheap, reasonably safe and quite effective. Its use is so widespread and routine that we tend to take it for granted and hardly even consider it a drug. Still, aspirin is capable of working mischief, especially when the physician fails to monitor the patient's total drug intake:

> Judy Mathis twisted her knee while playing touch football in her college physical education class. The next day the knee was sore and swollen, in spite of the aspirin she was taking, so she went to the college health service. There a physician determined that nothing was broken and wrote a prescription "to help it along." Judy had the prescription filled and took it along with her aspirin tablets.
>
> After two weeks the knee was still sore and in addition she was beginning to feel tired and "dragged out," so she returned to the health service. A second physician made a routine examination of the knee and refilled the original prescription.
>
> Two more weeks passed and, although the knee was improv-

ing slowly, Judy was feeling worse and worse, constantly tired and listless. At this point she went home for a weekend and consulted her family physician. When he saw what she had been taking, he immediately placed her in the hospital. The school physician had prescribed a coated tablet containing a large amount of aspirin. Together with her aspirin tablets, Judy had taken the equivalent of over 600 aspirin tablets in 32 days. She was weak from hemorrhaging in the gastrointestinal tract and had the beginnings of an ulcer.

The very commonness of aspirin had lulled not only the patient but two physicians as well into a dangerous complacency.

Although aspirin is an efficient pain reliever by itself, it is commonly combined with other ingredients to form dozens of different "combination of ingredients" drugs. Double blind tests have been inconclusive as to whether these additional ingredients make for improved analgesic action, but they do introduce some medical problems. A case in point is the ingredient phenacetin, long combined with aspirin and caffeine to form the once familiar "APC" tablet. It has been known for at least fifteen years that phenacetin can cause a severe kidney affliction and may lead to blood disorders known as dyscrasias. The Food and Drug Administration has so far seen fit to do nothing about withdrawing phenacetin, although some drug manufacturers, to their credit, have voluntarily removed it from their formulas. Still, numerous pain combinations regularly prescribed by physicians contain this ingredient, which pegs these physicians as being at least fifteen years behind on their pharmacological homework.

When we pass beyond the aspirin level and begin to talk about the strictly prescription analgesics, we enter a different category of drugs entirely. All of the presently known strong analgesics are opiates, and all are addictive. Furthermore it has long been established that there is a direct correlation between analgesic effectiveness and addictiveness: the better it works, the more likely it is to addict. For over a century, pharmaceutical science has attempted to produce a non-addictive analgesic and failed. (Heroin, for instance, is one such attempt.) The conclusion today is that the basic molecular structure which produces strong analgesic effect also produces addiction. Recently there has been promising research with some of the polypeptides, hormone-like compounds produced by the brain, but non-addicting analgesics based on these compounds are at least a decade away. For the present we are left with the incontrovertible fact that all the effective analgesics—from morphine to codeine—are addictive.

From this difficult fact arises perhaps the strangest paradox in medical practice: of all categories of drugs, the opiates alone are typically *underused* by physicians today. This underuse stems from the same source as the *overuse* of most other drugs, that is, from the average physician's superficial knowledge of pharmacology, which prevents him from making rational therapy choices in response to his diagnosis.

> Jeff Deering was a patient in a private hospital for a very painful injury. Since he had been a medical corpsman in Vietnam and his physician knew it, he was allowed to request a dose of analgesic whenever he felt he needed it. For the first twenty-four hours the pain was severe and he requested frequent and large doses of the drug. Then as the pain decreased he took smaller doses at less frequent intervals.
>
> When the dulling effect of the narcotic wore off, Jeff became aware of the eerie moaning from the next room. It was a sound he remembered from the field hospitals in Vietnam, the sound of a man dying from some painful, terminal condition. When he asked the nurse why the man was not being given medication for the pain, she replied: "We can't give him too much. His physician said he might get addicted, so we had to take him off it."

Jeff Deering was astounded by this attitude, but if he had spent very much time in civilian hospitals he would have known that it is more or less normal. Having had it drummed into their collective consciousness for the last half-century or so that all analgesics are addictive, most physicians have a knee-jerk reaction to the problem of addiction. A moment's reflection will reveal a deep-seated fallacy in this attitude: the problem of addiction is largely a social one, since obtaining the drug by illegal means is disruptive of the individual's life pattern. If the patient is a terminal case, bound to die in the near future anyway, then his addiction loses all social, and most medical, significance. In the case of a patient dying of inoperable cancer, the massive use of analgesics is simply common decency.

On the other hand, a patient such as Jeff, with a painful but not very prolonged condition, can generally be trusted to supervise his own analgesic intake. As the pain decreases he will want less and less of the mind-clouding drug and will be off it entirely before physical addiction can set in. Here a rational and an irrational approach to the use of analgesics were put into action by two physicians treating patients in adjacent rooms of the same hospital.

From these six categories of drugs, then, all but a miniscule fraction of prescriptions are written. The drugs themselves are an incredibly varied lot in terms of action, safety and side effects. The one thing they have in common is that they are all prescribed with about an equal level of disregard for their true medical function and utility. Quite clearly, most physicians in practice today are not managing to fill their dual roles of diagnostician and manipulator of the patient's condition. Instead, most physicians seem to have chosen—not consciously and often merely by default—to simplify their professional lives by relaxing their critical faculties in the area of drug choices. Given the strengths and weaknesses of their professional education, it is predictable that this should be so; nor does the existing professional hierarchy in American medicine leave the physician much choice.

4 The Information Gap: DRUGS, THE CONSUMER AND HOW THEY GET TOGETHER

A prescription is a little like the Brooklyn Bridge: just when you think you know who owns it, somebody else turns up with a claim of proprietorship. At first, the prescription exists as a confluence of observations and prior knowledge in the mind of the physician. Having gone through the mental gymnastics of selecting a course of treatment for your condition, he writes down his cogitations in the form of a prescription.

Once the prescription is in the patient's possession, it becomes, at least partly, his property, but this scrap of paper has no real value until it is surrendered to the pharmacist for filling. At this point the prescription becomes part of the pharmacist's files, where it must remain for varying periods of time depending on state or federal law. The pharmacist then becomes a part owner of the prescription as its custodian. (In pharmaceutical practice prescriptions are seldom destroyed or disposed of except by accident.) During this time the prescription may be subpoenaed by various regulatory agencies, but at all times the physician remains legally responsible for directing the use of the drugs prescribed. The pharmacist acts as a sort of valve, turning the supply off or on at the physician's discretion. Further, although the patient/consumer "buys" the medication in the same way he buys a roll of film or bar of soap elsewhere in the drugstore, it cannot legally be returned in the same way as the film or soap, once it has left the premises. (Some pharmacists do make exchanges or refunds, but the medication, to be legally correct, cannot be returned to his shelf and be resold.)

By convention the prescription is written on a rectangular piece of paper approximately 4 by 5 inches in size, although this is not a legal requirement. In my years behind the prescription counter

I have seen prescriptions written on all manner of materials: the backs of letters, on envelopes, on receipts (one for the purchase of a physician's new Cadillac), matchbook covers and the like. One unusual one was written for a physician's hunting companion on a regular prescription blank but, lacking a pen or pencil, the man had used the lead tip of a .22 calibre bullet!

Despite the fact that prescriptions may be written on any sort of handy material, they are generally written on some sort of pre-printed blank. The information these blanks contain tells a good deal about whose finger is in the prescription pie. The prescriptions in figures 1 and 2 came from a large group-practice clinic. Except for a few newcomers, the names of all the physicians currently practicing at the clinic are printed at the top of the blank. This listing, however, is of little practical value in trying to decipher the signature at the bottom of the blank. The list is not alphabetical, but in order of seniority; consequently it is fair to assume that it is printed solely for the status-enhancement of the physicians involved. It is certainly no help to the pharmacist whose file is customarily designed to accommodate the standard 4 by 5-inch blanks within narrow limits. Consequently, he must either fold this blank in half, effectively reducing the nominal capacity of his file from 1000 to about 700, or cut off the top of the blank. If he takes the latter course, he frequently cuts off the date as well.

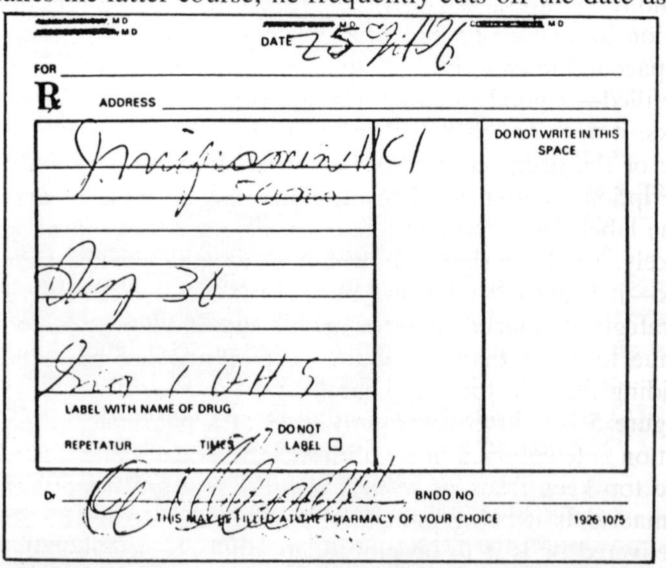

Figure 1. Prescription A (blank used by a group-practice clinic; physicians listing partially omitted).

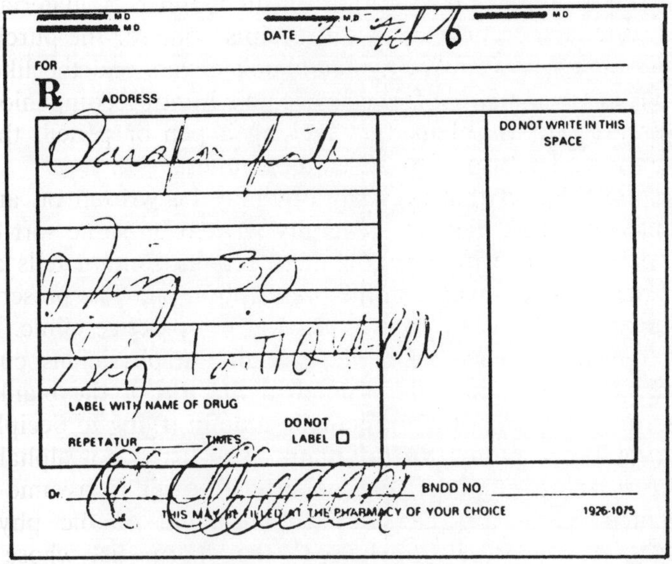
DATE

FOR

℞ ADDRESS

DO NOT WRITE IN THIS SPACE

LABEL WITH NAME OF DRUG

REPETATUR TIMES

DO NOT LABEL ☐

Dr BNDD NO.

THIS MAY BE FILLED AT THE PHARMACY OF YOUR CHOICE

1926-1075

Figure 2. Prescription B (bottom portion).

The prescription blank in figure 3 (from a physician in private practice) is more or less standard, bearing the physician's name, telephone number, address and narcotics registry number. In addition to a space to indicate the number of refills desired, there is a space to indicate the time span over which the prescription may be refilled—a good practice. On the other hand, unlike the clinic blanks, it does not routinely instruct the pharmacist to include the name of the drug on the finished label. It is a safe bet that most prescriptions written by this physician end up with no drug name on the label. Does the physician himself have these forms printed? Unlikely. Look at figure 4, which shows the reverse side of the blank—it bears the logo and name of a local pharmacy. This bit of strategically placed advertising will undoubtedly bring in enough revenue to more than offset the cost of printing the blanks and providing them to the physician.

Figure 5 is a form commonly used at a pharmacy when a prescription is telephoned in by a physician. The easily checked boxes at the top keep track of several matters that are important to the pharmacist. Is it being paid for by Medicare-Medicaid? Should it be delivered or is it to be picked up, and when? The "SIG" midway down the blank marks the spot for the physician's instructions

Figures 3 and 4. Front and back of prescription blank used by physician in private practice.

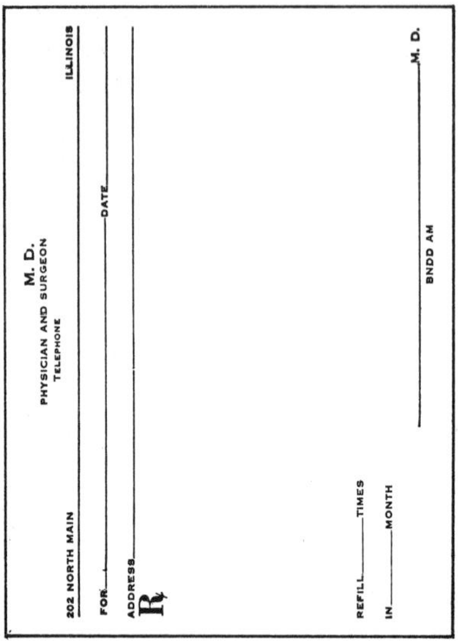

202 NORTH MAIN

M. D.
PHYSICIAN AND SURGEON
TELEPHONE

ILLINOIS

FOR ______ DATE ______

ADDRESS ______

℞

REFILL ______ TIMES

IN ______ MONTH

BNDD AM ______ M. D.

mini pharmacies
YOUR REXALL STORES
ILL.

Figure 5. Blank used by a pharmacy for telephoned prescriptions.

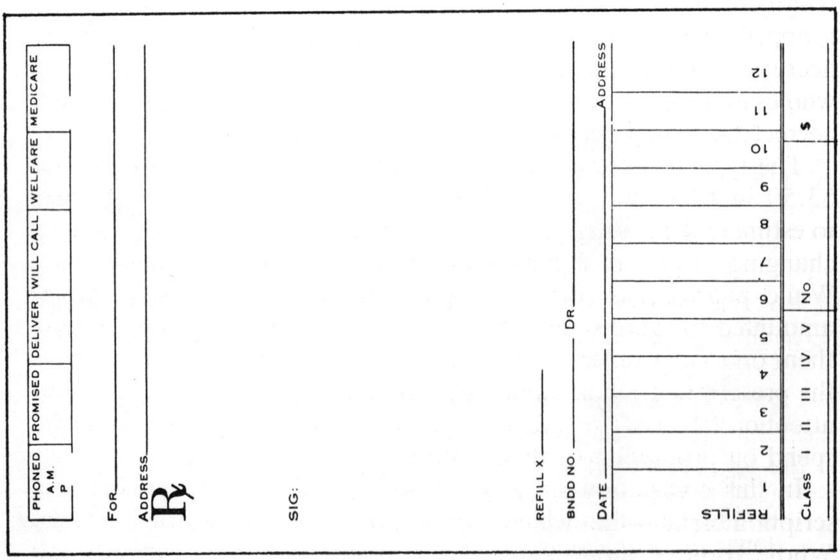

PHONED A.M. P	PROMISED	DELIVER	WILL CALL	WELFARE	MEDICARE

FOR ______

ADDRESS ______

℞

SIG:

REFILL X ______

BNDD NO. ______ DR ______

DATE ______ ADDRESS ______

REFILLS 1 2 3 4 5 6 7 8 9 10 11 12

CLASS I II III IV V No $

to the patient—it helps the pharmacist to get these in detail and isolate them from other information that may cause confusion. Note that there is no space to indicate a time limit next to the refill blank, but there is space at the bottom to record up to *twelve* refills: the pharmacist naturally wants as much repeat business as possible.

The "Class" box at the bottom concerns the narcotics controls placed on certain drugs. Classes I and II (drugs with the "greatest potential for abuse") cannot be prescribed by telephone—the pharmacist must have a legal prescription "in hand" before releasing them. Some pharmacists, however, will dispense such drugs on the strength of a telephone call and trust that the physician will supply a legitimate prescription later. It is illegal, but it means another sale: Listing classes III, IV and V is useful to the pharmacist since there are legal restrictions regarding storage, refilling and a host of other things that do not pertain to other drugs. The "NO." box provides a uniform location for the prescription number that enables him to retrieve and identify a prescription.

Finally, the $——— box is a matter of providing a uniform location for pricing information. Contrary to popular thinking, prescription prices are not often changed once they are established for a given, numbered prescription. However, things have changed in recent years. Whereas the market prices of drugs remained relatively stable during the last twenty-five years—prices either dropped or increased very slightly—we are now seeing few price decreases and many price increases. It is common practice for wholesale drug outlets to supply supplemental price listings which correct the computer-generated line item extension prices.

The typical prescription cost a consumer, on the average, about $3.50 in 1950 and about $4.00 in 1970. Today there is no way to estimate the average prescription price since pharmacists are now changing prices on a day-by-day basis to reflect increased costs. While pharmacists used to absorb increased costs, which never amounted to more than a matter of pennies, they are now passing them on to consumers. It is beyond the scope of this description of the prescription blank to elaborate further, other than to draw your attention to the $1 of every $4 taken in which drug manufacturers spend on promotion of their products.

In this connection we might mention still another type of prescription blank—that which is preprinted by the drug manufacturer. Whole pads of these blanks are supplied to the physician, with prescriptions for certain heavily-prescribed drugs already printed on them (tranquilizers, birth control pills and diuretics are often in this category). All the physician does is sign his name and (ideally) fill in the patient's name, address, and the date.

In short, the prescription blank—whether it comes from the clinic, the pharmacy, the physician or the drug manufacturer—is designed and printed primarily as a piece of professional advertising and only secondarily as a device for transmitting vital health care information. As such, the prescription blank actually bears a stronger socio-economic kinship to the business card or the letterhead than it does to, say, the punch card or the computer data tape. And small wonder. Use of the prescription as a device to control drug therapy has followed no rational pattern. It has simply been there since the days of the black-robed medieval physician and the apothecary or herbalist huddled in his back-alley shop filled with garbled herbs and bottles of malodorous tinctures. The working prescription has been more or less standardized by custom, but very little of it is controlled by law, or even by codified standards of practice. Certainly it cannot be said that it evolved to meet the needs of the time. In consequence, the reading and filling of prescriptions really is something of a black art—a mixture of experience, medical judgment, intuition and educated guessing.

Fraud, Forgery and Other Diversions

The legal requirements as to what information must appear on a prescription vary widely from state to state. The one thing that must always appear is the signature of the physician, dentist, osteopath or veterinarian, and, generally, the patient's name and address are required. (In the case of veterinary prescriptions the animal's name and species are generally mandated as well.) Beyond this, some states require a brief "description" of the patient (age, sex, weight, height or the like). When it comes to the actual prescription, the prescriber is on his own as far as designating the drug and how it is to be used.

It may come as a surprise to many, but prescriptions are almost never written in Latin, although I recall a recent one, written by a physician who didn't want his patient to know what he was taking, for "Acidum Acetylsalicylicum" (translated: acetylsalicylic acid or generally—now—aspirin. "Aspirin" was originally Bayer-Farben's trade name). Still, certain abbreviations of Latin phrases are used as a standard shorthand. For instance, b.i.d., t.i.d., and q.i.d. stand, respectively, for *bis in die* (twice daily), *ter in die* (three times daily) and *quator in die* (four times daily).

The valid information contained in the body of a prescription is expressed in four basic blocks: (1) the name of the drug, (2) the size and form of dose, (3) how many doses are to be dispensed, (4) how, when and how often the drug is to be taken. Under the best circumstances only three people handle a prescription: physician, pharmacist, and patient. Under certain conditions, however, the seven bits of information contained in the four blocks may be subject to interpretation by six (or more) individuals, making a minimum of forty-two points at which errors may creep in.

Under the best of conditions the pharmacist works overtime to gather the information needed to simply comply with the letter of the law. It is almost normal for the patient's name and address to be missing or incomplete, and at times even the "core information" of the prescription may be hopelessly garbled—as well as being essentially illegible. The pharmacist is generally the one who must make good on these information failures. Beyond the fact that the pharmacist—who ordinarily fills a minimum of 100 prescriptions in an eight-hour day—could do very nicely without the demands of such "busywork" on his time, there is a more important consideration involved in this haphazard collection of information: While the physician may know his patient quite well in a vital-statistical way (he must, in order to bill for his services), the pharmacist often does not know him from Adam. Consequently, even though the pharmacist gathers the required information about the patient, he has no way of knowing how the data applies; the person shuffling about on the other side of the counter may only be a neighbor of the person for whom the medication is intended. Unless he knows the patient personally, the pharmacist must constantly weigh intuitional character judgments against the danger of social popularity of the drug involved. An average person finding a prescription fluttering down the street might pick it up and deposit it in a trash container (if one were handy), but more likely he wouldn't notice it at all. On the other hand, a heroin addict finding an unfilled Valium prescription in a stolen wallet will probably use the prescription to obtain a supply of the drug. Even if he doesn't use it himself, he knows he can sell or trade it on the street to obtain a drug he can use.

Just in case you doubt that there could be much of a supply of unfilled prescriptions around, let me simply add that various authorities have estimated that between 20 and 40 percent of all prescriptions written in America are never filled by the person for whom they were written. How many of these prescriptions are subsequently filled by another person for his own use is anybody's guess, but the possibilities are frightening: in a single afternoon's stroll around a large midwestern clinic, I was able to pick up no fewer than thirty-five discarded prescriptions from the street, gutters and trash cans—and I only gathered those that were in plain view.

If a pharmacist fills a fraudulent prescription, he is the one held responsible. It is true that the individual bringing the fraudulent prescription to the pharmacist faces possible legal penalties, but the pharmacist faces the possible loss of his professional license. This tends to make him cautious to the point of being chronically suspicious of anything that appears to be out of the ordinary. The most seemingly inconsequential deviations—things the average person would never think of, let alone see—will cause his threshold of suspicion to plummet. In a way, filling a prescription involves balancing bits of information against one another, and though this may sound like the sort of operation a computer performs, you should know how different it really is.

Perhaps the most important key to a prescription is the physician's signature at the bottom of the blank. This signature is generally the only direct evidence contained in the prescription relative to its origin and authenticity. Depending on where he is doing business, the pharmacist must keep in his head the general appearance of the variable signatures of from a few dozen to several hundred physicians. Nor is this all: many office nurses write and sign routine prescriptions—if it can be said that any prescription is merely routine—for patients who have previously been seen by the physician. This means that the pharmacist must also be able to recognize the signatures of local physicians as written by their nurses, as well as being able to verify the authenticity of the nurse's initials which sometimes follow such a surrogate signature. Even this is not the end of the matter since a substantial percentage of all prescriptions are telephoned to the pharmacy—the pharmacist must be able to reliably recognize the voices of the local physicians and, more frequently, of their office personnel.

At first glance such a willy-nilly set-up would appear to be a forger's paradise. As a matter of fact, no one contends that the prescription system is foolproof, nor that it is impossible to obtain drugs by prescription illegally, nor that this is not actually done. A combination of factors, however, tends to make these control deficiencies self-limiting. An important factor is that most of the popular drugs in the illicit market—heroin, cocaine, marihuana, LSD—are not part of the prescription drug market anyway. Those potent, and more popular, street drugs such as Dilaudid, methadone, barbiturates, and amphetamines, which *are* prescription items, are now subject to stringent federal and state controls: a prescription for any one of these which was scribbled on any available piece of paper would immediately be suspect. In some states special forms are required, but the real deterrent is that such prescriptions are filed separately at the pharmacy. This makes them more "visible" and the pharmacist knows that this file will be the first one scrutinized if a state or federal inspector arrives on the scene and asks to see the prescription files. The only other prescription drugs that see much street use are the tranquilizers, some sedatives and certain "reducing pills," and, as was detailed in the last chapter, it is so easy to obtain a legitimate prescription for these drugs that forgery is hardly necessary.

Although the memory and suspicions of the pharmacist provide a certain braking effect on illicit prescription drug use, it is actually the "speak-easy" prescribing practices of the typical American physician which prevent the limitations of the prescription system from being severely tested with regard to forged prescriptions. Drug abuse expert Sidney Cohen has noted that many an addict has obtained a quick—and legal—prescription for opiates by doing a good imitation of someone with renal colic. For less controversial drugs (note that I did not say less addictive), less dramatic methods generally suffice—in most cases, simply asking for a prescription is all that is required.

I still recall, without much amusement, an incident of prescription fraud which involved me some years back. One evening I was behind the counter of a small pharmacy when a man I had never seen before hobbled up to the counter. Clearly in pain, he was doubled over with his hand clasped over the general area of his right kidney. He had, he claimed, just come from a physician's office and would I please hurry with his prescription—he was "really hurting." I became suspicious at once because, although the prescription (for the opiate Dilaudid) appeared to bear the correct signature, the physician was an older man who no longer held evening office hours. When I called his office, however, it was the physician who answered the phone. "Oh yes," he explained, "I had a desk covered with paperwork." The patient had come knocking at the door and since he was a stranger, the physician hesitated, but "He was holding the area of his left kidney like it was going to explode," the physician went on, "so I prescribed the Dilaudid to tide him over. Renal colic; you know how it is." When I told the physician that the patient had come to the pharmacy holding the area of his *right* kidney, he was silent for a moment. Then he said grimly, "O.K., give him the 'one tablet' treatment." I did.

In the prescription vial I placed just one Dilaudid tablet, but I charged him the full price for the prescription. As is usual in such cases, the man paid for the prescription and hurriedly left without looking at the bottle. A few minutes later he was back.

"Hey," he said, "there's only one tablet in here and you charged me four bucks for it."

"That's right," I replied, looking him straight in the eye.

He grinned sheepishly, turned and almost ran out into the night. Neither I nor the physician ever saw him again.

This sort of treatment may seem shoddy to outside observers, but it is one way in which some pharmacists and some physicians try to keep the lid on prescription drug fraud.

Getting the Right Drug in the Right Form

The most important failure of the prescription system, however, does not concern its inability to control fraud, forgery or other drug diversions—in this respect it somehow manages, like the British Empire, to "muddle through." The true shortcomings of the prescription system occur at two points, where it makes contact with the professional actions of the physician and the pharmacist:

> *Case 1:* When Susan Bachman complained of general nervousness, inability to relax, and insomnia, her physician wrote a prescription for "Combid tab. 10 mg, Sig: 1 Qid." Combid, a long-acting combination of an antispasmodic, isopropamide, and a phenothiazine tranquilizer, is not manufactured as a 10 milligram tablet. It *is* produced as a timed-release capsule containing 10 milligrams of the tranquilizer and a smaller amount of isopropamide and is intended for twice daily administration—the "bid" portion of the trade name reflects this. Two pharmacists, unable to receive a telephone clarification of the prescription from the physician, refused to fill it. A third pharmacist, who

didn't even bother contacting the physician, filled it using the capsule.

After taking the medication for two weeks, Mrs. Bachman was rushed to the hospital in oculogyric crisis, a grotesque and painful condition in which the neck muscles spasmodically wrench the head to one side, the eyes roll back and the tongue lolls. The condition could have been expected in this case because the phenothiazine in the combination has been a documented offender for two decades, and the dose here was about double what is normally prescribed. Most physicians do not prescribe it for simple anxiety in any case.

The physician who wrote this strange prescription has a reputation among local pharmacists for pharmacological ambiguity. He often changes his mind in the middle of writing a prescription and, rather than start over, he writes over, scratches out and generally makes hash of the prescription. Alternatively, he may confuse drug names and mix doses and dose forms, which is what happened in the case of the Bachman prescription. To the casual observer this would seem to be a situation guaranteed to create continual chaos and result in endless malpractice litigation. In fact Dr. Shannigan's garbled prescriptions were generally filled in a more or less acceptable manner for an outrageously simple reason: Shannigan owned a building which housed a drugstore owned, on paper, by his nephew; and Shannigan telephoned nearly all his prescriptions there. The pharmacists at Shannigan's store "understood" him and took it upon themselves to correct his prescribing errors as a matter of routine. Had Mrs. Bachman's prescription gone there, one of the pharmacists would simply have changed the dosage form from tablet to capsule and the dose from four a day to two a day. As it was, however, the prescription was written on a weekend, when Shannigan's store was closed.

When the other pharmacists in the community received the Bachman prescription, they were faced with the following dilemma: the prescription was obviously in error because of the contradictions; Shannigan, when telephoned by the pharmacists, refused to discuss the matter. The choices open to the pharmacists were thus: (1) Refuse to fill the prescription, (2) alter the prescription to conform with the manufacturer's recommended dosage (illegal), (3) fill the prescription as written as nearly as possible by using capsules instead of tablets (hazardous). The first two pharmacists to whom Mrs. Bachman took the prescription opted for choice

(1); they considered choices (2) and (3) to be professionally unacceptable since they entailed violating state laws and, with regard to (3) particularly, unacceptable risks for the patient. The third pharmacist opted for choice (3).

This turned out to be injudicious and short-sighted, for legal as well as medical reasons: not only did Mrs. Bachman develop serious side effects, but the pharmacist exposed himself to the prospect of being named co-defendant in any resulting malpractice action against Dr. Shannigan. Recent court decisions have established that *any* individual who "can be expected to know better" must take appropriate corrective action in the event of ill-conceived treatment, or share liability for its adverse outcome. (Just how far this protocol will be extended is not yet clear, but it obviously pertains to nurses, pharmacists and physicians.) Later on we will examine in detail the reasons why this doctrine of shared liability has not yet led to any dramatic increase in the pharmacist's therapeutic input. For the time being, it will suffice to note that Shannigan vented his spleen to the employers of the two pharmacists who had refused to fill his prescription. As a result, one pharmacist was fired outright; the other, who had been filling in part-time, was informed that the "rush" was over and his services were no longer required.

Needless to say, the percentage of prescriptions which contain errors as serious as those in Mrs. Bachman's is not large—a fact which is of no comfort at all to the patient who is injured by such an error. What is more disturbing, to the point of being frightening, is that the pharmacist—if he detects the error at all—often has no way of consulting the physician who wrote the prescription. We all have a pretty clear notion of how difficult it is to get hold of a physician and talk to him or her directly, which is what is needed for any sort of meaningful consultation. Not only are there generally at least two people blocking access—the office secretary and the office nurse—but physicians, being "busy" people, have priorities as to which calls they will bother to return. A pharmacist calling for a consultation usually ranks somewhere between the Fuller Brush man and a third cousin in Podunk who needs another loan to cover his gambling losses. The pharmacist, to a great many physicians, is a threat to his dominant position on the medical "team." He is not used to sharing the task of determining safe and effective therapeutic regimens; consequently, a call from a pharmacist is almost always interpreted as a signal that he, the physician, has failed—he erred.

The Misty Regions of Dosage Instructions

Obviously, physicians, like all other mortals, are subject to error, and at times the errors have virtually nothing to do with pharmacology:

> *Case 2:* Gerald Silverman has practiced as a pediatrician for some twenty-six years and, like most of his colleagues, has developed certain preferences in prescribing. Apparently out of concern for the problems of dosing small children, Silverman is fond of prescribing liquid medications. Where more than one medication is required, he routinely orders that the drugs be combined in a single bottle by the pharmacist. For one seven-year-old suffering from an upper respiratory infection and sore throat, he wrote a prescription for the mixing of equal parts of three preparations: a cough suppressant, an anthistamine-decongestant and an antibiotic. The pharmacist who received the prescription was puzzled: the usual dose for *each* of the medications involved, for a seven-year-old, would be one teaspoonful four times a day. Mixing equal parts of the medications and giving one teaspoonful of the resultant mixture would mean that the dose of each had been reduced to 1/3 teaspoon. In the case of the cough suppressant and the anthistamine-decongestant the results would be of little consequence. Subtherapeutic doses of the antibiotic, however, can lead to the emergence of resistant organisms. Worse yet, if the throat condition was caused by an organism known as a Group A streptococcus, failure to finish off the organism could lead to later complications such as rheumatic fever and a damaging kidney condition known as glomerulonephritis. It sometimes takes years for these complications to show up, and by that time the damage is done.
>
> A telephone call to the physician was an exercise in frustration: the error was so elementary that he could not seem to grasp the significance of the problem and he cut the call short by demanding that the pharmacist fill the prescription exactly the way it was written. Since the pharmacist was a social acquaintance of the child's father, he took the professionally dangerous step of filling the prescription and then explaining the problem in detail to him.

Even under the best of circumstances, dosage instructions are usually the most confusing part of a prescription. It is not at all unusual for a physician to write "One or two tablets, three or four times daily, or as needed." In the event of a drug reaction or interaction, the emergency room physician treating a patient who has been taking a prescription thus labeled is faced with the not-too-comforting fact that the victim may have been taking from zero to eight doses a day. There is even a pretty good chance that *more* than eight doses a day have been consumed.

Most physicians assume that "as needed" translates as "less often if the need does *not* arise." Most patients, however, interpret the phrase to indicate: "*more* often, in the event you feel the need." Over-the-counter drugs, be they laxatives, cough preparations or headache remedies, carry carefully worded warnings as to the maximum daily dose and the length of time over which it is safe for them to be consumed. But it is almost unheard of for a physician to include a warning such as "Do not exceed eight tablets in a 24-hour period," despite the fact that prescription drugs, are, by simple definition, more dangerous than anything sold over the counter (except alcoholic beverages).

There is another situation which is potentially more hazardous than faulty semantics in prescription instructions, and that is no instructions at all. Oh, there is always something there, usually "as directed," "as needed," or something equally meaningless. This usually means that as the physician scribbled the prescription, he simultaneously muttered, "Take two of these four times a day and apply the cream twice a day." By the time the consumer gets his prescriptions filled and arrives home, the odds are better than even that his memory will have him taking two of the tablets twice a day and applying the cream four times a day. Beyond this, a prescription with such instructions is almost completely immune to the scrutiny of even the most conscientious pharmacist. Under these circumstances there is no way the pharmacist can double-check the physician's instructions—either to protect the consumer from injury or himself from legal entanglement if the physician has made an error.

Among pharmacists (privately, of course) there is a wraith of suspicion that some physicians use the catchall "as directed" to ensure that there will be no scrutiny of their therapeutic adventures. There is at least a grain of truth behind this suspicion, as any emergency room physician could—if he would—testify, but the important point is that the current system of prescribing allows the individual physician to insulate himself from scrutiny by other professionals. It appears to make little difference that that scrutiny is intended to protect him as well as the consumer.

When the prescription system is working "normally," how effective is it? Does it assure that consumers take the prescribed drugs properly? One study, conducted by a group of clinical pharmacists, was not particularly encouraging. Five groups of consumers, each of which had been prescribed one of five common drugs, were interviewed concerning the manner in which they actually took the medication. In every case the prescription label bore a complete set of instructions (none were of the ambiguous "as directed" variety), yet, depending on the drug and the consumer's understanding of his treatment, from 9 to 35 percent of them had failed to take the medication as prescribed. Taking into account that a consumer who has failed to follow instructions is likely to conceal his "default," it seems safe to assume that the true rate of default in the "real world" could easily be twice that documented by this survey. Overall, a conservative "guesstimate," based on my experience behind the prescription counter, would be that *half* of all the drugs prescribed in the United States are not taken by the consumer in the manner the physician intended.

At times, too, the physician's directions—even though they appear superficially to be rational—are of questionable value to the consumer. The manner in which a great many asthmatics are instructed to take their medications is a case in point:

> *Case 3:* Billy Chavez is a four-year-old asthmatic. The first symptoms developed while his father was serving in the armed forces overseas. It took a while, but his condition was eventually diagnosed by a military physician. The medication prescribed in this case was a popular preparation containing theophylline, ephedrine, and a small amount of phenobarbital. Most states allow the purchase of this combination without a prescription and it is generally quite effective. As seems to happen with most asthmatics taking this medication, however, Billy continued to have attacks, and they nearly always occurred in the wee hours of the morning.
>
> When Billy's mother asked her pharmacist if a stronger preparation were available, one which might prevent the "residual," as she put it, early morning attacks, he very wisely avoided the issue of "stronger" versus "more effective" medication. Instead he countered by asking Mrs. Chavez the circumstances under which she administered the medication. Sometimes a parent will

give the medication only when it appears the child is about to have an attack, but this was not the case; Mrs. Chavez replied that she gave the medication exactly as the physician had indicated. She gave Billy a dose four times a day, and since mealtimes and bedtimes were convenient, this was when he was dosed: in other words, at roughly 8:00 A.M., 12 noon, 5:30 P.M., and 8:30 P.M. This left a gap of some twelve hours between the night and morning dose, and the pattern of Billy's attacks indicated that the drug effects had "worn off." He was literally out of control of the medication for a period of several hours.

There is a long-acting preparation available, but it is a fairly large tablet that must be swallowed whole, and Billy had not learned this technique, so the pharmacist recommended that Mrs. Chavez space the doses more evenly. Now that Billy gets his medication at 7:00 A.M., 1:00 P.M., 7:00 P.M., and 1:00 A.M., he rarely is bothered by the asthma. A full-blown attack may occur every six months, but he has gone without one for nearly a year now.

In this instance the pharmacist was on fairly safe ground in offering his advice. For one thing, the physician involved was not a local practitioner; he was located in an Air Force hospital 6,000 miles away. Secondly, although the drug in question is commonly prescribed by physicians, it happens to be a non-prescription item in the state where this incident occurred. Consequently, physicians feel less jealously protective of their "rights" in controlling its use; and a concerned mother would feel more comfortable in consulting a pharmacist about problems encountered with a drug that is so easily available.

Look-Alike, Sound-Alike Drugs

In most cases the entire process of information transfer effected by a prescription is so vague that the consumer may not have the faintest notion of where to begin when it comes to working out what went wrong:

Case 4: Elaine Carlson visited her gynecologist for her annual Pap smear. As the smear was being taken she engaged her physician in a conversation regarding another problem. She had stopped smoking after moving to the Midwest from Texas the year before, but she was still bothered by a nagging cough and congestion—"It sometimes takes an hour of hacking to get rid of the 'gunk' that seems to build up overnight." After asking more about symptoms—headache, nasal stuffiness, stiffness of neck and tightness of muscles in that general area—which often accompanied her cough, the gynecologist obligingly wrote her a prescription for an antihistamine for "symptomatic relief." Because of his specialty, this physician seldom had occasion to prescribe antihistimines, and he had to search his memory for the name of one. When he finally recalled one, Teldrin, he could not remember who manufactured it, whether it came as a tablet or capsule, or what the proper dose should be, so he simply ordered twenty and directed that they be taken "as needed for pnd"—his idea of a proper abbreviation for "post nasal drip."

When Mrs. Carlson stopped by her neighborhood drugstore, she decided she might as well have the prescription filled. It couldn't hurt and might help. The pharmacist glanced at the piece of paper and snorted in disgust. The handwriting on the prescription was abominable; it was so bad he could not easily decipher the name of the drug, and the idiosyncratic abbreviation "pnd" certainly didn't look like anything he had ever seen before. After some cogitation, the "pnd" scribble was translated as "pain." He knew that this particular physician was partial to the analgesic "Talwin," so it was an easy step to assume that pain and Talwin belonged together. As a result the prescription was filled using Talwin, and the label read: "Take as needed for pain."

Several days later, Mrs. Carlson awoke with a severe headache which did not respond to the usual two tablet dose of aspirin—in fact, it seemed to get worse. She knew full well that the skull is bone and that it couldn't really expand, but she felt as though it had ballooned. At this point she remembered the prescription bottle that was still in her purse. Retrieving the bottle, she saw the phrase "for pain" and without hesitation downed one of the tablets. An hour later the pain was even more severe and she felt as though, as she explained later, "It was forcing me out of my body." She began to have perceptual hallucinations—a frightening experience at best. Fortunately, a neighbor came to visit and, seeing Mrs. Carlson's condition, bundled her off to the nearest hospital's emergency room. The examining physician, having no idea as to the cause of Elaine's bizarre symptoms, gave her a complete examination, including a spinal tap. By the time he was done, the effects of the drug had begun to wear off, and, since there appeared to be nothing amiss, he let her go with the caution to "take it easy for a couple of days and call me if anything unusual happens."

In considering this case it would be easy to get sidetracked on the issue of whether or not the drug Talwin should even be allowed to remain on the market at all. Its incidence of side effects is thought to run as high as 20 percent, and the pattern, all too often, is very much like what happened to Elaine Carlson: the pain is intensified and central nervous symptoms ranging from simple drowsiness to frankly psychotic, suicidal behavior develop. As in this case, these alarming effects usually resolve themselves as the drug disappears from the bloodstream, a matter of a few hours. Mrs. Carlson, however, was left to endure several days of ghastly headaches, a result of the spinal tap, not to mention a bill for over $100 in emergency room fees.

The implication instead is this: under any reasonable system of information transfer, Mrs. Carlson would have known what drug she was supposed to get. Furthermore, she would have received the correct medication in the first place. Her physician would not have been content to prescribe whatever antihistamine he could remember by name, and her pharmacist would not have had to work from a dubious and undecipherable prescription. Finally, no matter what drug she received, she would have known why she was consuming it and what she might expect of it.

As it was, it was her great misfortune to be ensnared in a chain of errors with whose consequences she was completely unprepared to cope. She was caught like a rat in a trap when: (1) her physician prescribed outside his area of expertise; (2) her physician's arrogance and prejudice kept him from looking up information he needed but didn't have at hand; (3) her pharmacist, faced with an ineptly written prescription that he couldn't adequately decipher, foolishly did the best job of deduction he was capable of doing (his culpability was inexcusable and bordered on criminal negligence); (4) her physician had isolated himself, making it difficult for pharmacists to consult him—he was almost in quarantine; (5) her physician failed to take her into his confidence concerning the exact nature of the prescription; (6) she had to endure several hours of horrifying psychic aberration; and (7) she was subjected to well-meaning, but unnecessary emergency room treatment—had she been able to tell the examining physician what drug she had taken, he could have been less concerned about the possibility of, among other things, a "stroke."

Talwin and Teldrin are by no means the only pair of look-alike, sound-alike drugs a pharmacist must beware of confusing. Papaverine and pavatrine are a couple of old-timers that used to be regularly confused; chlordiazepoxide (a minor tranquilizer) is sometimes confused with chloramphenicol (an antibiotic), and chlorpromazine (a major tranquilizer) has been known to be dispensed in place of chlorpheniramine (an antihistamine). It is common practice for pharmaceutical journals to publish lists headed, "One Hundred Drugs Most Commonly Misread" or "Fifty Potentially Lethal Mistakes in Prescription Interpretation." Probably the all-time classic list was published in *Pharmacy Times* (March, 1971) and since reprinted in a standard textbook dealing with clinical pharmacy. It contains *700* look-alike/sound-alike drugs! Below are a dozen pairs of drugs from this list. I have placed the general use of the drug in parenthesis after each name; even if you are not a health care professional you will have little difficulty imagining the sort of mischief that could result from any one of these mix-ups.

Ambenyl (antihistamine)—Aventyl (psychic stimulant)
Ananase (proteolytic enzyme)—Orinase (insulin substitute)
Bentyl (antispasmodic)—Aventyl (psychic stimulant)
Chloromycetin (antibiotic)—Chlor-Trimeton (antihistamine)
Compazine (major tranquilizer)—Compocillin (antibiotic)
Daricon (antispasmodic)—Darvon (analgesic)
Demerol (opiate-analgesic)—Dicumarol (anticoagulant)
Dilantin (antepileptic)—Delalutin (hormone)
Diuril (diuretic)—Doriden (sedative)
Donnatal (antispasmodic)—Dianabol (hormone)
Doriden (sedative)—Doxidan (laxative)
Dyrenium (antihypertensive)—Pyridium (urinary analgesic)

Frightening though such lists may be, it's a sad fact that they are of little practical value—the printed word is of little use when it comes to comparing the look-alike that is scribbled or the sound-alike that is garbled. Another factor that will be discussed later in the chapter is the time "crunch"—even if a pharmacist had a cautionary list close at hand, he would be hard-pressed to make use of it as he frantically scrambles to fill as many prescriptions as quickly as he possibly can.

There are times when even the most hard-boiled pharmacist contemplates the prescription system in astonishment, wondering how it manages to deliver the desired end result, in spite of a nightmare tangle of bewildering, and, all too often, meaningless inconsistencies. As with a nonsensical Rube Goldberg device, it may be a long and tortuous path from the cry of the baby to actuation of the mechanical hand that rocks the cradle, with endless opportunities for disaster along the way. It is small comfort that most people believe that the system is generally effective, because it is a fact that no one really knows how well things are going. Most health care professionals, figuring that they can look out for themselves, don't want anyone rocking the boat; more than one has privately admitted fear at what might crawl out if the rock were turned over.

Sometimes the System Works

Still there are bright spots, areas in which the prescription system manages to work quite well indeed. The best example I know of such an area to be viewed with optimism is one involving the glycosides of digitalis. There are several of these compounds, but there are two that are very popular: digoxin and digitoxin. Both are venerable and still very useful in the treatment of certain heart conditions. From the clinical point of view, one essential concern when it comes to the prescription of any digitalis preparation is the precise regulation of dose. The drug has a very narrow "therapeutic range." That is, there is a very small difference between the size of an effective dose and a toxic dose. With most drugs there is only a look-alike or a sound-alike hazard, but with digoxin and digitoxin there are both. It would seem that dangerous mix-ups would be common. As a matter of fact, they are not, and there are a variety of reasons for this, but none of them have very much to do with any error-resistant qualities inherent in the prescription system.

One factor that tends to keep the digitalis preparations from being confused is the peculiarity of dose size. Digitoxin is generally made available as tablets of 0.05, 0.1, 0.15 and 0.2 milligrams, while digoxin is produced as 0.125, 0.25 and 0.5 milligrams. The pharmacist who receives a prescription for a 0.125 milligram digitoxin tablet knows instantly that something is amiss. Because we operate in a free enterprise system, however, there is nothing to prevent some drug manufacturer from adding a 0.125 milligram digitoxin tablet to his line. Though this is not likely to happen, heaven help the consumer taking digitoxin if it ever does.

A second line of defense against errors is the patient himself. Digitalis tends to be taken for long periods of time, and as other consumers recognize other products through experience, so the patient taking digitalis learns to recognize "his" medication. Each manufacturer's digitoxin tablets are the same physical size, but each is colored differently. Digoxin tablets, on the other hand, are generally of different sizes, and the consumer, who has usually been impressed with the importance of compliance, is likely to notice the difference.

Finally, digitalis has going for it a combination of factors which no other drug possesses: (1) It is one of a very few drugs of its sort that is highly effective, (2) it is known to be extremely hazardous if misused, (3) it is usually prescribed by or in conjunction with specialists (generally cardiologists, whose prescribing habits are carefully circumscribed—they are less prone to pharmacological adventure and tend to have a better understanding of those drugs they do use), (4) it has been in use for a very long time (as a folk remedy since the dawn of time and as a specific drug for 200 years).* Because of these factors, the typical physician has great respect for digitalis and tends to use it with great care.

Few other drugs fare so well from the consumer's standpoint. Fortunately (depending on your point of view), most other drugs—and the antimicrobials are an excellent example of this—have a wide therapeutic range, which is to say that they are not generally toxic except in massive overdoses. Most other drugs are not prescribed for such specific use nor is the dose so carefully calculated (one pharmacologist-physician maintains that a properly dosed cardiac patient's body contains close to one third of a lethal dose of digitalis). By contrast, whole categories of drugs such as the

* The cardiac glycosides have been found in a great number of plants. The leaf of the common foxglove, *Digitalis purpurea,* the seeds of Strophanthus Kombe, the fleshy bulb of the "sea onion," the root of the lily of the valley, and the kernel of the nut of the yellow oleander are a few examples. It was in 1785 that a physician, William Withering, published an account of ten years of experience with foxglove. He was aware that the drug was effective in certain forms of "dropsy" (generally, an accumulation of fluids in the extremities), but he failed to make the connection between the drug's diuretic and cardiac effects.

The drug was used for nearly eighty years after Withering's treatise before its effect on the heart muscle was discovered, and until the twentieth century, an alcoholic extract of the leaves or the powdered leaves themselves in capsule form were the popular dose forms. In the last forty years, digitoxin and digoxin, stemming from the isolation of the several active glycosides contained as a mixture in the leaf of the foxglove, have become the most popular preparations—generally in tablet form. The action of the single glycoside is far more predictable than that of a mixture.

antimicrobials, sedatives, tranquilizers (both minor and major), diuretics and antihistamines tend to be prescribed with almost reckless abandon, aimed shotgun fashion at conditions whose causes and importance the physician has only the vaguest notion.

History, too, is on the wrong side of the already plummeting balance: the vast majority of highly effective drugs have been introduced since the end of World War II; a substantial number of physicians—and pharmacists, for that matter—received their training before that time. Those who have been trained since that time, at least until about 1965, are probably no more able than their aging colleagues, if, indeed, they are as able. One need only recall that the disciplines of anatomy and physiology are, so far as the basic elements are concerned, respectively about 300 and 150 years old; for all practical purposes, modern drug therapy is less than 40. Easily 90 percent of the drugs in use today did not even exist 30 years ago!

Clearly, the present system works more or less adequately for those drugs which require only minimal therapeutic manipulation, that is, for specific, long-term therapy in which the physician is aware of the need for careful monitoring and the consumer is at least minimally aware of the importance of the medication to his continued well-being. Where either of these elements is missing, the prescription system, with its relatively insignificant input from the pharmacist, does little to protect the consumer. There are no other effective mechanisms to regulate either the way the physician prescribes or the manner in which the consumer utilizes modern drugs.

A Prescription a Minute

A tenuous professional relationship is not the only factor which prevents the pharmacist from influencing the physician to perform in a consistently rational manner. The environment in which pharmacy continues to be practiced tends to prevent the pharmacist from scrutinizing too closely the prescriptions he fills. The purely economic facets of the problem aside (they will be dealt with in depth in a later chapter), there is a related fact of life for the pharmacist about which few people, including the vast majority of pharmaceutical educators, have any knowledge, but which has a direct bearing on the way a pharmacist handles prescriptions. First, the economic health of any pharmacy relates directly to a factor which I will call "prescription density": each pharmacist must fill a relatively large number of prescriptions per unit of time. If the pharmacist is the store owner, then the more prescriptions he fills, the more money he makes; his fixed costs are the same whether he fills one prescription per day or one hundred. On the other hand, if the pharmacist is an employee, as most are, then he and his salary are a part of the fixed costs. The employee pharmacist makes the same salary regardless of whether he fills one prescription or one hundred. Obviously, the owner will press the employee pharmacist to produce at the highest rate possible. Note that I did not say "at the highest rate possible consistent with safety!" I have worked for people of the latter sort, God bless them, but they are a very small minority and there are fewer every year.

Some years back it used to be common sport for pharmacists to boast (in the letter columns of certain "journals") about the number of prescriptions they had managed to dispense in the span of an eight-hour shift. One would write in to claim that he had filled 200. Next month some one would be claiming he had filled 280. I haven't bothered to read this sort of trash for several years, but the last I recall, some idiot was claiming over 300, with an hour off for lunch. He may actually have done this, but remember that there are only 420 minutes in a span of seven hours, and that tallies to less than a minute and a half for each prescription.

In the last decade there has been a gradual increase in professional awareness in the clinical arena of pharmacy, and as a consequence the appearance of this sort of letter has tapered off. This is not to say that some pharmacists do not still indulge in such dangerous excesses or that they do not still write letters about it. What it probably does mean is that the editors are embarrassed by such foolishness and prefer not to publish them.

Admittedly, the percentage of community pharmacists who fill over 200 prescriptions a day is small—not because they wouldn't *like* to fill that many, or couldn't be pressed to fill that many, but because there isn't quite *that* much business to go around. The average, however, is in the neighborhood of 100 a day per pharmacist, and the pharmacist who fills less than 50 a day will probably soon find himself looking for another line of work. A physician who runs seventy patients through his office each day is generally viewed with suspicion (the perception of some is that he's either an incredible hack or he's "cleaning up" on one of the public aid or old age assistance programs, and they may be right on both counts), but in a country such as ours, which has more than 300,000 physicians and fewer than 130,000 pharmacists, the pharmacist's work load tends to be dictated by numbers as well as economics.

Given that an eight-hour day contains 480 minutes and the average pharmacist fills 100 prescriptions a day, this works out to an average of 4.8 minutes devoted to each prescription. Would that this were so! The pharmacist almost always has other duties besides filling prescriptions. Making non-prescription sales, telephone answering, keeping track of inventory, writing orders, supervising other personnel (some states require that the manager of a drugstore be a pharmacist), handling complaints and the like can easily chop two hours out of the available time. Result: about 3.5 minutes per prescription. Still adequate, but getting tighter. Nor is this the worst: prescriptions seldom come in at regularly spaced intervals; they tend to come in in batches: a spate at opening time, a batch in the middle of the morning, a rush at noon, another more prolonged rush from about 2 P.M. to 4:30 P.M. and a yet more intense rush of shorter duration at about suppertime. At any time—but usually in the midst of a rush—there may be a call from a nursing home requesting refills for two or three dozen prescriptions and, to add insult to injury, most of the prescription numbers are likely to be jumbled. Thus there are a couple of times each day when the pharmacist is filling prescriptions at the rate of 50 or 60 an hour—*one a minute*. During slack periods he still works at a frenetic pace because this is the way he "buys time" to handle his other responsibilities and maybe, if he is lucky, take a couple of minutes to compose himself over a cup of coffee.

Interpreting a Prescription

When all the motion is broken down in this way, the result is that, on the average, the pharmacist has from 2 to 2 1/2 minutes to devote to your prescription. It is pertinent for you as a consumer to ask just what a pharmacist does in this brief time. By way of illustrating, in a general sort of way, what goes on when a real prescription is filled, I have taken the liberty of reproducing, in figures 1 and 2, a pair of prescriptions written for a relative of mine who visited a physician for what was diagnosed as a case of "nerves." He brought them to me for evaluation before having them filled (I was not working as a pharmacist at the time), and with his permission I have subjected the prescriptions to the following procedures: (1) I processed the information contained as though I were going to fill them, recording the steps as I perceived them;

(2) I evaluated the prescriptions for general pharmacological pitfalls; (3) I took the prescriptions to one of the better local pharmacies in my area and observed how *they* filled them; (4) I called the office of the physician who had written them and, without revealing that I was a pharmacist, asked several questions relevant to important information failures in the prescriptions. This, then, is the story of two prescriptions.

To most pharmacists, prescription interpretation is so automatic that they do not even recognize the various steps and priorities they assign in the process. I had rarely paid any attention to it myself, even though I have filled between one-half and three-fourths of a million prescriptions in my career. Where I *have* tried to slow down to identify individual steps or blocks of steps, as I did in the case of these two prescriptions, the result is a sort of Gestalt perception of the entire prescription as a simultaneous display of information. This eidetic image contains landmarks that are like beacons coded for priority, although, curiously, they are not the priorities one would expect. Instead, these priorities are determined by the prerequisite obligation of accurately deciphering a noisy, distorted signal coming from the physician. Here, then, is one way I might read and process the prescriptions in figures 1 and 2.

First, my eye goes to the first two lines of the body of the prescription—but not directly to the drug name. In fig. 1 I note the "50 mg" on the second line. This appears to indicate a tablet or capsule. If it were a liquid, injectable, suppository or other dose form, the "set" would be different. In fig. 2 no size is given—possibly a tablet or capsule made in one size only.

With this tentatively established, I now "see" the drug name. In fig. 1 my eye catches, in order, "I", "p", "mine" as my mind flashes "Imipramine HCl", then "50 mg." I scan that top line in reverse as a double-check on my automatic perception. In fig. 2 I catch the "forte" first. Few drugs have this suffix and the only common one that might apply in such circumstances (this is determined by several peripheral bits of information and influenced by my acquaintance with the consumer) is Parafon. Again I scan the top line in reverse, but a caution triggered by the size of dose of fig. 1 and an impression of "different" about the combination causes me to read again from left to right.

If the handwriting had been difficult and had not revealed, to a satisfactory degree of certainty, the name of the drug, I would have had to backtrack, combining what I had decided about the dose form with the instructions and looking at the signature to see who had written the prescription. (The prescription form had already alerted me to a large block of peripheral "bits" that would also have come into play.) Each physician has a fairly limited range of drugs from which he does the great majority of prescribing, and after you have seen a few hundred prescriptions from an individual practitioner, you can quickly narrow the span of products he is likely to prescribe as, for instance, a 50 mg tablet at bedtime. In any case, it is at about this point that I take note of the physician's signature. Does it look like it should? If it is different, is it *too* different? As astonishing as it may seem, a physician's signature can tell you how sure he feels of himself, if he is angry, if he has a hangover—a great many intimate things that are sometimes important as you interpret a prescription.

All of these considerations take place as I reach to my left breast pocket for my pen—a matter of a few seconds. Now I assemble the entire prescription in my head: "30 Imipramine, 50 mg" and "30 Parafon Forte." Pen in hand, I now check to see that the patient's name and address are at the top of the prescription. In this case they are not, so I ask the patient and fill it in. Sometimes the physician does scribble something here, but as often as not it is illegible and I still must ask the patient. If I have not identified the physician's signature by one means or another, I ask the patient at this point and give some indication as to how long it will be before the prescription is ready: "This will be ready in just a minute," or "This requires compounding and will take about 15 minutes," or "Our order with a fresh supply of this just came in, but I've been too busy to unpack it. Could we deliver it this afternoon?"

The next step is to place the prescription and label on the counter and, using a numbering device, to stamp the same number on each of them. As I am doing this, I am rereading the instructions and composing the statement I will later type on the label. I then go to the stock shelves, take down the stock bottles, return to the prescription counter and reach for empty containers of appropriate size. This last is so automatic that I can't explain how (at least in the case of tablet vials) I know the correct size, but 99 out of 100 times I'm right. After counting and bottling the tablets, I type the labels. For the imipramine there is little difficulty: "i HS" comes out very nicely as "Take one tablet at bedtime." (There is a slight problem with the quantity since it could be read as 30, 36, or 38. I was conservative in deciding on 30, but some pharmacists would be greedy and dispense 38.)* Deciding what directions are appropriate for the Parafon Forte prescription is more difficult: I must decide whether the physician has written "Q4H" or "QID"—"every four hours" (six possible doses a day) or "four times a day" (every six hours) . . . I chose "QID," since it is a more reasonable dose, even though the scrawl looks *slightly* more like "Q4H." In any case these instructions will have little bearing on how the patient uses the drug, because the physician has confused the issue by adding "PRN" (as needed).

When it comes to the matter of refills, neither prescription is a problem since the physician has indicated nothing and in my state such prescriptions cannot legally be refilled. However, it would be a simple expedient for me, or anyone else, for that matter, to enter some indication making it refillable. I have seen prescriptions with nothing but a check mark in the general area of the "Repetatur" box refilled for several years. Perhaps the most remarkable perversion I have seen involved the extensive refilling of a prescription on which the physician had written two prescriptions. Cramped for space, he had written over the refill box. A crossed "t" was interpreted, almost triumphantly, as an indication that the physician desired refills for both prescriptions "ad lib," and they were refilled frequently for several years.

Returning to filling the prescriptions, the typed label must now be attached securely to the drug container. (Incidentally, *never* accept a prescription with a label loose inside the container. Not only is this practice illegal, it is also very dangerous. Imagine the problems of an emergency room physician faced with treating a child who has swallowed the contents of a prescription bottle—and there is no label to be found.) If one of these prescriptions had been for a pre-packaged preparation, say an ointment, a prudent pharmacist would peel off the manufacturer's label. Many consumers are puzzled or angered at this peeling. What is the pharmacist trying to hide, they wonder; what information is being kept from them? The answer, in most cases, is not much. The manufacturer's label usually contains little more than the drug name, a listing of contents, and sometimes an abbreviated version of the package insert.

---

* There is little doubt that the physician intended 30 tablets be dispensed for several technical reasons, the most important being that 30 is locally considered to be a month's supply of most drugs given at the rate of one a day. It needs to be pointed out, however, that the other prescription also calls for 30 tablets, and if there is any logic to *that,* I prefer not to pursue it.

Often the label refers the reader to the package insert or other technical sources for *all* information. (The package insert, incidentally, is written for the physician and presumes an expertise most consumers do not possess.) If the original label is left in place and the typed prescription label affixed over it, many consumers will remove the prescription label in order to read the manufacturer's label. With the prescription label removed, the prescription is essentially *unlabeled*. Depending on the circumstances, the law sees such containers, not in the possession of a "professional," as being either mislabeled or misbranded, and the person possessing it may find himself in a nasty spot. So, the pharmacist peels off the manufacturer's label first.

Once the label is attached, the prescription is essentially filled, so far as the traditional dispensing mechanics are concerned. The pharmacist must still determine the price to charge the consumer, and this is generally done using a set formula provided by the store owner. One such formula might read: "Average wholesale price (AWP) + 20 percent + a $2.00 professional fee."

With the price calculated, I would be faced with the question: what do I say to the consumer? If I were working for a mass merchandising drug chain, the question would not arise, since I would not directly confront the consumer. Instead, the prescription would have been received by a sort of clerk-receptionist, handed to an apprentice, who is seldom more than a typist who has been taught to read prescriptions, and I as a pharmacist would have been primarily involved in packaging the final product and scanning the prescription to see if the label is consistent. Under other, more nearly ideal circumstances, I might well answer any questions the consumer might wish to ask concerning the use of the drug, but here there is a series of barriers: a tangible one of wood and plastic, and psychological barriers that are difficult to assess. Beyond this there is the fact that the data collected by the physician is absent—without it, the pharmacist is not in the best position to advise the patient.

So much for the hypothetical filling of these two prescriptions. What happened when they were actually filled? I took them to a community pharmacy which I regard as one of the better ones in my city. It is owned by a pharmacist, who also fills some of the prescriptions, and it maintains drug profile records, although they are far too fragmentary to be of any real value. The prescriptions were taken at the counter by an apprentice pharmacist (one who has not yet completed his five years of training and therefore is not authorized to work without a pharmacist's supervision). The apprentice read the prescriptions aloud to the pharmacist at work in the adjacent work area. This pharmacist filled the containers on the basis of this oral communication, then handed them to the apprentice who had typed labels in the meantime. The pharmacist did not check the labels against the prescription. (Although I only knew the man slightly, he was aware of my professional status. This may have made a difference in his mind, but were our positions reversed, I would have double- or triple-checked my apprentice on any prescription!) In reading out the prescriptions, the apprentice interpreted the ambiguous dose in prescription 2 as "QID," instead of "Q4H." As I noted earlier, I would tend toward this interpretation for superficial pharmacological reasons, even though it seemed more likely that the physician actually wrote "Q4H."

When I arrived home with the filled prescriptions, I placed a call to the physician's office, told the receptionist that I was a close relative of the patient and explained that there was some question about the dosage of one of the drugs the physician had prescribed. She promised to "ask Doctor about it" and return my call. This was at 10:20 A.M. When I had received no call by noon, I tried four times to call between 12:00 and 1:00 P.M. No answer. Apparently everyone was out to lunch. This is a crucial fact, because there is always a substantial rush of prescriptions to be filled during the noon hour, and it is precisely at this time that it is virtually impossible to contact *any* physician. Finally, at 1:30 P.M. I was able to reach the receptionist, who put me through to the nurse. I explained the problem to her, and after some shuffling of papers she explained that the Parafon Forte should be taken four times a day.

I then asked if she would check two other things with the physician: (1) what did *he* think the proper dose should be? and (2) would it make any difference if the patient had finished taking a prescription for the drug Marplan two days before? She said she would check and I was placed on "hold." The question regarding the Marplan was definitely a loaded one. This drug belongs to a group of drugs called "monoamineoxidase inhibitors," or MAOIs. Some of them are used to control blood pressure and others are used as antidepressants, like the imipramine, and by themselves they are relatively safe. When an MAOI is combined with imipramine, however, the results can be disasterous. In the words of one pharmacology text, "Severe toxicity may be seen when given during exhibition of MAO inhibitors: circulatory collapse, hyperpyrexia, death. May cause accumulation of a substance normally destroyed by MAO." Furthermore, this effect can occur up to two weeks after the MAOI is discontinued—that's the meaning of the phrase "during exhibition of, etc."

A little over five minutes later the nurse was back on the line. Her reply: "The Marplan isn't something we ordered. We'd have to know who ordered it, and for what." This sort of reply is utterly irrelevant, since the reason for taking Marplan could have no bearing on its potentialy lethal interaction with the imipramine. Concerning the dose of Parafon Forte, she said that the physician had ordered it to be taken "four times a day, or every four hours if they were indicated." She didn't answer my second question either, but she did tell me what I had suspected: the physician intended my nephew to take the Parafon Forte four times a day at four-hour intervals—more or less. In his "innocence" he left his directions open to several interpretations. The label ought to have read: "Take one or two tablets at 8 A.M., Noon, 4 P.M., and 8 P.M., if needed." I cringe at this last because I have frequently been censured by store owners for interpreting "prn" to mean "if needed" under similar circumstances: they would prefer to see it written "*as* needed," since this tends to increase the patient's consumption of the drug, leading to more refill business.

This, then, is the saga of two prescriptions. They were neither very complicated nor very arcane, yet it is possible to pinpoint several vague areas where error and misinterpretation could bring their consumer to grief—even without opening to question the actual medical soundness of prescribing them in the first place.

My nephew had gone to the physician complaining of nervousness, depression, stiff neck, "knotted" muscles and the like. The Parafon Forte was apparently intended for the physical symptoms since it is considered to be a muscle relaxant and might help prevent the muscle spasms causing the "knotting" and stiff neck. The minor tranquilizer diazepam, however, is generally recognized to be superior for this purpose, in addition to being somewhat cheaper. The imipramine is a "mood-elevating" or "antidepressant" drug intended to relieve the depression. As with most drugs of this sort, it has limitations—the main one being that no one is quite sure whether it really works or not. There are some who suspect a placebo effect rather than a pharmacologic effect. In any case, it is generally conceded that *if* mood-elevating drugs of this type *do* work, they do not begin to exert a pharmacologic effect until they have been taken for weeks or, in some cases, months. Not one of the professionals involved here saw fit to inform the patient of this fact.

In summary, although the drugs prescribed are superficially justifiable, in view of the patient's symptoms, there is not a great deal that can be expected of the therapy. The problems behind the symptoms are probably of psychological origin and are self-limiting, which is to say that no matter what therapy is prescribed, they will disappear in time. Since his graduation from college a year ago, my nephew has been unable to find a job fitted to his talents and abilities (not unusual these days). Consequently, he has been working at menial jobs, for low pay, and is predictably depressed and anxious about his future. Under the circumstances, it seems that a few chapters from Marcus Aurelius or Dale Carnegie would do about as much good as these drugs, and at considerably less cost: the two prescriptions came to $9.48, with a courtesy discount —they would have otherwise cost about $14.40.

We Can Do Anything With Nothing In No Time At All

What we can learn from the story of these two prescriptions is, in a way, not what the health care "team" can do for you, the consumer, but what they can *not* do. Mainly, neither the pharmacist, nor anybody else, can provide you three basic and vital guarantees you have every right to expect to receive along with your prescription:

(1) The pharmacist cannot guarantee that the medication he delivers is "exactly what the doctor ordered." Prescriptions are simply subject to too many sources of error and misinterpretation to afford a reliable level of control as drugs are dispensed.

(2) The pharmacist cannot guarantee that the physician's prescription is a pharmacologically rational response to your condition, or even that it is safe for you as an individual to consume.

(3) Even though it is likely that the pharmacist knows a fair amount about the drug—its action, dosage, side effects, possible interactions with other drugs and contraindications—it cannot be guaranteed that he will feel free to counsel you in the use of the drug, even if you could manage to slow him down or isolate him long enough to ask him about it.

In short, the prescription system is a remnant of medieval medical practice, a bit of tenth century technology which is (in its basic design) inadequate to cope with the demands of modern therapy. Expecting a prescription, in typical circumstances, to adequately control the use of a modern drug is somewhat akin to asking a nuclear physicist to conduct his experiments on subatomic particles with the aid of Galileo's water clock and a wooden measuring stick. No rational scientist would undertake to do research on such terms, but the state of our physician-dominated health care system is such that the glaring technical inadequacies of prescription-directed drug therapy are rarely questioned.

What does the pharmacist think? Here is the best answer I have been able to find:

We, The Unwilling
Led By The Unknowing
Are Doing The Impossible
For The Ungrateful.

We Have Done So Much
For So Long
With So Little
We Are Now Qualified
To Do Anything
With Nothing.

In No Time At All.

Anon.—From the handwriting
on the wall of a
hospital pharmacy.

5 Drugs in the Hospital

Barry Miles and his wife Judy were asleep on a cold January night when he was roused by a fit of coughing. His nose and throat were strangely irritated, but a faint, almost unnoticeable crackle and an eerie flickering brought him closer to full consciousncss. Somcthing was different about the room. Smoke! That was it. Throwing back the blankets, he dashed groggily for the door. Without any thought of possible consquences, he threw the door open and was engulfed in a cloud of smoke and a sheet of flame: the oil space heater had developed a leak and the living room of the small frame house was now a blazing inferno. That blast of smoke and flame that had come through the suddenly opened door seared Barry's lungs and throat. Blinded and in the grip of a mind-blanking panic, he let out a croaking scream that woke his wife as he collapsed to the floor. Somehow Judy Miles managed to slam the door shut, buying a few extra minutes, then, badly burned about the head, shoulders, arms and hands, she dragged her husband through the large window that had been blown out by the first explosive rush of superheated air that came through the door. It seemed to take an eternity, but neighbors arrived on the scene quickly, and the pair was rushed to the community hospital for treatment of their second- and third-degree burns.

After the burns were dressed, the emergency room physician ordered the administration of antibiotics to prevent the development of a pseudomonas infection, a frequent occurrence following severe, extensive burns. The pseudomonas organism is common in most modern hospitals—the water in floral arrangements found in almost every hospital room generally teems with them—and they are nearly impossible to eradicate. Since Mr. Miles was unconscious, he was to receive one gram of carbenicillin intravenously four times a day. Mrs. Miles, though very painfully burned, was conscious and as alert as it is possible to be after a heavy dose of opiates, so she was to receive the same dose of the drug orally.

Anyone who has worked in a hospital which has an emergency treatment facility knows that emergency situations tend to happen in clusters, and this night at the hospital where the Mileses were treated there was a deluge of disaster. Before the Mileses were brought in at 1:00 A.M., the emergency room had already funneled a long procession of victims into various units of the hospital for further care. There had been two badly injured motorcycle passengers, a pedestrian from a hit-and-run accident, nine people from a three-car smash, an elderly man with a moderately severe coronary, six knuckleheads who had done their best to terminate one another in a barroom brawl with knives and blunt instruments of whatever sort they could lay hands on, three gunshot victims and two drug overdose victims. Amid this mayhem the expected complement of law enforcement people milled around; each of them had reports to fill out and each of them was in a hurry to get back to his beat—they plucked and teased at the nurses and aides each time one appeared in the busy corridor. It was just one of those mean nights, and the hospital pharmacist, who was as busy as everyone else, had no opportunity to confer with the emergency room physician until 6 A.M.—five hours after the Mileses had come in.

The pharmacist was mildly curious as to why the physician had ordered the carbenicillin as he had, since, properly used, the drug should be given in very large (and expensive) doses to be effective for the treatment or even prophylaxis of pseudomonas. When the tired pharmacist asked about his reasoning, the exhausted physician replied that he was fearful that the smoke and heat-damaged respiratory tissues, particularly with Mr. Miles, might be infected by any stray organism and that a pseudomonas seemed the most likely one to guard against. Almost as an afterthought he asked why the pharmacist was concerned. The pharmacist had to inform him that to produce a blood level that would do the job effectively, he would have to give from 30 to 60 grams or more of carbenicillin a day instead of a mere 4 grams. A dose of carbenicillin of that magnitude would cost the patient between \$100 and \$200 a day. He then added that when the drug is given orally, its absorption characteristics are such that attaining a blood level of any consequence was out of the question—the oral dose would be excreted so rapidly by the kidneys that more than half of a given dose would be in the urine in a very few minutes. (The drug company detail man who had told the physician about the wonderous properties of the drug had neglected to mention these things.)

Faced with this information the physician had to balance costs and certain hazards that accompany very high doses of the drug against the probability of an infection by pseudomonas. There was no doubt that the oral form was inappropriate and there was considerable doubt that the intravenous form was feasible at effective levels. In the end, the physician decided on other, more appropriate therapy, but not before his patients had been without adequate protection for nearly a day.

Taking "Hospitable" Out of "Hospital"

If you were cared for by a physician at all in the last year, the odds are about one in three that he treated you in one of America's 8,000-odd hospitals. Chances are good that such an institutional encounter cost you rather a lot of money. In spite of health insurance—although many experts say it is *because* of such insurance—you paid something out-of-pocket in most cases, because basic room charges are nudging $170 a day and a typical confinement runs between three and four days. What did you get for your money, in terms of professionally collaborative health care? Does the institutional orientation of the hospital provide better regulation of prescribing practices, or better monitoring of drug therapy than is typical of treatment provided outside its confines? The answers to these questions will inevitably involve some consideration of the hospital as a social and economic phenomenon—in any event they will be equivocal in some cases and extremely disquieting in others.

In the medieval world a "hospital" was a place of lodging where members of religious orders took care of sick or injured persons who were too poor to purchase the services of the physician and apothecary in the customary way. The word "hospital" is related to our words "hotel," "hostel," "host," "hospitable," and "hospitality," and it is interesting to note that, even at the present time, hospitals and hotels share a marked architectural kinship. In fact, until the last century, the two buildings were virtually indistinguishable, and an edifice which filled one of these functions in one generation might well be converted to the other in the next.

Medical care in the early hospital was, generally, largely custodial. The religious personnel who attended the sick and injured were, except in rare instances, outside the regular ranks of medicine (composed of apothecaries, barber-surgeons and physicians), although it is also certain that some medical practitioners did occasionally provide care to the hospital inmates, either on contract or as an act of charity. Those individuals who could afford the services of a practitioner were generally treated in their homes. After all, the practice of medicine required nothing that could not be conveniently packed into a satchel and brought to the patient's bedside. The only reason for gathering the poor together into hospitals was that it was cheaper and more convenient to treat them that way—two or three in a bed and dozens of beds in each "room." It was actually far safer to be treated at home, away from the danger of contagion.

The enormous advances in the technology of medicine which began to appear in the early part of the nineteenth century brought about substantial changes in both the function and the clientele of of the hospital. Crude surgical procedures were refined and became more sophisticated with the advent of anesthesia (around 1840); a greater degree of sophistication in the treatment of disease was made possible by the refinement of Leeuwenhoek's discoveries about microbes dating from the late seventeenth and early eighteenth centuries. Starting with the discoveries of Cagniard-Latour, Schwann and Kutzing in the 1830s, and building on the work of Berkeley, Bassi and Schonlein in the 1840s and 1850s, Tyndall and Pasteur lent credence to Lister's introduction of "antiseptic surgery" (about 1864), by their work in the last quarter of the nineteenth century. But it was not until the waning days of the century that bacteriological science, spearheaded by Joubert, Koch and Pasteur, firmly proved the microbial cause of human disease.

The introduction of x-rays, oxygen therapy, orthopedic traction and diathermy at the end of the nineteenth and beginning of the twentieth centuries, to name but a few developments, all made a large part of the practice of medicine dependent upon the existence of large physical plants to house the equipment and provide the special environments necessary for treatment. The hospital, correspondingly, became larger, less hotel-like and more specialized for its function. Frequently the hospital grew into a "medical center," a complex of buildings to house a whole galaxy of medical services, and generally this took place in large cities with nearby professional schools and excellent transportation. Likewise, the general secularization of society, coupled with the private philanthropy that arose in the later stages of the Industrial Revolution, has generally resulted in the large modern hospital's being controlled by secular, rather than religious, groups.

Despite these massive, sweeping changes, however, at least two very important features of the medieval hospital still haunt our modern, antiseptically white, chrome and glass healing pavilions. First, the organization and control of the hospital is not the *direct* responsibility of a medical practitioner. True, a rare physician serves on the hospital board, but he is seldom active in the practice of his profession. Relatives of practitioners, prominent business and civic leaders, as well as other individuals having economic ties to medical practitioners, *do* serve on hospital boards. Their attitudes, like their legal responsibilities, are corporate-oriented and they are inaccessable to a typical consumer. Second, few physicians are paid employees of the hospital, although many of those who are have iron-clad contractual arrangements. Generally, physicians are free agents who are granted "privileges" at the hospital. (It would seem that the term "privilege" would indicate the possibility of control through either suspension or revocation, and, indeed, a physician's privileges can be suspended or revoked by the hospital administrator or board. In nearly thirty years of close observation, however, I have *never* seen, or heard of, the revocation of the hospital privileges of a physician who was less than sixty years old, unless it was forced by an agency outside of the local medical community.) When it comes to providing medical services to the consumer, these distinctions and attending conditions often lead to a disjointed and impersonal delivery system—one which is alarmingly prone to errors.

Standing Orders: "Take This . . . Please."

Nowhere in the hospital care system are these errors more likely to occur than in the delivery of medication, and these errors may easily begin within seconds or minutes after admission to the institution. Let us say that you have been admitted to a hospital, shown your room, handed a hospital gown and told to occupy the bed next to the window. A few moments later the medication nurse enters, bringing you two tablets in a paper cup and a glass of water. "Here," she says, "take this, please."

"What is this?" you ask curiously.

"It's your medication," is her inevitable response. A pause.

You're trying to decide how to respond to that—clearly it is medicine, but is it really intended for you—this soon?

"Did Dr. Smith order this for me?"

"Yes, this is on Dr. Smith's orders."

Confused, but reassured, you swallow the tablets and the nurse departs. As you set your glass on the bedside table, it suddenly occurs to you that Dr. Smith couldn't possibly have ordered the medication you have just gulped down—his office nurse told you a little over an hour ago that he was in Louisville on business. "He'll be back late tonight, so you go ahead to the hospital. The arrangements have already been made, and he'll see you there first thing tomorrow morning." This situation—your belly is already warning—is *not* going to help your ulcer.

What the medication nurse failed to tell you (and no one is apt to volunteer such information—you'd have to ask the right question of the right person at the right time in the right way) is that you received the medication, a sedative and an analgesic, on Dr. Smith's "standing orders." In other words, Dr. Smith (who happens to be a gastroenterologist) has left orders at this hospital that *any* patient of his who enters the hospital with symptoms of a gastric ulcer is to be given the two tablets you received—and that they will be repeated every four hours until he changes those orders. So far the hospital has only the sketchiest of records on you, no physician has examined you regarding your present condition, and—depending on the drug distribution system used in your hospital—the hospital pharmacist (if, indeed, there is one) may not even know that you have been admitted, let alone that you have been given medication. Of course, there is something else you are not yet aware of: you are going to be given a mild tranquilizer shortly and a strong sedative at "bedtime," thereby insuring that the nurses will not have any "trouble" from you during the night. If you happen to live in the "wrong" state, you will find that you do not have the option of refusing to take these medications—it is a simple matter to load a syringe with medication, insert a suppository, or force a stomach tube down the throat of an unwilling patient. This does not happen often, but in mental institutions especially it is not uncommon for such methods to be used as a form of punishment for "uncooperative" patients—particularly if the treatment produces pain, as some injected medications do.

This sort of situation prevails in a great many American hospitals. It is difficult to even estimate how many hospitals allow the use of standing orders (there are apparently so many other mysteries about hospitals that nobody seems to have gotten around to collecting data on this one), but a general rule of thumb is that the only hospitals which do *not* allow standing orders tend to be the large teaching hospitals and possibly some others which employ "in-house" physicians. In other words, whenever you enter your community hospital, you stand a fair chance of receiving standing order medication.

The chances of this happening are particularly great if you happen to be admitted as the result of a "common" ailment and have been seen by a specialist for treatment of your affliction. The hypothetical example given earlier involved a gastroenterologist and an ulcer patient. One could talk, almost interchangeably, about the cardiac patient and his cardiologist, the individual with a chronic bladder infection and his urologist, or the mother-to-be and her obstetrician. In such cases, if the patient has been rushed to the hospital, either with or without the physician's prior knowledge, the physician generally has a fairly good idea of the circumstances, even without bothering to go to the patient to make an examination. It must be understood that in such cases the physician's knowledge of his patient's condition, even though it stems from extensive experience, is only statistical: "*if* a lady in the ninth month of pregnancy has been taken to the hospital, *then* there is a good probability that her signs of labor"—and this is particularly true if she has already had children—"will soon result in the termination of her pregnancy." The consequence of this statistical sort of assumption is that the medication regimen arising from the physician's standing orders will be appropriate in only a certain percentage of cases.

To illustrate how this works, let us examine the standing orders of obstetricians practicing at one 250-bed community hospital. There are eight obstetricians practicing here, but there is a total of ten different sets of standing orders since two of the physicians have left *two sets* of orders, one for patients who may require caesarean sections and the other for "normal" deliveries. (It is uncertain how the decision is made as to which set of a physician's orders will be used in the event of doubt; sometimes a perfectly normal delivery is concluded before the physician who expected to do a "section" arrives at the delivery room.) Typically, one physician's orders call for a "packet" of medication to be sent to the floor for a patient. (This hospital uses packages very much like home freezer bags that can be sealed with a hot wire device and pressure-sealing plastic bags.) One such packet is made up of:

2 capsules methprylon 300 mg (a sedative), one to be given at once.

1 suppository bisacodyl 10 mg (a cathartic), to be inserted at once.

6 capsules dioctyl sodium sulfosuccinate 60 mg (a stool softener), one to be given with a full glass of water every six hours.

6 tablets propoxyphene napsylate 100 mg (an analgesic), one or two to be given as needed for pain.

Most of the packets contain a similar set of medications—basically a sedative, bowel evacuant, stool softener, and an analgesic, but the situation, as far as the pharmacist is concerned, is hardly that easy. There are dozens of sedatives, dozens of analgesics, several stool softeners, and a great many combinations of similar drugs made by different manufacturers. Instead of a mere four drugs, it takes closer to *fifty* at this hospital to fill such packets for eight physicians.

How well do such pre-packaged regimens meet the medical needs of the typical woman who delivers at this hospital? Judge for yourself. The only item in the ten sets of packets upon which the eight physicians came close to agreeing was the cathartic suppository, and the fact that about the only alternative they had was an enema probably determined this. The dioctyl sodium sulfosuccinate (stool softener) is a longer term item and its effects, if it were effective at all, would not be seen for many hours, perhaps even days. At any rate these two are the only ones that might legitimately be considered concensus items. It is of interest to note that neither of the drugs in question exert their actions as a result of being absorbed—the significance of this is that there is little chance that the as-yet-unborn child would receive a dose of drugs second-hand which might injure it.

When it comes to the drug propoxyphene, the situation is different since no one has ever been able to substantiate with any consistency that it is as effective an analgesic as its original manufacturer-distributor claims. It certainly is *not* a weight-for-weight equivalent of the old standby codeine, but it is most unusual for an obstetrician to use codeine in such situations—they prefer more potent analgesics, such as meperidine.

The sedative methprylon raises several questions simply because it is a sedative. Meperidene and the other potent opiates are generally distributed in a separate drug-handling system and go to a nursing station as a stock item, thus often becoming part of a different set of standing orders. There are sometimes copies of such orders hidden in a file drawer in the pharmacy, but since that facet of control of the drug's use is not strictly a pharmacy function, it may be that only the pharmacy director is aware of them. It is then possible that with a combination of the methprylon and the strong opiates, given on two different sets of standing orders, a woman in the delivery room may be "bombed out of her skull," totally oblivious to what is happening.

Clearly, some patients are happier if they *are* heavily sedated during such an "ordeal," but there are many who object to this. In recent years there has been a great deal of interest at the consumer level in the Lamaze method of prepared childbirth. There is no need to recount here the actual method except to say that it involves a certain amount of concerted effort. There are breathing and muscle training exercises which are used at certain stages of the delivery. In many cities there are series of classes held which involve both the husband and wife, and though they are not expensive, if there is any charge at all, they require considerable interest and motivation. It comes as a shock to many first-time parents to find that the husband may be barred from the delivery room even though the physician has authorized his presence. Even though the physician may have intended to go along with his patient's "faddish" notions, he is apt to forget to warn the personnel in the delivery room. The result is that before the physician arrives the poor patient has been heavily sedated and wouldn't know the difference between Lamaze and La Leche—she is in no condition to use her tediously taught and practiced training:

> Becky Lynch wanted to have her second baby by the Lamaze method, so she visited five obstetricians before she found one who would go along. Every visit, she reminded her physician, and every time he assured her that she would get no more than one "shot" of 50 milligrams of meperidine. The rest would be up to her. Her physician was as good as his word except that he forgot to tell the anesthetist he would not be needed, and, at

what appeared to be the first sign of pain, the anesthetist clapped a mask over Becky's face. Unfortunately, the irate Becky tried to fight the anesthesia and as a result she was quickly taken to a light plane of surgical anesthesia. When she came around after delivery, she was so angry and ill that she nearly became dehydrated from vomiting.

It is a sad sidelight of this story that Becky had five children before she was able to deliver a baby without being similarly sedated. Since this happened over ten years ago, it is a wonder that she did manage, but she finally found a woman obstetrician who had several children of her own.

Beyond all this, however, there should be a general concern over the mindless dumping of *any* potent drug into the bloodstream of a pregnant woman. Until a few moments after birth, the baby and mother share a common blood supply and many of the drugs given the mother—this is particularly true with the respiratory depressing opiates—appear rapidly in the baby's blood. On the other hand, the six propoxyphene tablets in the standing order packet best illustrate what can only be described as mindless medication that appears to be the result of what has been called the masculine misconception of childbirth (if men had babies and all that). The simple fact is that the drug is of dubious value since double-blind testing indicates that it sometimes does not perform any better than a placebo.

As we leave the "standard" drugs which appear in standing order packets and go to the more idiosyncratic entities, the situation becomes even more ambiguous, pharmacologically speaking. One oral surgeon, for instance, includes eight 250 milligram tablets of penicillin VK in every packet. This amounts to only a two days' supply—not enough to wipe out most serious infections, but probably enough to allow the emergence of "wild" and resistant organisms. In fact, since this is a standing order, there is no presumption of infection, only that some infective organisms may creep in. (The operating field being the oral cavity, it is referred to as "dirty surgery" since there are almost always some potentially virulent organisms present.) This is what is known as the "prophylactic" use of an antibiotic, shotgun treatment without any substantial evidence of game in sight. There is some controversy about this sort of prescribing, but very little documentary evidence that it is at all appropriate. Not only does the patient become a possible mutation generator producing resistant organisms which may cause future problems (as discussed in Chapter 3), but he is also exposed to the unnecessary risk of a reaction to the antibiotic that could end fatally (remember that no one has yet taken a drug history when the standing order is filled), plus the unnecessary expense (drugs, you will discover, usually cost considerably more in the hospital than at the neighborhood pharmacy).

At times, too, the standing orders may simply reflect the physician's prejudices, rather than any medical necessity. There is a physician at one hospital whose specialty is internal medicine, but who, from time to time, will delivery a baby. His standing orders present a very thorny problem: his packet contains twelve 5 milligram tablets of DES (diethylstilbesterol, a synthetic sex hormone). When given shortly after delivery, this drug, depending on how much is given and for how long, will reduce or stop the new mother's production of breast milk. It makes no difference to this man that a substantial number of modern mothers wish to breastfeed their babies, all of his maternity patients receive the DES on his standing orders. He never asks about what the mother wishes, he presents this order as a *fait accompli.* When there is no milk the mother generally has no idea as to why it dried up and uses a bottle for feeding.

There are a great many other possible complications which may arise from the fact that the hospital is not actually the physician's "base of operations," but more of a "rendezvous point" where certain physicians and certain patients get together under what are, supposedly, ideal medical conditions. What might happen, for instance, if your regular physician is not available when you must enter the hospital? This sort of thing seems to happen most frequently in maternity cases, but is commonly seen in all areas during the prime vacation months. One unseen and seldom considered hazard that may contribute its part is the fact that vacation scheduling for key personnel in most hospitals is haphazard—they rarely get more than a couple of weeks, but in small and medium-size hospitals many departments are dependent on a single "key" person and there are no trained replacements. Consider the possible consequences of the following case in which the OB man happened to be on vacation:

Vera Markham, age twenty-two, was awakened at 1:30 A.M. by a sharp, cramping pain which she took to be a signal of the onset of labor. This was Vera's first baby and she hadn't the faintest idea as to how much time she had to get to the hospital. Her physician's nurse had tried to tell her about timing the intervals of contraction, but as with most "first timers," her apprehension drove all thought of timing the contractions from her mind, so she shook her husband awake. He, in turn, placed a call to Dr. A——, Vera's obstetrician. Dr. A——'s answering service reported that he was out of town until Monday, but Mrs. Markham should go to the hospital where Dr. B——, who was taking Dr. A——'s calls, would be notified.

At the hospital, Vera was admitted and, since she was admitted as Dr. A——'s patient, the medications on his standing orders were ordered from the pharmacy. Dr. A——'s packet included six 300 milligram methprylon capsules (sedative), one cathartic suppository, and twelve propoxyphene napsylate compound tablets (analgesic).

When Vera's labor began to progress more rapidly, Dr. B—— was summoned and he arrived in time to assist the birth of an eight-pound, three-ounce boy at 5:45 P.M. Before leaving the hospital, Dr. B—— ordered 100 milligrams of secobarbital (a sedative) every six hours and pentazocine (an analgesic) every four hours. Since he was not aware of Dr. A——'s standing orders, he made no mention of them and Vera received both A's and B's medications. As a result, Vera's accounting of the next forty-eight hours is that she knew *something* was going on—people kept putting things in front of her, asking questions that she couldn't understand and, from time to time, she was given this cute little doll which kept slipping from her grasp. It was so terribly frustrating and yet she couldn't summon the will to really care for more than a moment or two. Vera's husband had heard about something called postpartum psychosis from one of the guys where he worked, and though he hadn't the faintest idea as to what this involved, he saw his wife in a zombi-like state that frankly worried him. He finally stopped Dr. A——, who had just returned, in the hallway outside his wife's room and demanded an explanation. Dr. A—— didn't have an answer so he replied that he hadn't had a chance to see his patient's chart, but that it wasn't too uncommon for a woman to be pretty groggy for a couple of days.

It was a very concerned and angry physician who, after reviewing Mrs. Markham's chart, went looking for the unit supervisor, Mrs. Patterson. He didn't find her because she had left on vacation and would not be back for another three or four days. After ordering all medications on Mrs. Markham to be discontinued immediately, Dr. A—— made a bee-line for the hospital administrator's office where he vented his spleen. The Administrator informed Dr. A—— that several key people in Nursing had taken their vacations at once and he had been forced to allow the transfer of less well qualified individuals or face the prospect of closing down the unit—"I'm sorry about your patient, Doctor, but these things will happen."

These things, unfortunately *do* happen, but who pays for the damage? In almost every case it is the victim who pays. For the Markhams it was two extra days in the hospital while Vera was being "detoxified." Of course, the poor nurse who had been transferred from an orthopedic unit to the supervision of the obstetrical unit spent a terrifying half hour in the administrator's office.

At this point, since I do not deal with the nurse's situation in depth anywhere else, it should be explained that they are considered to be the lowest individual on the medical totem pole, and as such they absorb an incredible amount of abuse. I have seen physicians throw things at them, shove them, spill things on them unnecessarily, purposely knock things out of their hands, nick them with sharp instruments, and generally treat them in the meanest and most petty ways imaginable—simply because they, the physicians, can do so without fear of reprisal. One reason there are few male nurses is the fact that few men in our culture will take this sort of abuse without reacting strongly and most physicians are well aware of this. But beyond this, because of such intimidation, nurses, whether male or female, are far more prone to error than would be the case if they were treated as they should be—as important colleagues who have as much to contribute to good health care as any other professional. Obviously, all physicians do not abuse all nurses, but it happens often enough that it makes a significant contribution to the sort of care a consumer receives in *every* hospital in the United States. In the case of Vera Markham, no one knows whether it was the nurse's ignorance, carelessness or intimidation that resulted in the double medication. The poor woman took the verbal abuse without a word, left the room when dismissed, burst into tears outside, took two strong tranquilizers and went back to work.

There are a great many other things that could be said about this whole matter, but there is one observation in particular that needs to be made: had Dr. A——'s packet contained one of the combination opiate analgesics (as some do at this hospital) instead of the propoxyphene napsylate compound, Mrs. Markham could have been in far more trouble.

The Drug Room System

From the standpoint of well-regulated drug therapy, a few questions are in order: Is there a pharmacist involved with drug dispensing and control in the hospital? How adequate is the hospital's drug record system? (In some cases it might be more appropriate to ask if there is any system at all.) How accurate is the hospital's drug delivery system? Although there are certain uniformly disconcerting facts in each of these areas, the answers will depend to a large extent on which particular hospital we happen to be talking about.

There are three basic systems of drug distribution in use: drug room, floor stock and individual order. If there were only one hospital using the drug room system in the United States, it would be one too many. The same is true of hospitals using only the floor stock system. Many hospitals use a combination of the individual order and floor stock systems—the better organized the hospital, the more use it will make of the individual order system. The best will use a system known as unit dose, with a central pharmacy and satellite pharmacies located as close as possible to the nursing units they serve—the ultimate goal of this system is to eliminate the floor stocks of drugs completely. (An idealized system of this sort will be described in detail later in this chapter.)

If you should ever find yourself a patient in a hospital which uses the drug room system to distribute drugs, my candid advice is to get out, if you are able, as quickly as possible and take your chances elsewhere. Unfortunately, you will probably never know because, again, it is a matter of asking the right person the right question at the right time in the right way. To have any sort of a fighting chance, however, you need to have some idea of how the system works: Hidden somewhere in the deepest recesses of the institution will be a locked (one hopes) storeroom. Inside will generally be a small work table, and the walls will be lined with rough wooden shelves or metal shelves that were discarded by some other department. The room is usually illuminated by a single bare light bulb dangling from the ceiling, and, if it is not too far below ground, some light may filter through a grimy window or two. Presiding over this hole-in-the-wall there is usually an ancient crone wearing what may look like a nurse's uniform. Whether she has nursing "credentials" or not is a matter of indifference since her primary function is not medical, but clerical.

Let us say that the medication nurse on Unit B finds that she has two or three patients whose charts contain physician's orders for tetracycline 250 milligrams, a common antibiotic. Since she can find none of the drug in the jumble of the unit's drug cupboard, she writes out a requisition (on some scrap of paper if she can't locate a requisition form quickly) for 200 capsules of tetracycline 250 milligram and dashes off to the drug room. There the drug room clerk will shake what appears to be 200 capsules out of, hopefully, a bottle labeled tetracycline (not oxytetracycline or chlortetracycline or perhaps something else similar), put them into a container of some sort, scribble a label of sorts, attach it to the container and hand it to the nurse from Unit B. Of course there is always the chance that a full bottle of 1,000 capsules will be handed over—it makes things easier for the clerk.

Several control problems are immediately evident to even the most casual observer. How did the medication nurse decide that she needed 200 capsules? She guessed, and it was not even an educated guess, because she had no way of knowing how long the patients for whom the drug was ordered might remain in the hospital. For that matter she didn't have the faintest idea why the drug was being given to her patients, so it might well be that the order would be stopped at a moment's notice on any or all of the patients. She does know, however, that if she runs short she'll have to make another time-consuming trek to the bowels of the hospital. But, worse, the drug room is only open from 8 A.M. to 4 P.M., and if one of the later shifts runs out of the drug, it will be her fault and she will hear about *that*. If, as is usually the case, there are a large number of capsules left over, no one will complain. Under such conditions it is not uncommon to find three or four containers of the same drug pushed back into dark corners of various cupboards on a nursing unit. At this point we now have the makings of a first-class tragedy.

Tetracycline was chosen for this example because it is what is known as a "dated item." This means simply that a time limit has been established for the shelf life of the drug and a date is stamped on the manufacturer's (or distributor's) label. After this date, the label warns, the drug should not be used, but more often than not the clerk in the drug room and the nurse on the floor have no idea why this is so. The drug clerk almost never takes the trouble to mark the expiration date on the repackaged drugs she puts out, so the nurse may not even be aware that the item is dated. This being the case she will not be the slightest bit concerned about giving drugs that have been on the unit for several years—and this is the tragedy, because she may well be passing out pure poison instead of life-saving drugs.

Several years ago, physicians saw a condition that went by the name of Fanconi's Syndrome, which was considered to be a rare hereditary metabolic disorder. In fact, the condition occurred so seldom that many physicians wouldn't see one case in a lifetime, but this changed. Some years after the tetracyclines were introduced, physicians began to see far more cases of Fanconi's Syndrome than anyone had reason to expect under normal circumstances. It took time and sound detective work to discover that there seemed to be a focal point: a statistically significant number of people with the condition had taken tetracyclines. It wasn't long before it was demonstrated that tetracyclines degrade as they age and it was these degradation products which were the culprit in many cases that were then known as "acquired Fanconi's Syndrome." Treatment of the disorder, to paraphrase one author in the *New England Journal of Medicine,* is "usually ineffective" . . . patients generally die of renal failure.

The Floor Stock System

A slightly more effective distribution system is the floor stock system, but the hazards discussed so far with respect to the drug room are still present. The only essential difference between this system and the drug room system is the presence of a professional whose knowledge of drugs, their uses, care and storage, tends to slightly reduce the more obvious hazards. I'm speaking of the pharmacist, of course, but the degree to which the existing hazards are reduced depends upon his ability, experience and motivation. Generally, a pharmacist sees that stock bottles on the wards are more or less uniform, properly labeled, and that the stock is fresh. Too, he usually tries to keep the amounts of drugs on each unit at a manageable level, not too much and not too little.

The original hope in this system was that the drug supplies located on each floor would contain only those drugs in actual use or for which there was a high probability of continuing need, and that there would be controlled amounts—drugs would be "managed." What in fact happens is that every medication nurse makes every effort to secure as large a supply as possible of every drug for which she might conceivably have some use, no matter how remote the possibility. At first glance this might appear to be ascribable to altruistic motives or the desire to be efficient. After all, isn't it better to have everything at hand so there is no need to run to the pharmacy (or the drug room) to get a supply if, or when, a drug is needed? It is sad, but true, that the most compelling reason for nurses to become pharmaceutical packrats is that physicians can be so downright mean about delays. No matter that the drug in question is a rare item for which there has been no demand for a decade, if the medication nurse cannot produce the drug immediately when a physician asks for it, she is quite apt to find herself the target of a torrent of abuse. Though such occurrences are not as common today as they once were, they make a deep and lasting impression, and, to avoid a repeat performance, a victim will frantically scurry around gathering drugs to add to her already overflowing cupboard.

The actual prescribing routine in these two systems is almost unbelievably casual. The scene: it is 9 A.M. on Unit A and Dr. Blue (known to the nurses as "the Bear") emerges from the elevator and starts his rounds. Passing the nursing station, he pauses to scoop up the charts for his patients, grunts an unintelligible word or two which is only intended to attract attention, then stalks down the hall in the direction of his first patient's room. If at all possible any nurse on the scene will drop what she is doing, grab the "medication" or "order" book and dash off in pursuit. (This is often complicated when several physicians arrive at once, which is not unusual since many physicians spend their early morning hours in the hospital and their afternoons in the office.) As the physician examines a patient, he adds his current observations to the patient's chart and may, as he writes, say: "Let's continue the penicillin on Mrs. Jones, give her some 30 milligram codeine with the aspirin if she needs it, and change that 100 milligram seconal to half gram chloralhydrate with a repeat in four hours if she needs it."

The problem here is that the nurse isn't sure that all this is going into the chart along with orders to change a dressing, order a lab test, and get the lady to "dangle" her legs over the edge of the bed for half an hour, so she does her level best to take it all down and—ideally—to get the physician to sign the orders just as he would sign a prescription. Most of the time the physician doesn't bother to sign the orders, but even if he does, he rarely reads what is written, so there is no verification of the accuracy of what the nurse has taken down. When the orders do not go into the physician's notes, the nurse's record is all there is to work from. In this case the nurse must transcribe, for the physician's signature later, what she has managed to set down.

If no nurse had been available when Dr. Blue took off on his rounds, he would have simply scribbled his orders, probably signed the chart, and dumped the charts on a convenient flat surface in the general vicinity of the nursing station on his way out. He assumes that his orders will be noticed and that they will be carried out. Soon. Eventually, of course, they will come to light and hopefully one of the nurses will be able to decipher his writing, but it is not certain that everything will come out as he expected.

From the nurse's standpoint the limitation of the medication book is that she cannot use it directly to guide her drug administration routine. For this, the information needs to be organized according to patient and medication time, so she does this on a "medication sheet" and fills out small cards which can be hung on a board whose rows and columns of hooks represent patients (horizontal) and medication times (vertical). Thus if Mrs. Jones is to get her penicillin at 8 A.M., Noon, 4 P.M., and 8 P.M., four tags with her name, room and bed number, and a description of her medication are hung on hooks beside her name at the appropriate times.

At noon, the Meds (for "medication") nurse will remove the tags in that time column, place them on a tray, set a paper cup above each card and place each patient's medication in its cup. Once the nurse has completed these "setups," she starts making her rounds of the patients to administer the drugs. You'll recall that I mentioned the treatment some physicians accord nurses a few pages back, and if you give this situation a little thought, you will see that our Meds nurse is carrying a rather delicate burden—almost like leaves on outstretched palms in a brisk wind. I have seen people bump nurses making their med rounds hard enough to send this tray and the nurse flying. Unfortunately, I have seen experienced nurses scrape up the mess, sort it out haphazardly, and continue. I have seen less experienced nurses do the same thing, and beyond the fact that the medications had been all over the floor, I shudder to think what sort of mix-up they might have perpetrated had I not grabbed a broom and helped sweep up and destroy the spilled drugs. An "accident" of this sort means another complete setup, so that the last patient on the route may well receive his medication closer to 1:30 than 12:00.

The Unit Dose System

It *could* have been Chaplinesque scences of this sort which led pharmaceutical manufacturers to begin packaging many drugs in what are known as "unit doses," but the fact is that hospital pharmacists spent years forcing them to do so. In this system, each dose of medication is individually packaged in a plastic-and-cardboard, foil or heavy paper unit, oral liquids are packaged in foil or glass cups, and injectable drugs come in plastic and glass disposable syringes. In this way each dose is identifiable even to the manufacturer's lot number until the moment the drug is administered.

At first glance, this system would appear to be a packaging engineer's dream—and the individual packaging does, in many cases, add to the cost. Nevertheless, most clinical pharmacists, and those physicians who have taken the trouble to look into the matter, agree that unit dose is probably the only system on the scene which holds any promise of reducing the chaos of present dispensing methods. For instance, Dr. Byron Barnes of St. Louis College of Pharmacy estimated that the typical patient in one hospital received one of every ten doses of medication in error. Dr. Barnes, as Dean of the College, probably is unable to work in hospitals extensively, and as much as I dislike saying so, his estimate, though based on sound data, is probably low. Some hospital pharmacists allow that the error rate nationwide may be one dose in five, or higher. Dr. Barnes's estimate was based on a study done at Massachusetts General Hospital, which is a large teaching hospital (at the time it had 1,067 beds) that makes extensive use of computers and is certainly to be considered a trend-setting operation. In the late 1960s this institution averaged 3,000 physician orders and 10,000 drug doses and treatments each day. In light of more recent studies of other institutions, it is certainly a reasonable assumption that a 10 percent error rate in such an institution as Massachusetts General would translate to a much higher rate in a more typical (as far as an average consumer might find) institution.

Although there are some differences in studies, there is a shocking report that surfaced in the fall of 1975 illustrating just how bad the situation can be. The findings of the study were reported to Congress by the Comptroller General of the United States as "Potentially Dangerous Drugs Missing in VA Hospitals—Different Pharmacy System Needed." The General Accounting Office (GAO) studied eleven VA hospitals, nine of which used ward stock system and two of which used unit dose distribution systems. At the nine ward stock institutions, from 24 to 57 percent of the drugs checked could not be accounted for after their withdrawal from the pharmacy. In the institutions using a unit dose distribution system, the rates varied from 9 to 12 percent missing—better, but far from good. The GAO's recommendation—and this gives some idea of just how large a quantity of dangerous drugs may be floating around—is: "Drug losses could be reduced and patient care improved in VA hospitals by converting the *164* hospitals presently using the ward stock system to the unit dose system" (emphasis added). Clearly, this indicates that an additional unit dosing cost of 10 percent (this includes amortization of initial equipment investment and small extra costs of certain unit dose packages) would pay handsome dividends, at least for the VA.

The unit dose system is still relatively new, and there is not really enough data at this point to be able to say anything authoritatively, but from what data is available it is not unreasonable to expect it to reduce errors by half. And with experience the *able practitioner* should not be surprised if the rate of error were reduced to 1 percent or less. The factor of risk to the consumer is lessened for several reasons, the most important of which is that the pharmacist is given greater responsibility for the control of medication dispensing. This brings us to the most central factor: *competence*. There are a great many possible variations of unit dose—there is, as yet, no single preferred construct, although there are some basic elements—but, and this cannot be stressed too often, it is the competence of the pharmacist *in collaboration* with the nurse which makes this system work.

Here is an example of how unit dose might be utilized: A patient is admitted to the hospital and is examined by his physician; the physician makes note of the admission and writes his orders on a two-part NCR (no carbon required) form. As soon as the physician signs the form, a nurse or ward clerk tears off the portion he has used (the sheet is divided into sections with perforations for this purpose). One copy becomes part of the patient's chart (this sheet is not perforated), while the other is sent to the pharmacy by messenger, pneumatic tube, or other such device. (Some institutions have a central pharmacy with "satellite" pharmacies located on or very near the nursing units they serve, but for the sake of simplicity, let's assume this is a small, 100-bed hospital where the central pharmacy does it all.)

At the pharmacy, the pharmacist fills the prescription, but instead of simply putting the drugs into a container and dispatching them, he proceeds differently. First, he enters the drug information on a distribution sheet (each sheet covers a unit of from 25 to 50 beds which can conveniently be served by one nurse), then he labels a compartmented plastic or metal drawer with the patient's name and room number, and finally he puts the unit dose package of the drug into a compartment in the drawer which indicates the hour at which the dose is to be given the patient. Let us say that Mr. Jones is to receive 1 gram of sulfisoxazole at 8 A.M., Noon, 4 P.M. and 8 P.M. It is now 8 A.M., so the pharmacist puts two 500 milligram unit dose packages in the 8 A.M. and Noon compartments and sends the drawer to the nursing unit where the first dose will be given and the tray will be inserted into its appropriate slot in the "medication cart." Since there is one such cart for each nursing shift, he will then prepare a second tray and put the medication in the 4 P.M. and 8 P.M. compartments. A third tray for the night shift will be inserted, labeled but empty, at least for the moment, in the third cart. The night nurse (11 P.M. to 7 A.M.) will open the drawer as she makes medication rounds and, finding it empty, will know (as a double-check on her own medication sheet) that Jones has no medication coming.

Physically, the heart of the delivery system is a specially constructed wheel cart which can be locked when it is not in use. There are several types, but essentially all use tiers of trays which can be secured from theft and, to a significant degree, prevent mixing or spilling the medications. Thirty or forty-five minutes before shift change, an orderly can exchange a filled cart for an empty one. Since only the Med nurse and the pharmacy have keys (a different key for each unit) there is little risk as the cart is taken to the floor, and if some clumsy individual wishes to mess up the Med nurse, he would be more apt to injure himself than spill the medications—the cart would have to be damaged before the medication could get scrambled.

On the floor, the medication nurse can look over her medication list and, as added insurance, open each drawer as she makes rounds —this could be every hour. A look in the drawer reveals which patients are to receive medication and simultaneously provides access to the medication itself. A change of carts at each shift change provides convenient times for medication changes three times a day. Interim or emergency doses can, of course, be sent up from the pharmacy at any time—in seconds if there is a pneumatic tube system.

There are a great many advantages to this system, but only a few need to be mentioned. For one thing, it saves nursing time since there are no setups to be made; it's all done at one time in the pharmacy. (I do recall more than one nurse—when I set up an early unit dose system—who persisted in taking the blister-packed medication from each drawer, popping it into a paper cup after opening the pack, and placing the cups on tags on a tray! Obviously, a bit of retraining is sometimes called for.) Not only does reducing the time required for the nurse to dispense medications mean that patients will receive their medication more nearly on time (I have personally set up unit dose carts for a twenty-four-hour supply of medications for 100 patients on three nursing units and double-checked them in a little over one hour),* it frees the nurse to care for her patients. The system is also more or less accident proof: since the doses are segregated by hours and patients, a slip or hard jolt cannot scramble the medications. And each dose is labeled right up to the moment it is delivered to the patient.

Overall, the really important advantage of unit dosing is that it places greater control of dispensing in the hands of the pharmacist. And it affords him the opportunity of greater involvement in therapy—it is almost impossible for a pharmacist *not* to know what drugs are going to which patient, even if the institution does not use a patient profile form. In this system prescriptions (signed direct copies of physician's orders as they appear on the patient's chart) must go to the pharmacy for a supply of medication to be dispensed. Even though a patient profile form may not be used, a composite

---

* Assuming it takes a nurse an hour to set up medications and then administer them four times a day on each of the three units, and assuming that it took an hour and a half for me to do the setup for all units for a twenty-four-hour period and half an hour for the nurse to administer them each time, the hospital has saved at least 6 1/2 hours of nursing time. It is true that an hour of a pharmacist's time costs more than an hour of a nurse's time, so some unit dose hospitals have trained nurses to do the job. However, the task of filling the cart has been better done by technicians whose work is double-checked by a pharmacist—it is done more rapidly by people with less training, some think, because it is a very tedious, mechanical task.

record of some sort must be assembled to assure a continuing supply for medication. Even the most simple tabulation presents the pharmacist with the opportunity to at least summarily check for drug interactions and inappropriate dosage. Unfortunately, in current practice the *typical* hospital pharmacist is no more likely to make such checks than the typical community pharmacist would be.

As the Comptroller General's report to Congress documents, the unit dose system does seem to effectively reduce pilferage, spoilage, loss and, possibly, the unauthorized administration of drugs. Where the drug room/floor stock system is used exclusively, there always seem to be large quantities of drugs for which there is no accounting, and there appears to be a strong temptation for nurses—as well as aides, orderlies, janitors and anyone else who can gain access to them—to administer drugs to friends, patients and themselves ad lib without regard to the possible serious consequences. Whenever I have had the occasion to work in a hospital that makes extensive use of floor stock drugs, I have deemed it a professional responsibility to periodically inspect and thoroughly check such stocks and determine, as much as possible, what happens to them after they reach the floor. This sort of thing is unpopular with many nurses, but it happens to turn up some very dangerous situations.

A few years back, I was carrying out such a routine inspection on the wards of a large mental institution when I came across an unlabeled quart Mason jar half-filled with white tablets of roughly the same size and shape. One of the nurses explained that these were "headache tablets" that were given to anyone complaining of a vague ache or pain. I was able to identify two sizes of glutethimide (a sedative), sulfisoxazole (a soluble sulfa), aspirin, aspirin compound, and a few tablets that looked and tasted like an aspirin compound with codeine. When I confiscated this witches' brew and destroyed it, the nurse asked what she could do now. To my reply that she should use the tablets in the stock bottle labeled aspirin, she protested, "But I'm supposed to be able to account for those!"

On another memorable occasion, I discovered a large bottle of oxycodone "compound," an opiate-analgesic combination. This medication had not come from the hospital pharmacy because we had never stocked the item. Instead, it had been brought into the hospital by a terminal cancer patient. When the patient died, one of the nurses simply squirreled away the remaining tablets. Not being familiar with the product, she looked it up in the *PDR (Physician's*

Desk Reference). This only served to confuse her; when she saw the name of one of the opiate salts was "terphthalate," she interpreted it as "taurocholate" and assumed it to be a mild laxative because it contained "bile salts." By the time I arrived on the scene, she had used half the bottle, giving two tablets at bedtime—she was nonchalantly dispensing an addictive opiate, which is known to constipate some people, as a laxative!

While the unit dose system offers a certain amount of relief from this sort of surreptitious "prescribing," it must be emphasized that it is neither foolproof nor immune to tampering. This is so chiefly because of the physician's ambiguous relationship with the hospital, which makes it all but impossible to get him to follow a set of rules if he doesn't particularly feel like doing so. At the risk of seeming to contradict some of my earlier statements, the same holds true of the nursing staff—good nurses are in short supply. Aside from this, the full advantages which might accrue from the unit dose system are seldom, if ever, realized. It is an extremely rare hospital that will permit, let alone encourage, the clinical practice of pharmacy. Pharmacists are not encouraged to take drug histories, to keep patient profiles, to monitor therapy or consult with physicians on matters concerning drug therapy. As a result, consumers continue to be victims of the most irrational sorts of drug therapy in the hospital as well as outside its confines.

The Tangle on the Patient's Chart

From time immemorial, physicians have written drug orders on patients' charts. Typically, the orders are intermingled with the physician's clinical observations, test results, and orders directed to all manner of other technicians and professionals which are written day by day in no particular order. Unfortunately, these ingrained habits carry over into unit dose prescribing. At the heart of the unit dose system is the two-part NCR order form on which the physician writes drug orders. Under normal circumstances it is logical to tear off the top portion to send to the pharmacy and leave the sheet below intact. In many cases, however, nurses and physicians demand that the copy that was actually written by the physician remain with the chart, so the bottom sheet is generally the one sent to the pharmacy. To the pharmacist, there is no actual difference, but what all too frequently happens is that the bottom sheet is torn beyond the perforations, or gets folded over, or the physician will see some empty space and start writing an order on a sheet where the lower part is not in place. This means that part or all of an order may never arrive at the pharmacy. A nurse checking the chart and finding only the original will assume that the copy of the information has been received by the pharmacy. The following incident illustrates how tragic the results can be:

> Del Berger had been mildly ill for two days with what seemed to be a deep chest cold, but late Friday afternoon he ached so badly and was so feverish that he called his physician. The physician listened to his description of symptoms, then told him he'd order a prescription and that he would call the x-ray department at the hospital and order a chest film for the next morning. Mrs. Berger drove to the drugstore and picked up not one but three prescriptions: cephalosporin capsules, aspirin compound with codeine tablets, and a cough syrup. At 7 P.M., Del coughed up some blood and was having difficulty breathing, so Helen called the physician again and was told to take Del to the emergency room as soon as possible. Dr. Cord would meet them there in twenty minutes.
>
> By 8 P.M., Dr. Cord was convinced that Del had pneumonia and should remain in the hospital for a few days. Since Cord hadn't eaten his evening meal and had promised to take his wife to a party at 9 P.M., he told the admitting clerk to admit Berger and wrote an order for the cephalosporin to be given intravenously every six hours, then departed. Cord was out of the hospital before the clerk had time to enter a diagnosis for Del, so she consulted a nurse in the emergency room who told her to put "PAP" as the diagnosis—it was one of Dr. Cord's favorite diagnoses. PAP stands for "primary atypical pneumonia," and in Cord's case it covered a multitude of sins, because the real diagnosis could be established later and changed on the record without anyone asking questions.
>
> Fortunately for Del this particular diagnosis triggered a response in one of the floor nurses who knew that any of Dr. Cord's patients entering the hospital with this particular diagnosis received a particular series of tests. It was sort of expected that the nurse on the floor would order them automatically so that most of the results would be available when Cord came to see the patient the next morning. Normally a Culture and Sensitivity test was not a part of the battery of tests, but Del produced more bloody sputum, so the nurse took it on her own initiative to order the culturing of this for organisms.
>
> In the lab, a quickly stained sample of sputum indicated that the organisms were mainly Gram-negative rods. It would be

another thirty-six to forty-eight hours before the identity of the organism would be known with any certainty, but it was immediately clear to the technologist that Gram-negative rods generally are not as sensitive to the effects of penicillin or cephalosporin as they are to other antibiotics. Since it was the custom of the physicians at this hospital to prescribe an antibiotic, usually a cephalosporin, before the lab results were available, the technologist immediately called the floor nurse to explain the situation. Dr. Cord, however, could not be reached through his answering service.

At 10:15 P.M., Del Berger's condition began to worsen—his temperature rose to 105° and he appeared to be going into shock. Fortune smiled, at least for the moment, as the nurse spotted one of Dr. Cord's colleagues (he was part of a group practice) in the corridor and he consented to see Berger. In light of the lab technologist's information and Del's deteriorating condition, new orders were written. The first change was from the use of cephalosporin to kanamycin—an antibiotic more likely to be effective against Gram-negative rods.

The floor nurse returned Berger's chart with the new orders to the nursing station and went immediately to give her report to the incoming 11 P.M. to 7 A.M. shift. The hospital used NRC pharmacy orders, so she was confident that the next shift would soon have the drugs since the ward clerk merely had to tear off the second sheet at a perforation and dispatch the order to the pharmacy. What she was not aware of, however, was that the physician had started writing directly after a preceding order that had already been removed and sent to the pharmacy—there was no second sheet to take the impression. This meant that the order to stop cephalosporin and the orders to start kanamycin were never sent to the pharmacy.

There is no reason or rational explanation for the fact that no one on the 11 P.M. to 7 A.M. shift inquired about the order to stop the cephalosporin therapy and start kanamycin therapy. The fact is that there is nothing to indicate just what *did h*appen—the bottles of cephalosporin for intravenous administration continued to be sent to the nursing unit, and they were used on *some* patient, but not, according to his chart, on Del Berger. Del Berger's chart did indicate that he had been given kanamycin, in spite of the fact that there was no record of the pharmacy delivering any of the drug for him—the pharmacy wasn't even aware that the drug had been ordered.

It was never satisfactorily explained whether Del had actually received the kanamycin or not, but the following afternoon

Dr. Cord arrived on the scene again. Not all of the test results were in at that point, but Cord was aware that Berger had a kidney problem and the use of kanamycin could be hazardous, so he ordered tests to evaluate the situation. He was not particularly alarmed because Del's condition appeared to be improving and there were no signs of toxic effects from the drug, so he wrote an order to continue the drug. *This* order reached the pharmacy just as the 3 P.M. to 11 P.M. shift came on duty, and as a result it lay in the incoming order box for nearly an hour. When the pharmacist finally came to these orders (further delayed by the fact that such orders in this hospital were considered to be "routine"), all of the "update" or "continue" orders were assigned low priority for attention, the assumption being that an adequate supply of the drug was already in the nursing unit. Finally, at 9 P.M. the pharmacist, having no other pressing work, began to check the order to continue kanamycin for Del Berger and was confused to find no indication that an order had ever been delivered to the pharmacy to *start* giving the drug. He did, however, find the cephalosporin order that was never cancelled. Assuming the later order to be mere confusion on the physician's part, the pharmacist ignored it.

In the meantime, the lab returned the results of kidney function tests which indicated real trouble—Berger's kidneys were functioning at only about 10 percent efficiency. This meant that any drug which is nominally removed from the body by the kidneys would be removed at a far slower rate. Both cephalosporin and kanamycin are such drugs. In most hospitals information regarding a patient's lab tests is not routinely sent to the pharmacy, so the pharmacist must take it upon himself to obtain the information; more often than not this means leaving the pharmacy to view the patient's chart.

At 2:00 A.M. Sunday the situation began to come to a head. But before going further into Del Berger's part in the drama, it is essential to understand the staff scheduling priorities of this particular hospital. Hospitals have several groups of employees who work a rotating shift, and the largest of these groups is the nurses. The shifts run from 7 A.M. to 3 P.M., 3 P.M. to 11 P.M., and 11 P.M. to 7 A.M., and the least popular of these shifts is the 11 P.M. to 7 A.M. It's true that fewer nurses are required for this shift, but there are a very few nurses who prefer to work only this shift, and there are seven days in a week. This creates a problem. It is not unusual to find a nurse working twenty-one nights in a row on the 11 P.M. to 7 A.M. shift, then taking a week off and returning to work the 7 A.M. to 3 P.M. shift or 3 P.M. to 11 P.M.

shift for three or four months on a more rational five-day-a-week schedule. Even so, someone must work Saturdays and Sundays and since it is easier to find part-time people who will work a day or two during the week, the schedule of the regular staff is generally juggled to accommodate. At least that's what this hospital did.

The "charge" nurse on 4-West where Del Berger occupied room 462, bed 2 (he had become 462-2 instead of Del Berger) had only worked twelve nights in a row in the current month, but she had worked the last fourteen days of the previous month, making a total of twenty-six days straight; she was "completely wrung out." She had been assigned a new LPN, and, hoping to keep this "eager beaver" out of her way, she told her to take rooms 460 to 473—the rooms farthest away from the nursing station. Fortunately for 462-2, the eager beaver began to review her patients' charts to familiarize herself with her charges. At 1 A.M. Sunday the LPN came across 462-2's kanamycin-cephalosporin problem when the supply of cephalosporin came up from the pharmacy for 2 A.M. administration. She found a record of the cancellation for the cephalosporin and a new order for the kanamycin, but no supply of kanamycin. The patient's chart indicated that he had been receiving the kanamycin although none had been ordered for him from the pharmacy—a puzzling situation.

Earlier in this chapter we talked about the phenomenon of "squirreling" drugs on the nursing station. When a drug is no longer in use it is supposed to be returned to the pharmacy, but nurses, fearing they may not have a drug the instant it is needed, often cache their own little supply. It wasn't possible to discover in minute detail what really happened in this case, but a good guess is that the cephalosporin was probably given and entered in the patient's chart as kanamycin until this point. The charge nurse, hoping to avoid trouble, now found some kanamycin for the LPN to give. The LPN had never worked this nursing unit before, so she decided it was wise to simply give the cephalosporin to the charge nurse and administer the kanamycin. After all, it was 2 A.M. Sunday morning and *she* certainly didn't want to be the person to place a telephone call to Dr. Cord—or any other physician for that matter—at that hour.

By the time Dr. Cord saw Del Berger, late Sunday evening, four doses of the kanamycin had been given and there were some signs of toxicity, but Cord was in a hurry so he barely glanced at his patient. Early Monday morning when Cord took a closer look at Berger, he saw the signs of toxicity very clearly. At the same time he studied Del's chart more closely and discovered the results of the Culture and Sensitivity test as well as the result of the kidney function test. The organism causing the illness was an Aerobacter, which is very sensitive to chloramphenicol, slightly sensitive to kanamycin and not sensitive at all to cephalosporin or any of the penicillins. Also, kidney function was only about 5 percent of normal, so Cord decided to change medication—now giving the chloramphenicol.

At this point the people in the pharmacy discovered that their records of Berger's medication were different from those on the chart at the nursing station, but instead of investigating—"We were too busy at the moment, besides which, the error happened on the 3 P.M. to 11 P.M. shift"—the pharmacy director simply left a note for the pharmacist on the later shift to "check it out." The matter would normally have ended there, since the pharmacy director was notorious for his failure to follow up such notes, except that the pharmacist on the later shift was not the same person who had been involved in the situation as it occurred.

Tuesday morning the director found a typed report on his desk that, from the pharmacy's standpoint, detailed precisely what had caused the "error," what changes were required to prevent such errors in the future, and what damage had been done the patient. When the director saw that Del Berger's kidneys were no longer functioning and that he had lost 90 percent of his hearing—clearly a possible malpractice situation stemming from the kanamycin incident—he decided to bury the report unless someone made an issue of what had happened. No one did.

Del Berger now visits the hospital twice a week to spend several hours on an artificial kidney machine, and since hearing aids are of no value where there is extensive nerve damage—such as kanamycin is known to cause—he is learning to read lips. It is unlikely that he will ever know his injuries were *not* the result of the infection. When asked about the experience, he says, "I'm lucky to be alive. That's the main thing I care about."

Who Is Running This Hospital?

When it comes to preventing tragic snafus such as this, the major stumbling block is that the hospital's administration cannot tell a physician to shape up and follow directions without risking a major confrontation. One unfortunate reply that plagues the insistent administrator is: "Just who in the hell do you think is running this hospital?" The implication is clear, and the administrator, who is *charged* with the responsibility of running the institution, seldom has the stomach to force the issue lest he put his job and quite probably his career on the line. Unless the institution is the only hospital for a hundred miles and he has the solid backing of a tough, independent hospital board, there is little chance the administrator will come out unscathed. The reason: the physician is not an employee of the hospital, but a free agent, and it is he and his physician colleagues who write the rules that govern the medical staff. The hospital is far more dependent upon the good will of the physician than the physician is on the good will of the hospital. The balance in the relationship is clear from the flow of health care dollars: the physician himself receives about $.25 of the health care dollar, but he directly controls the expenditure of about $.51 the consumer puts out at the hospital and $.09 the consumer spends for drugs. That's $.85 or 85 percent of the health care dollar, and that is *Power,* considering that 10 percent or more of America's GNP goes for health care!

It is rare that a physician loses his hospital privileges. The administrator frequently threatens to temporarily suspend a physician whose charts and medical records are not current (there is usually a three- or four-month leeway), but the physician usually has staff privileges at several local hospitals, so he laughs and takes his patients to one of them. Eventually he does bring his records more or less up to date, and the suspension, if there was one, is quickly lifted. The hospital administrator knows full well that his threats are hollow—he is a paper tiger.

As rare as a suspension is, a revocation of privileges is, as I noted earlier in this chapter, far rarer—it almost never happens. And when it does, it comes about by demand of other physicians and it is either a result of an outside agency (a felony is committed), senility (the man goes blind, insane or presents a danger that even his patients have begun to talk about), or it is to be a punishment for transgressing one or more of the unwritten rules of the profession. In the early days of Health Maintenance Organizations (pre-paid group practices such as the Kaiser Permanente plan), physicians who went to work for the HMOs frequently lost or could not obtain privileges at local hospitals. Their colleagues in the community considered it "unethical" for a physician to work regular hours for a salary instead of being paid on a "fee for service" basis (it posed an economic threat and might become popular with consumers).

Given the administrative structure of the American hospital and the physician-oriented conservatism of the Joint Commission on Accreditation of Hospitals (JCAH), which is an adjunct of the AMA, it is hard to imagine things being any other way. Typically, the authority structure of a hospital moves down the ladder from a board of directors, to an administrator, who in turns directs (it might be more accurate to say coordinates) a staff of professional, paramedical, administrative, and clerical personnel. In general, the only employees of the hospital who are professionals are the nurses and pharmacists (if there are any). Paramedical personnel include lab technicians, therapists, x-ray technicians, orderlies and the like. Physicians do serve on administrative committees like the tissue, infection control, and pharmacy and therapeutics committees, but these bodies, if they function at all, are little more than a means of keeping people in line. It is more or less incidental that the medical practices which these communities monitor happen to take place in the hospital, since the hospital is only intrinsically involved in either the investigations or the decisions of its committees. (It might be more appropriate to use the word "accidentally" here in spite of the fact it is the antonym of "intrinsically"—this is, as you shall see, an essential dichotomy.) The hospital is responsible for assuring consumers of the competence of its employees and services but in fact has little means of doing so.

Whatever form a hospital administration takes (and there are many variations, too complicated to discuss here), there is always a committee responsible for the rules which govern the medical staff; it may have any number of titles, but it is inevitably composed of physicians (there may be exceptions where an "outsider" is placed on such a committee, but in nearly forty years of observation I have never heard of one), and this committee, regardless of its title, is the power behind the throne. The only instance I am aware of in which the power of the rules committee is abridged to the slightest degree is where the physicians are employees of the hospital, as in governmental institutions. Even then, the power wielded by the rules committee transcends that of all other committees *combined*—every important committee in the hospital, because of the nature of the beast, requires extensive physician involvement.

Still, there is someone who is more fundamental to the hospital than even the physician. Who? You, the consumer. According to figures available in May, 1976, you spent $118.5 billion on health care in 1975, of which 25 percent went to physicians and dentists, 9 percent was spent on drugs and 51 percent was spent on hospitals and nursing homes (8 percent was for the nursing homes). For all these dollars you are allowed to be a *passive* participant because the hospitals have neither the means nor the inclination to represent your needs.

Standing orders, discussed at the beginning of this chapter, are allowed because the physician insists upon it. I don't insist that such orders are "bad," but they *are* used under conditions over which too little control is exercised; there are no safeguards. The hierarchy of physicians dictates hospital policy in other areas as well. Without their approval you do not have the advantage that could accrue to you from such things as the practice of clinical pharmacy—if the "right" physicians had agreed to it in 1970, as many as one out of four American hospitals could have clinical pharmacy programs today, and by 1980 seven out of ten hospitals in the country would have some clinical personnel available.

No sane person denies the need of strong physician involvement, but consumer groups are now beginning to question the manner in which unilateral decisions, made by physicians for so long, serve the consumer. A good case in point is the current drive by certain consumer organizations and health insurers to require consultations with a second surgeon before elective surgery is performed. The data being compiled by these persons is more than adequate to indicate that physicians should (and easily could) have written such mandatory consultations into hospital rules decades ago. One can only speculate as to how many of the almost automatic tonsillectomies of the 1930s, '40s, and '50s would *not* have been carried out had consultations been required. The same may be said of appendectomies, hysterectomies and similar procedures, but, at the risk of repetition, such consultations did not serve the best *economic* interests of the medical and dental professions or the institutions in which they practice. Hospitals, collecting, as they appear to have in 1975, $.43 of every health care dollar, certainly had no incentive to pressure physicians into enacting such rules. ($51 billion divided by 8,000 hospitals equals a bit under $6.5 million per hospital.) Some call it coincidence—I do not—but there appears to be a direct correlation between medical incompetence and the increased use of hospital facilities. Unnecessary surgery, profuse laboratory tests that are both inappropriate and expensive, *documented* irrational drug use often resulting in reactions, all of these increase both the duration and cost of a consumer's stay in the hospital.

The Losses Have To Be Made Up Somewhere

This economic conspiracy against the American consumer tends to be obscured by the mystique surrounding hospitalization. We have been led to equate the American hospital with the epitome of modern medical practice. It goes without saying that such miracles of modern medicine as open-heart surgery and organ transplants would be unthinkable without the modern hospital. But what most consumers fail to realize is that it is highly unlikely that they will ever *need* open-heart surgery or an organ transplant. At least three-fourths of all hospitalizations are for mundane, even unnecessary, purposes: a patient is to be observed for changes in condition, tests are to be made, or, quite simply, a consumer will be hospitalized because whatever is to be done will be paid for by an insurance program only if it is carried out in the hospital. As long as there is a bed available, few hospitals exercise any control over admissions. The one general exception to this may be the teaching hospital, which will sometimes reject patients if their problems are not sufficiently exotic to be of interest—"Hah! A classic case of kyphoscoliosis with a full-blown respiratory acidosis! What a pity we don't take that up until next semester. Send it to County." In the community hospital, however, the rule is to fill every available bed and keep them full. Empty beds in a hospital, just as in a hotel, mean lost revenue.

Once a consumer is "captured" by the hospital, the fleecing begins. Basic room charges are only the starting point; the remainder is made up of charges for drugs, lab and x-ray tests, convenience items, dressings and other services—even the television sets produce revenue. Profits from these are used to offset perennial losses from open-heart units and other medical showpieces. The hospital is not about to curtail the utilization, irrational as it may be, of the profit makers which support the prestige-building, but often unnecessary, revenue losers. What is so professionally disheartening is the way in which the medical staff eagerly cooperates in this grand theft. Perhaps I would take a different view if my income were in the six-figured bracket, but that's pretty doubtful. One of the reasons is expressed in these words of a laboratory technician working in a large private hospital near Chicago:

> In two years I must have personally analyzed specimens from about 500 spinal taps. Every time a patient came in complaining of a stiff neck, wham, they'd hit him with a spinal tap. I don't

> recall a single one of those tests coming up positive for meningitis —or anything else. When I asked one of the physicians about this, he explained, "Look, this way, if the guy does come down with meningitis later, they can't sue me. I can say, 'Get lost. I did my job. I ran all the tests.' " The lab director called me on the carpet for even daring to ask about the taps. He pointed out that the hospital made nearly a $20 clear profit on each procedure. That's ten grand just from the ones *I* ran, and there are three shifts with five technicians on each shift. And that's not the only test they do that with.

If that isn't enough, I can recall one hospital where I was given the price of $1.25 each for a cephalosporin antibiotic capsule; I knew that a pharmacy a few blocks away only charged $.65 apiece for them, but at 2 A.M. the poor consumer didn't have any choice. It's a wonder they didn't think to give out a day's supply of four capsules and make a flat charge of $20. Considering that health insurance companies routinely pay just about anything the hospital's business office puts on the bill, such a flat fee billing for "emergency medical supplies" would probably be paid unquestioningly.

The hospital pharmacy does not, as a matter of fact, have to resort to such underhanded tactics to turn a tidy profit. For one thing, hospitals purchase their drugs in large quantities. This and the fact that most qualify for special non-profit institutions discounts gives them an advantage, but in many areas groups of hospitals, both non-profit and those operated for a profit, pool their purchasing power to obtain even better discounts. As a result we find hospitals frequently qualifying for much better prices than the typical community pharmacy. Just how extensive this has become is illustrated by one recent study of 107 drug items: community pharmacies paid less than hospitals for exactly 7 items; for the remaining 100 they paid more—as much as 70 percent more! One community pharmacist said this of the situation: " 'Special price' seems to be a basic tenet in every pharmaceutical manufacturer's community-marketing dictionary. There are, to mention a few, the pharmacy price, the dispensing physician price, the clinic price, the small-chain price, the large-chain price, the private hospital price, and the unbelievable state and federal government price." (Before you rush to inform your Congressman of this, you should know that this—and much more—was given as testimony before the Subcommittee on Activities of Regulatory Agencies of the House Select Committee on Small Business in 1967.)

Beginning with lower costs for the drugs, the hospital pharmacy then goes on to compound its economic exploitation in much the same way the large chain drug outlet does, except that the hospital seldom passes any of the savings along—the large chain outlet passes enough savings along so that its prices are 10 or 15 percent lower than the typical community pharmacy. (Actual costs are as much as *50* percent less.) The fact is that the drugs which cost the hospital less to buy and less to deliver may cost you, the consumer, as much as *forty* times what you would pay for them in the neighborhood pharmacy. I have seen aspirin tablets that can be purchased in almost any retail outlet for less than half a cent each sold in hospitals for as much as $.20 each. Gouging of the sort illustrated in the instance of the cephalosporin capsules is the rule rather than the exception. (As I recall, those capsules cost the community pharmacist $.50 each, while the hospital paid only about $.43.)

In light of the fact that the hospital pharmacy generally doesn't have (or need) a fancy facade or a great many expensive fixtures, and considering that hospital pharmacists are generally paid less than their counterparts in the chain and neighborhood stores, why the need for all this? The simplest answer I know is that some way must be found to pay for the $3-$5 million open-heart surgical facilities. (My town has four hospitals and three of them have such units; the sad fact is that *one* is probably more than is needed for a service population of about 250,000.) Of course, the money hunger does not end there, but suffice it to say that the typical hospital is probably less efficient (which is to say that it is more wasteful) than the federal government. The losses must be made up somewhere.

This Pharmacy May Be Hazardous to Your Health

How exactly does all this fit into our investigation of health care quality, since it seems that I have dealt extensively with the dollar aspect of hospitals? Surely performance fits into this picture to justify the existence of a pharmacy in the hospital. It is true, hospital pharmacies provide services which simply could not be performed by the community pharmacy. You cannot, for instance, call the typical community pharmacy and ask them to compound intravenous medications, but most hospital pharmacies *are* now responsible for the compounding of specialized intravenous medications. At one time this task was performed on the nursing unit, but the increasing complexity of modern drugs and a better appreciation of the problems involved demanded that someone with extensive expertise take over the task. The logical person was the pharmacist, and because the drugs were already in the pharmacy, it was possible to sell the idea. This may sound casual, but what really happened was that over a decade or so some very competent people in teaching hospitals, bolstered by the American Society of Hospital Pharmacists, carried on a veritable crusade. Once the idea was firmly entrenched in the large teaching institutions, it spread to the smaller institutions. There are still a great many hospitals without such programs, just as there are a great many which have programs which are no improvement on the older system.

The danger is, as it always has been, that the IV solutions will become contaminated. The problems involved with contamination of a solution that goes directly into the veins of a patient are indeed formidable (not that such solutions may not already be contaminated as they come from the manufacturer, but I will not here attempt a discussion of that very important facet of the problem). In recent years physicians have felt the need to "feed" some of their patients intravenously, and the procedure, which goes by several names such as "supplemental alimentation," "hyperalimentation," or more commonly, "TPN" (for "total parenteral nutrition"), is a high risk procedure. Perhaps the greatest danger lies in the fact that generally a tube known as a catheter is inserted into one of the veins of the arm or a vein in the area of the collar bone and is threaded into a large vein which carries a large volume of blood (the vena cava). This is a vein whose contents are very quickly emptied into the right auricle of the heart. Under normal conditions the blood from the right atrium is pumped into the right ventricle, which in turn pumps the blood to the lungs. In the lungs the blood is oxygenated and returned to the left atrium, which then forces it into the left ventricle from which it is pumped all over the body. Because the brain is such an important organ, it receives much of this "fresh" blood, and it receives it immediately after a small (by comparison) amount is drawn off by the coronary arteries. After this there is a priority of sorts that sends a considerable flow of blood to the liver and kidneys. Thus, any infectious organisms or foreign particles introduced by either the solution or the catheter stand a very good chance of ending up in the lungs, heart, heart muscles, brain, liver or kidneys. This can, and far too often does, result in injury to tissues or infection. The greatest hazard appears to be from infection, although there are several other dangerous possibilities that have been documented and speculated upon in the literature of health care.

There are many different sorts of these nutritional solutions, as the names indicate, but it is important to know that all such solutions contain high concentrations of nutrients that are essential to microbial growth. I have seen situations where bottles of these solutions were hung at room temperature for periods of from eighteen to twenty-four hours as their contents seeped into a patient's vein—this despite standing orders and repeated warnings that the bottles be replaced at least every twelve hours. Under such circumstances, any organism that finds its way into the solution has at least a passable chance of surviving and multiplying. There is some evidence that the high concentration of glucose found in such TPN solutions inhibits most organisms, but it is not true of *all* organisms. Ten years ago, I used a medium remarkably similar to TPN solutions to grow a common mold, Aspergillus flavus. Spores of this common bread mold can be found almost everywhere, but I was using very special cultures known as NRRL 3000 and NRRL 2999. One of these cultures, when grown on this liquid medium, produced the most powerful cancer-causing compound known—Aflatoxin B-1. Of course, the other one did not and no matter what I tried it would not; however, I did isolate several "wild" strains from moldy bread, peanuts and corn that did.

Since the introduction of the techniques that make continuous intravenous feeding possible, a great many systemic infections have been reported as being associated with this procedure—and some fatalities have resulted. As far as I know, the possibility that someone might develop a malignancy as a result of Aspergillus flavus growing in one of the bottles and producing Aflatoxin has never been investigated, but it does not seem to be very probable that it has happened. It is, nonetheless, recognized that great care must always be used to protect patients against invasion by these organisms.

To make matters worse, some organisms are deadly regardless of whether they are alive or dead. The reason for this is that they may produce toxins that are released when they die and their cell walls rupture; or, and this is particularly true of those organisms known as "Gram-negative," chemical fragments of the cell wall react in a way that causes the red blood cells to release a compound that acts on certain control centers of the brain to cause body temperature to skyrocket. This is known as a pyrogenic reaction and the substances from the organisms are known as pyrogens. It may very well be that this is a protective mechanism, but it can be catastrophic for a patient's body temperature to shoot up eight or more degrees in a matter of an hour or so. Such situations were seen far more commonly in the 1930s, 1940s and into the early 1950s than they are today. A combination of better understanding of the mechanism involved and improved aseptic technology has brought us to the point where there is virtually no excuse for a human being to experience a pyrogenic reaction. Nonetheless, both pyrogenic reactions and systemic infections do occur in modern hospitals, and almost without exception the cause is incompetent aseptic technique within the hospital. It takes very small amounts of pyrogen, only a few nanograms, in fact, to cause a reaction. (One nanogram is 0.000000000001 gm., or a *trillionth* of a gram.)

> Dan Brown, age fifty-five, was admitted to Memorial Hospital (250 beds, located in a city of 68,000 population) for observation and testing. He had become unconscious for no apparent reason and on the way to the hospital went into convulsions. Tests made during the next few days indicated a brain tumor, and a craniotomy was scheduled. After the operation, laboratory tests were conclusive that the tissue was not malignant, but the surgeon had found the lesion to be too extensive to remove all at once; it would have to be done in two stages. Following such surgery it is not unusual for a patient to be semi-conscious for several days, and Dan's surgeon, knowing that a second operation was needed in the near future, decided on a course of intravenous feeding. On the fourth post-operative day, Dan Brown's temperature began to climb. At noon Dan was obviously in trouble with a temperature of 106.4°F, and although the rate at which it rose slowed, it didn't stop. By 8 P.M. the thermometer read a shade over 108°F and at 1 A.M. Dan Brown convulsed and died.

During the course of the "in-house" investigation that followed this incident, some astonishing facts came to light regarding the preparation of sterile solutions in this hospital's pharmacy:

(1) Solutions were commonly prepared in a large open room directly beneath a high velocity (unfiltered and undiffused) air vent.

(2) The work surface was the top of an old wooden table that had been discarded by the dietary department because it was "too unsanitary."

(3) One pharmacist was known to smoke, frequently spilling ashes, as he prepared sterile solutions.

(4) The Assistant Director of Pharmacy Services, during demonstrations of aseptic techniques, re-used sterile equipment that should have been discarded as contaminated, failed to disinfect seals of sterile bottles before puncturing them with a sterile needle, routinely removed gaskets designed to maintain aseptic integrity, and poured the solutions from bottle to bottle.

This same information, and more—"Pharmacists A and R never wash their hands before preparing sterile solutions, etc."—was contained in a report written several months before Brown entered the hospital—by one of the staff pharmacists, at the request of the Assistant Director!

Partly as a result of Brown's death and the resulting investigation, certain changes were made in the procedures for dealing with sterile solutions. The main modification was the installation of a "laminar flow" hood, a system which provides a "clean" work area which is kept clean by the constant flow of highly filtered air. *When used with proper aseptic techniques,* a properly maintained laminar flow hood can almost eliminate the chance of contamination in the preparation of intravenous solutions.

An interview with the representative of the company which supplied and installed the hood reminds me of a statement of H.G. Wells that human history becomes more and more a race between education and catastrophe—the new hood probably *increased* the chance of contamination to a considerable degree:

> We installed the unit on a weekend, so it wasn't till Monday that I heard about the first problem. I'd about expected it, but not that soon. Don't get me wrong, I'm not completely blameless, but they overbought—the unit was just too damned big for the room where they wanted it installed—and I didn't try very hard to discourage them. What the hell, I get 10 percent . . . anyhow, they turned the hood on and in ten minutes the heat build-up was enough to drive anyone out. After half an hour the thermal overload kicked out and that was it. I got back down there the next day and talked the maintenance people into sticking two eight-inch ducts in and reworking the return line on the air condi-

tioning. It was an awful job and took a month. Well, it did the job just fine, but I could see right off that one of those ducts was creating a turbulence right at the work-face. I didn't have to use smoke, you could see the dust particles being drawn into the work area. I hate to think what it cost, but I showed them how to rig a shield, that they wouldn't bump their heads on as they worked, to divert the blast from that duct. It looked like everything would work out O.K.

Six months later, I went in with a technician for a routine check—it's part of the service. By that time the HEPA [high efficiency particulate air] filter and pre-filters should have started to fill up, but the air flow indicator didn't give any indication of this. The technician shook his head and I knew something wasn't right when he flipped the switch and opened the filter compartment. Some idiot had removed an inspection plate and by-passed the flow through the pre-filters. Naturally, this made the HEPA filter load up, and flow was down to almost nothing in a few days, so the dummy took a ball point pen—you could still make out the ink smears—and poked holes in the HEPA. My God! Well, this voided the warranty, but I did a little arm twisting and my boss let me replace all the filters. I gave the director a little lecture and then we put a seal on the inspection plate and took off.

I was sure everything would be O.K. after this, but sure enough, when I checked back a couple of months later, that air flow indicator was top of the bubble and it shouldn't have been. This time the technician checks the inspection plate first, only the seal is still intact, so he shut her down and opened her up. This time we find someone has reached up inside and punched a whole mess of holes along the top of the HEPA where you can't see 'em. Well, we pulled the filter and find that somehow a good two-thirds of the thing was covered with a blue-green mold—someone had slopped a whole mess of some sort of nutrient solution on it and a few spores came through. Well, the solution was enough to cut the flow, but those things grew like wild and I suppose that was when the holes were punched. This time I sent a bill for $150 and hoped *that* would make them more careful. I heaved a sigh of relief when they cut that place from my territory along with another county, but I hear they have had several systemic aspergillosis cases since. I hope I don't get called as a witness—Jeezus, what a mess.

Needless to say, the air coming through the holes in the HEPA filter was loaded with organisms and the mold growing on the back produced spores by the billions. This was not the end, however, as further horrors came to light. The filtered air in the room was so pleasantly clean that the assistant director of the pharmacy moved a small desk in and made the sterile room his office. This brought dozens of people tramping through the room. (Note: a person in motion emits approximately 10 million particles 0.3 microns and larger per minute; 60,000 of these may turn out to be bacteria.) Because the HEPA filter in the hood removed smoke, most of the staff came to the sterile room to have a cigarette during coffee breaks. Since the HEPA filter traps particles 0.3 microns and larger with 99.99+ percent efficiency, it is small wonder that it rapidly became clogged.

As the hood salesman indicated, the holes punched in the filter to increase air flow took a toll: two narrow escapes from pyrogenic reactions, half a dozen cases of systemic aspergillosis, and two deaths that were listed as "hyperpyrexia," but which were indistinguishable from pyrogenic reactions (since the victims were public aid patients in their seventies, no one looked closely). In the cases of the survivors we must not overlook the facet of prolonged stays and costs: either the patient, an insurance company, or public aid was billed for more drugs and days in the hospital than would have been necessary in normal circumstances.

Another outrageous aspect of the entire matter is that the hospital expended nearly $100,000—90 percent of this was for the modifications—for a piece of equipment that may never work as it was designed to. If the proper sized hood had been purchased for the area in which it was intended to be used, the entire setup should have cost no more than $10,000. Understand that this is just a rough estimate, but this pharmacy was probably a break-even proposition that year, and you can be sure that $100,000 was made up somewhere else. They didn't learn much from the experience either, because they still cannot provide an acceptable level of safety in the finished TPN solutions because not one of the pharmacists appears to understand elementary aseptic techniques—this means that every compounded solution that leaves the pharmacy is suspect.

There are explanations for this ineptitude that I don't think much of, but they do have some merit. In hospital practice, as in community pharmacy practice, the pharmacist is often a drudge who works a shift and draws his pay. Too rarely is he a professionally independent practitioner, both able and allowed to make professional judgments concerning the work he is called upon to perform. In an effort to remedy this state of affairs, elements within the profession of pharmacy and a *very* tiny contingent of far-sighted physicians have sought to introduce the pharmacist to the clinical level of patient care. The efforts have been scattered, sporadic, occasionally well-conceived and successfully executed, but altogether too often doomed to failure because funding, interest and able personnel were lacking.

The Hospital Clinical Pharmacist

The clinical pharmacist's role basically involves interaction with both the consumer and the physician in all phases of drug therapy—a far cry from the typical pharmacist's role of receiving and filling the physician's written or verbal transmissions. Theoretically, the practice of clinical pharmacy in the hospital works something like this: when the consumer enters the hospital as a patient, one of the first medical professionals to see him is the clinical pharmacist. (Obviously, emergency treatment will have priority, but even here the clinical pharmacist contributes his expertise since drugs are such an important aspect of modern health care.) From the patient the pharmacist obtains a drug history: an organized compendium of drugs the patient uses, allergies, sensitivities, idiosyncracies, chronic conditions, missing organs and the like.

Depending on the situation, the pharmacist may simply add his impressions of the patient's condition with regard to drug therapy and insert the information into the patient's chart. He may contact the physician to discuss an immediate problem, or it may be left for the physician to digest the information in the drug history and contact the pharmacist. In any case, the information is available to the physician as well as the nurse or any other individual involved with the patient's treatment. In some institutions the pharmacist makes rounds with the physician, while in others formal consultations take place, but the important thing is that there is a starting point for collaborative interaction of all the people involved in treatment, including the patient. Even if no formal consultation takes place, the fact that the data collected by the pharmacist is entered in the patient's chart is often enough to provide a basis for rational drug therapy.

Ideally, of course, the physician and pharmacist will collaborate to provide the consumer the best possible sort of therapy, with each contributing his expertise. From the collaboration will come a treatment plan and a comprehensive monitoring of the patient, not just by the pharmacist and physician, but by everyone. In some cases the decision will be *not* to use drugs and the monitoring could catch early signs that drugs may be indicated, just as the reverse might be true where drugs *are* initially indicated.

Clearly, the clinical pharmacist will not have time for the mechanical dispensing function, but dispensing can be performed by technicians. Such technicians are already being trained and used effectively, although this is complicated by the fact that many states require direct supervision by pharmacists on a one-to-one basis. The relocation of the clinical pharmacist to a point closer to the patient which allows him to protect the patient against reactions, interactions and irrational therapy, also removes him from the required one-to-one supervision of technicians, and some accommodation must be made.

Properly constituted, the practice of clinical pharmacy in the United States offers the only real hope for rehabilitating our present drug delivery system both in the hospital and in the community pharmacy. As we have seen, however, the medical numbers game is stacked against any easy, straightforward solution. We need to know who the clinical pharmacist is, where he comes from, and, most important of all, how many we have at the moment and what the future prospects are.

There is as yet no formal degree requirement for the position of clinical pharmacist (there are some professionals who still refuse to acknowledge either the existence or the need), but it is probably destined to become the domain of the Pharm.D. degree (Doctor of Pharmacy) along with, perhaps, the Master of Science degree in such areas as clinical pharmacy, drug information, pharmacy administration and so forth. Both degrees require from six to seven years to complete, but the Pharm.D. is a professional degree while the M.Sc. is a post-graduate academic degree. The training of these professionals really only started about a decade ago, and though more schools of pharmacy are hopping on the bandwagon each year, the supply of such professionals is very limited. At the present time it is estimated that only about 500 specially trained clinical pharmacists enter the profession each year. This amounts to only about 10 percent of the nation's output of new pharmacists. It is difficult to be certain of exact figures, but somewhere between a third and a half of these individuals are siphoned off by teaching, research, or community practice. Hence, the available pool of such individuals does not offer a reliable indicator of the number of qualified clinical pharmacists available to America's hospitals.

This is one situation in which on-the-job experience is vastly more important than any academic degree. A Pharm.D. or a M.Sc. is not now and should not become a criterion for practicing clinical pharmacy—every *competent* pharmacist has the capability of becoming a *clinical* pharmacist. Quite a number of pharmacists who hold only a bachelor's degree have already been able to bootstrap themselves into clinical positions by virtue of non-credit postgraduate work, on-the-job experience, or a combination of the two. Overall, based on membership in the relevant professional organizations, subscription lists of clinical journals, and some very scanty employment figures, I would estimate that at the present time there are only approximately 5,000 pharmacists in the United States *qualified* to engage in clinical practice.

Since there are some 8,000 hospitals in America, the practice of clinical pharmacy obviously cannot reach into all the places it should—every hospital. As a very rough rule of thumb, every hospital should have at least one clinical pharmacist on its staff, and any hospital with over 100 beds should have another practitioner for each additional 100 beds. It goes without saying that every large hospital should have at least a skeleton crew of clinical pharmacists for the evening and night shifts. In all probability it would require *at least* 30,000 of these highly trained professionals to meet the minimum requirements of every American hospital. Without some drastic reorientation, at the present rate it could easily take us from *thirty to fifty years* to achieve this goal.

How is clinical pharmacy received where it is presently being practiced in institutions? Reports vary, but where the practitioner holds a Pharm.D. degree, the reception, by physicians at least, has been tolerant, but rarely wildly enthusiastic. I have seen the mere fact that the clinical pharmacist with the Pharm.D. degree is called "Doctor So and So" lead to an amusingly ready acceptance by physicians who thought he was a physician with special training. It is a pity that the typical physician will not accept an allied professional, whose expertise exceeds his own in a somewhat limited sense, unless he can address him as "doctor."

Acceptance of the clinical pharmacist by the hospital has been more ambiguous and harder to assess. This is understandable since a clinical pharmacist on the staff—like the open-heart surgical facility—is primarily, at least at the outset, a prestige generator rather than a revenue generator. Where a clinical pharmacist is in residence, drug use may actually fall off rather than increase. Since his primary responsibility is rational therapy, he rides herd on the adventurous prescriber. On the other hand, not only is the clinical pharmacist paid a premium salary as he goes about, as one administrator put it, torpedoing drug sales, but he is also forever insisting on improving pharmacy services in ways that do nothing to increase revenues. But what this administrator, who had half-a-dozen malpractice suits in litigation, was too short-sighted to see was that a single $100,000 award (five of the six were settled for sums well in excess of this) more than justified the clinical pharmacist's salary. I guess it *is* difficult when insurance companies set their rates on the basis of general experience rather than specific performance. Nonetheless, patients in this hospital were far better protected after the clinical pharmacist arrived, and the day may not be too far off when insurance companies will be backed into a corner and forced to recognize the damage they are doing our health care delivery system by blithely paying for incompetence.

Finally, the prestige the clinical pharmacist brings to a hospital is totally different from the sort an open-heart surgical unit brings. It is not the sort of prestige that can be easily conveyed to the consumer, who is, after all, footing the bill. Of course, the fact that the federal government (which is doing its own special sort of damage to our health care system) will not provide grants for the hiring of clinical pharmacists, but will pay a large part of the multi-million dollar construction costs for an open-heart surgical unit, does not help matters either. The clinical pharmacist doesn't make for impressive newspaper articles, nor can he be switched on at a moment's notice to trot through his paces for visiting dignitaries.

The result of all this is that, although being against clinical pharmacy is like being against motherhood or Santa Claus, hospital administrators are not falling all over themselves in the rush to install clinical pharmacists. In fact, many administrators are covertly doing everything possible to ward off the day when they must recognize their need—or should I say the consumer's need—for clinical pharmacy. Most physicians, by the way, are slightly nonplused by the entry of a new, high-powered professional into what has, heretofore, been their unchallenged bailiwick. The result has been that physicians—who can do just about as they please in the hospital—have not been tripping over each other on the way to the administrator's office to demand the universal establishment of institutional clinical pharmacy practice.

Clinical pharmacy, as it is currently practiced, is not above criticism (God help the consumer if it ever is). Like all emerging professions it has had its share of teething problems. Not only are there no accepted educational prerequisites (aside from a license to practice pharmacy), but the most likely candidate, and certainly the most vocal—the Pharm.D. degree holder—has a degree from programs that are barely out of the realm of educational experimentation. Some programs grant the degree after a year of combined classwork and internship (beyond the five-year bachelor's degree), while others require as much as three years (two years of classwork and clerkships and one year of internship). Nor is the level of instruction always above reproach. I recall with horror one Pharm.D. who blithely gave a diabetic patient glucose in an IV solution that called for sucrose, then asked me if the two chemicals were not identical. Upon learning that they were not the same and that glucose could have dangerous consequences, he sent *me* to retrieve the material. Some former GI may well owe his life to the fact that *some* pharmacists are aware that even elementary organic chemistry is important to the work they do.

In short, the educational situation with regard to Pharm.D.'s is nearly as chaotic as that which prevailed in American medical schools fifty or sixty years ago with regard to the M.D. degree. At least a partial cure of the M.D. chaos was effected by strong-arm intervention on the part of the AMA—after the famous Flexner Report told the whole world about it. Unfortunately, American pharmacists have no such clout. After all, there are only about 130,000 of them, they do not earn $100,000 or more a year, and worst of all, they seem not to be joiners—there are several relatively small and ineffectual professional organizations. The American Society of Hospital Pharmacists and the American Pharmaceutical Association, the two largest and most important professional organizations, do not claim—and never have—a combined membership that represents more than one out of three American pharmacists. Under the circumstances there is not apt to be any extensive reform, however badly needed, of any facet of pharmaceutical education. (This very blunt statement will be clearer after I discuss some of the deep philosophical divisions in Chapter 6 as I deal with the pharmacist.)

Preparing a Defense

From time to time, I find myself wondering whether or not the mass of information I am endeavoring to pass on to you, the consumer, is relevant, but what concerns me most is that I find it difficult to convey complex technical information so that it can be easily translated into remedial action by a typical consumer. A neighbor who happens to be a newspaper reporter asked me: "Given the prevailing practice environment, what can I do to protect my family?" In Chapter 8, I deal with pharmacists and physicians in community practice, but this individual was acute enough to realize that health care in the hospital is different. Indeed, care in the hospital is a different ballgame and it is played in a different ballpark. The rules are not the same. The rules are not written for you, the hospital structure is concerned mostly with economics, and it is far more difficult for a pharmacist to help you even if he has the inclination and the courage. Still, there are some things you can do to avoid being fleeced, or, worse yet, led to the slaughter. Here are some points to consider:

(1) Remember that when you choose your physician you are, to a large extent, selecting your hospital as well. *Ask a prospective physician where he hospitalizes his patients.* If he has privileges at more than one hospital, you will want to know if he has a system for determining which patient goes to which hospital. Ask, too, if he will treat you at the hospital of your choice. If he says no or indicates that he would prefer another hospital, ask him why. It is possible that he has a good reason for not using one hospital and he might explain—every bit of information helps.

(2) Remember that *this process must generally be repeated for each additional physician* whose services you use. For instance, your personal medical roster might include an internist, orthopedist, gynecologist, urologist and a cardiologist. It is a lot more convenient and possibly safer if all or any of them could treat you at the same hospital if the need arose.

(3) Checking out a hospital and its organization is a difficult and time-consuming task. You *cannot* depend on the Joint Commission on the Accreditation of Hospitals as a criterion. I have seen the JCAH (which is an adjunct of the

AMA) approve hospitals that I doubt could have met standards for an abattoir. There are definite limits to what you can, as an individual, find out about how a hospital is really run. *You might try placing a call to the director of pharmacy services and asking:* (a) what sort of drug delivery system does the pharmacy use? (drugroom/floor stock, individual order/unit dose, or a combination) and (b) is there a clinical pharmacist in the house or available for consultation, and are his services used extensively? You might, even if you get proper answers here, check with your community pharmacist and one or more of your physicians. The presence of a unit dose system and/or clinical pharmacist are clues to a proper drug control system, but not guarantees. On the other hand, if there is no clinical pharmacist and the hospital uses floor stock entirely, you can assume the worst—drug use and delivery are almost certain to be inadequately controlled.

(4) *If the hospital of your choice has a clinical pharmacist, casually ask your physician about this.* If he starts to make contemptuous snorting noises, it may mean that the clinical pharmacist is ineffectual, or that your physician is hidebound, or a little of both. Without additional evidence you probably cannot determine which is the case, but it does indicate that *something* is amiss. A hopeful sign is a response which indicates that all sources of health care expertise are considered and welcome. The clinical pharmacist—and by the same token all other professionals who might make significant contributions to your care—should at least be accorded a measure of professional respect by the physician.

(5) If you are being treated for a chronic condition that is likely to result in your hospitalization, *get a few things straight with your physician beforehand.* Question him about any standing orders he may have which are likely to involve you, to be sure there is no conflict or incompatibility. As you do this, remember that he needs an accurate drug history that you must help keep current—it is in your best interest that you not withhold any information. Unless you make prior arrangements with your physician concerning medication, there is little you can do once you are admitted to the hospital, until your physician arrives on

the scene. In many states your rights and your freedom of action are seriously abridged once you are admitted to the hospital. You may not have the right to refuse medication, and the more bureaucratic the institution, the more apt you are to find its personnel resorting to stomach tubes, injections and the like to medicate you against your will. Should your physician decide that a change in one of his standing order medications is advisable, make certain that this change is communicated to the hospital *in writing.*

(6) When you enter the hospital, *make a point of asking for a copy of the American Hospital Association's "Patient's Bill of Rights."* You may not get one, but keep asking, and make sure that as many people as possible hear your request. If you do obtain a copy, read it thoroughly and keep it in clear view at your bedside. If nothing else, it may convince the staff that you are one patient to be treated carefully and with respect even though the hospital has not decided to conform to the document.

By the same token, it is wise to read any releases or waivers that are shoved before you. Do *not* be afraid to cross out or refuse to sign anything you do not understand or which appears not to be in your best interests. A surprising number of hospitals will ask you to sign contracts that some consumer protection lawyers contend would never be enforced by a court of law. If the hospital does not back down, make note that you are signing the document under protest and demand a photocopy.

(7) Emphasize to your physician that *you are quite willing to be treated or tested in his office or on an outpatient basis* at the hospital, reserving actual hospitalization for serious conditions. This generally means that you will end up paying out-of-pocket for some items such as minor surgical procedures and diagnostic testing that would be covered by insurance if performed while you are hospitalized. However, as the saying goes, there is no free lunch. What the insurance company pays today eventually comes out of your pocket in the form of increased premiums—over the long haul it's a game in which you, the consumer, can't hope to win. If you have a choice, shop around for health care insurance. A few enlightened companies have come to realize that it is in the best interest of both insurer and

insured to pay for minor surgery and tests performed in the physician's office.

Will these steps get you better health care? They are steps in the right direction, but the sad fact remains that when you need the services of a hospital, you are not usually in any condition to shop around, argue with clerks, nurses and the like, quiz pharmacists or coerce physicians. You can take some preventive measures in advance, but in an emergency situation you are left to take what you can get.

It should be crystal clear at this point that before we can achieve any significant improvement in the delivery of drug-related health care in the hospital, the practice of hospital pharmacy must be substantially overhauled, but for this to happen there will have to be sweeping changes in the entire hospital. Unit dosing and clinical pharmacy offer real hope of controlling both the irrational prescribing activities of physicians and the distribution and administration of drugs in the hospital. Unfortunately, the economic orientation of the American hospital, and its domination by a hierarchy of physicians, make widespread implementation of these changes in the near future highly unlikely.

6 *The Pharmacist?* WHO'S THAT?

Social conditions can be such in the pharmacy that the pharmacist has psychologically little hope for other than a meaningless existence. Indeed, social conditions within a structure [*such*] *as the pharmacy may be such that employee pharmacists find it very difficult to maintain personal ego-autonomy.*

Clayton T. Shaw
(Soc. Sci. Med. 6:109, 1972 in Drug Intel. Clin. Pharm. 7:232, 1973)

The language is sociological jargon—cold, distant and Latinate. Shaw was doing what so many hundreds of social scientists set about doing in the late 1960s: he was investigating a minority within the American social system. It is unmistakable that American pharmacists constitute a minority, both within our culture at large and within the caste system of our health care professions. What is not so clear to consumers is that pharmacists are a minority in the most oppressive sense of the word. Pharmacists are not an oligarchic minority like physicians, college presidents, or the wealthy, but a minority in the same sense as Chicanos or blacks —economically stagnated, under-represented and, for all practical purposes, *invisible* to the majority.

Who, pray tell, is the pharmacist anyway? Your first impression of the person behind the prescription counter of either the corner drugstore or the local hospital is likely to be correct, for, ironically, the "typical" American pharmacist is a white, male Protestant of European descent. Looking more closely, as one group of researchers did, we find that, in addition to being almost the quintessential WASP, our "typical" pharmacist was reared in a community of 50,000 population, or less, and graduated from a public high school in a class of more than 200 students. Further, he was in the top 25 percent of his class, his favorite subject was either biology, chemistry or mathematics, and, had he not chosen to study pharmacy, he would likely have chosen medicine or teaching. His father typically has only a high school education and, as often as not, the aspiring pharmacist needed financial assistance to complete his education.

These humble socio-economic origins subsequently tend to determine the general course of the pharmacist's career. He leaves his college of pharmacy, not just flat broke, but in debt as much as $5,000-$6,000. Because he generally has a year's apprenticeship yet to serve (at low pay), is unlikely to have extensive "family money" at his disposal, and has "limited professional prospects," bankers see him as only a so-so risk. What all this means is that it is almost a foregone conclusion that the neophyte pharmacist will start his career working for someone else. His employer is almost certain to be either (1) a pharmacist from the "good old days" who has "made it" to the extent of owning his own business, or (2) a mass-merchandising drug chain which is owned, and ultimately controlled, by heaven-knows-who somewhere off in corporate never-never land. Nor is it very likely that the pharmacist will manage, in the course of his career, to progress from employee to employer, with the possible exception of becoming the manager of a store owned by someone else. In this case he would be, at best, a surrogate employer and still an employee himself—probably subject to greater stress and constraint than if he were to remain simply an employee pharmacist.

Even the most cursory investigation of economic systems is sufficient to demonstrate that an employee's remuneration and advancement are contingent upon performance of those tasks designated by his employer. Generally, the employee has little latitude; he is not free to alter in any significant way the manner in which the designated tasks are performed—except in the direction desired by the employer. An example, more simple than most, may help illustrate what I mean: When I was thirteen, I wanted to earn money to buy a camera, so I took a job as a caddy at a local golf course. The going rate was $.45 for nine holes and $.75 for eighteen, but the customary tip usually raised this to $.50 and a dollar respectively. One day, however, I discovered that some golfers were extraordinarily big tippers, but that, in return for the big tip, you had to deliver extra service. That day, I happened to draw one of these big tippers and was promptly pulled aside by one of the other, older caddies who offered me a dollar to trade golfers with him. He explained that he wanted to be in the same foursome with his buddy. I didn't really believe this, but I accepted the deal, and then demanded the real explanation. He hesitated a moment and replied, "Well, kid, I guess ya gotta learn the facts of life sometime. This guy and the guy my buddy has always play partners against the other two, and they play for big money. They always win and their caddies get 10 percent of what they win—I never got less than a fin and a couple times mor'n a sawbuck. 'Course, we help out with a hand mashie now'n then, but what the hell."

"Hand mashie now'n then," indeed! This kid would pick up a ball his golfer had hit into an unplayable lie and do anything but put it on a wooden tee. His minimum bag of tricks took five strokes off his man's scorecard. Even though I was only thirteen, I knew this wasn't right and it bothered me. To make it worse, the people involved in the match were friends of my family. I was so wrapped in thought about the situation that I forgot to mark my player's drive on the first tee, and on the third hole I almost stepped on his ball as we walked down the fairway. At this point a great many people would have been angry, but my man happened to be a priest, Father Tolson. He inquired about my health, and when I told him I wasn't ill, he replied that something had to be wrong, so I outlined the problem for him and asked what he would have done. "Well, son," he replied, "that's an interesting problem, and one that you have to answer for yourself, but bear in mind that most people seem to believe that if something isn't immoral or illegal, an employer has a right to expect the matter done. The trouble arises from the concept of what is moral."

Forty years later—nearly thirty of them spent in the practice of pharmacy—I am still alternately saying "thanks" and "no thanks" to Father Tolson. Yes, it is a question of deciding how much you can morally do to improve your employer's score, or profit margin. And no, it is not that simple. It is never a simple moral decision for an employee, because it is not a decision weighed out in the calm atmosphere of an ethics or sociology class. I remember one of my daughters reading aloud a course description that involved the study of both sociology and ethics, and it went something like this: "Would you like to understand social and ethical phenomena through observation and analysis rather than through reading texts? This course is designed to allow you to 'participate' through a variety of techniques. Behavior can be observed and recorded on video tape, you will learn computer analysis of different kinds of data, model building, and simulation techniques—all will be used to challenge and stimulate you as"—and on and on. When I was in my teens, I'm certain I would have been as excited by this as my daughter was. However, I have learned in the interval what a great many others have: an employee who is weighing his employer's demands against his own personal values and standards *inevitably* does so while sweating under the palpable threat of an economic sanction. A misstep under such circumstances is irrevocable and, unlike the computer analysis or video tape, cannot be easily or quickly erased and redone.

The Pharmacist's Right to Refuse

For the employee pharmacist the ethical/economic bind is, for the most part, both simple and direct. As I have already noted in discussing the problems of prescription filling and dispensing, the economic success or failure of a pharmacy depends almost exclusively on the density of its prescription business. Most expenses, including salaries, can be fixed at a predictable level, so that turning a profit hinges on filling the greatest possible number of prescriptions per hour, day, week, month, etc. For the *employer,* the pharmacy is a tool for making a living, and productivity is the name of the game. Any pharmacist, since he is better paid than the rest of the "help," who does not contribute his utmost to this end is an economic polutant which must be purged from the system.

What effect does the pharmacist's economic subservience have on the sort of health care that you receive? Several years ago, a young pharmacist applied for an opening at a hospital where I was director of pharmacy services, and his story clearly illustrates what can, and all too often does, happen:

> When I got out of school last year, I was nine months shy of having enough apprenticeship to become fully registered, so I tried to find a position in a hospital. At that point I wanted to be a community practitioner rather than a hospital pharmacist, but it seemed that the experience of working in a hospital would be

valuable. I applied at several hospitals only to find that most of them wanted experienced people, and the only way it seemed that I could get that was to enter a one- or two-year internship. To make a long story short, I ended up taking a job in a store in a small town, because by that time all the good positions were taken.

The man who owned the store was a semi-retired pharmacist in his late seventies—he only filled prescriptions when there was no one else to do it—and he introduced me to a young fellow about my age, John Wade. It turned out that John was the store manager and an apprentice himself, so I asked Mr. Ward, the owner, if that wasn't apt to cause problems since neither John nor I could legally work alone and state law required that there be one registered pharmacist for each apprentice. Lord! I thought he'd have a stroke right then. He told me that the store belonged to him, he'd worked thirty years to make it what it was, and *nobody* was going to tell him what to do or how to do it. This outburst really shook me up, so I just shut my mouth and went to work filling prescriptions.

Three weeks later, I received a letter from the state board informing me that I had passed the examinations and because of my military service time I was being granted a license. However, I would not be able to reciprocate that license to another state until I retook the "practical" portion of the exam the next year. This solved one problem, but in the meantime I discovered that John had never gone to pharmacy school and probably never would; he had simply been apprenticed when he got out of high school and what little he knew about pharmacy he had gotten by filling prescriptions. It wasn't that John couldn't do a passable job of filling most of the prescriptions—actually he could probably take care of 80 percent of them without supervision—but the trouble was that he didn't seem to have any concept of professionalism. I think he was a lot like Mr. Ward in his contempt of legal niceties.

Either one of them would fill a prescription that was eight or ten years old even if the guy who prescribed it had been dead for several years. At times they'd substitute—I don't mean use a different company's brand of the same drug, but actually use a completely different drug with, as they'd say, "similar indications." But the thing that scared me most was the way they'd "write" prescriptions for people who had never seen a physician. They would ask the customer what he wanted, then they would take a prescription blank and write a prescription up as though the physician had called it in by phone. Of course, I knew by this time that if the physician ever learned of the "prescription," he could be told that he had called it in, and even if he couldn't remember having done so, he'd end up thinking he had. I guess you'd be surprised, but they did the same sort of thing with public aid customers. If public aid didn't pay for a certain drug, they'd put down the name and quantity of some other drug that was authorized for payment, but give the first one. (They always "took" a little extra on these to cover the "extra" service.)

Knowing this was going on was bad enough, but it all came to a head one day when a friend of Mrs. Ward's came in and asked for some "hormones." She didn't have a prescription, because her physician had refused to write one for her, but she wanted some "hormones" because her friends were "all taking them" and they seemed to help them. I offered to call her physician and talk to him, but she just got mad and stomped out of the store. I know it wasn't right, but I hoped that John or Mr. Ward would handle the matter and I wouldn't know about it. That isn't what happened, though. About ten minutes later, the lady came back with Mrs. Ward and, pointing at me, she practically shouted, "That's him—make him give me some of those hormones, Willa."

The first thing that happened was that I just got cold all over, then I repeated my offer to call the lady's physician. Well, that wasn't good for anything. Mrs. Ward ordered me to give the lady some hormones. I knew from the tone of her voice that she wasn't going to take no for an answer, but I couldn't figure out any sort of compromise, so I just told her I had to have a prescription. At that point I might not have looked too closely at any sort of paper they might have shoved under my nose. Now, both of them stormed out and I knew I was in for trouble.

About an hour later Mr. Ward came in the back door of the store and I could hear him cussing to himself—a very bad sign. "What in the G—d— hell did you do?" were his first words.

"About what?" was all I could manage. I still wasn't sure what he was referring to.

"My wife just had a heart attack and you're responsible. What did you do?" was his angry response.

This was, to say the very least, a frightening state of affairs. Even though I knew Mrs. Ward's physician had examined her earlier in the week and pronounced her in excellent health, it was always possible . . . I found out later that this old gal used some device of this sort whenever she was thwarted, but that she really *was* in good health.

Anyhow, I'm here looking for a job because she wanted me fired.

Most of us who had been practicing pharmacy in that corner of the state were pretty well aware of the way in which Ward ran his store, and several of us had filed reports with the state pharmacy inspector. The inspector's reply? He didn't feel right about depriving a man of his living, so he would drop by and give Ed Ward a verbal warning . . . almost certainly without making any record of it.

I could probably write a chapter on the abuses that transpired at Ed Ward's store, and it would be a very long one, so I should hasten to add that the patently illegal, flagrant "prescribing" (known in the trade as "counter prescribing") and other "irregularities" that went on at Ward's pharmacy are probably more extreme than what goes on at your corner drug store. Nonetheless, it is consistently true that *all* such profit-motivated unethical behavior on the part of pharmacists arises from the same general set of circumstances. The crux of the matter is this: at the same time that the pharmacist's economic survival is dependent on filling as many prescriptions as possible, the only way in which he can have any significant, beneficial impact on the existing health care system, generally, is to *refuse* to fill those prescriptions which, in his reasoned, professional judgment, are clearly inappropriate or dangerous.

As I go deeper into consideration of professional education and information dissemination, my use of the words "reasoned professional judgment" will assume a different dimension. I will also further clarify the reason I choose to ignore the weak, but legitimate, option of trying to reason or negotiate with the physician in an effort to remedy such dangerous or inappropriate situations. In view of the information I have already provided, it ought to be clear that the effect of reasoning and negotiating on the physician is to put the pharmacist in the same position as that of the buzzing gnat —the noise attracts a half-hearted, but potentially lethal slap.

Refusing to fill a prescription, on the other hand, is more like a bee's sting. No matter what legitimate device the pharmacist uses, he finds himself in conflict with both the physician and the store owner—you could have filled ten prescriptions in the time you spent "fooling around" trying to get Dr. Jones to see the light! Consequently, the pharmacist, regardless of whether he is an employer or employee, may find his hands tied even if he has excellent grounds for questioning a prescription:

Ralph Bloomburg had been employed as a pharmacist for two years at the suburban outlet of a small drug chain in New Mexico. When one pharmacist at the company's downtown store fell ill, Bloomburg, along with the other pharmacists at the new store, found himself working one day a week at the older store to fill in for the sick man. The second time he worked his shift at the older store, he received a telephoned request to refill a prescription which he could not locate in the files. When he called the store's other pharmacist, he was told, "That's kind of an old one, you'd better look through the 'dead' file in the basement."

After a protracted search, Bloomburg managed to find the original prescription. Written some ten years earlier for a public aid patient by a physician who had died shortly afterward, the prescription bore a notation of a number in a more recent file. That number was still in the basement and that prescription also had a similar notation. After eight new numberings, the current prescription was located in a file that had been started three years earlier.

The "active" prescription revealed that a Mrs. Maria Montoya, or someone using her name, had been receiving 112 tablets of 500 mg glutethimide every two weeks. A quick check of earlier numbered prescriptions indicated that this had been going on for nearly six years. The current prescription had been refilled so often that several additional sheets had been stapled to it to record the refill dates. On the original prescription it had been noted that the successor of the dead physician had authorized continuation of the prescription. There was also a notation, apparently in the handwriting of the original prescriber, that Mrs. Montoya could have as much of the drug (a sedative) as she wished because she was dying of pancreatic carcinoma.

A telephone call to the second physician disclosed that:

(1) He had never examined Mrs. Montoya before approving the prescription.

(2) The diagnosis of cancer of the pancreas had been made by the dead physician and there was no way to check its accuracy. (As long as the pharmacists continued to fill the prescription without calling the physician, he had no way of knowing her fate—she apparently simply quit "doctoring" after her original physician died—but he "guessed" she was dead.)

(3) In spite of his assumption that Maria was deceased, the

physician was not the least perturbed. He saw nothing wrong with filling the prescription, and he was not disturbed by either the amounts of the drug or the frequency with which it was being dispensed: "Out there in the barrio those people all pass the stuff out to the relatives."

The physician did finally agree to cancel the prescription, and asked Bloomburg to have Mrs. Montoya call his receptionist for an appointment. What happened, however, was that whoever was having the prescription refilled simply took it to the other store where it was refilled without question. For his efforts, Bloomburg earned a reprimand from the company vice-president, who was not a pharmacist and who did not share Bloomburg's concern over the possible dangerous side effects that often accompany the excessive use of glutethimide.

This sort of abuse is *quite* common: the pharmacist's employer almost invariably regards refill business as pure "gravy" which no businessman in his right mind would do anything to discourage. In my years as a practitioner I have seen a great many prescriptions refilled until the paper on which the original was written had literally disintegrated with age. I have also seen individuals go to tragi-comic lengths to interpret a prescription as being refillable. In one instance, a physician had written two prescriptions on a single blank, with the result that he had covered the entire face of the sheet with writing. A carelessly crossed "t" in the general area of the "refill" box was regarded as carte blanche to refill the prescriptions whenever the patient requested them—which she did with regularity for nearly three years before one conscientious pharmacist called the prescriber's attention to what was happening.

It goes without saying that an employee pharmacist is often expected to have a certain moral elasticity when it comes to refilling prescriptions. Some pharmacists I know can match ink colors with almost spectroscopic accuracy and have, close at hand, pens which match the colors of those used by local physicians. It is the easiest thing in the world to put a check or cross in the "refill" box in perfectly matching color, then proceed to refill the prescription for years. Such antics are foolproof because precious few physicians can tell, ten minutes after writing a prescription, whether or not they made the prescription refillable. Those *very* rare physicians who do make copies of the prescriptions they write, or who never allow their prescriptions to be refilled, stand out like a sore thumb—their prescriptions are beyond the pale and only a very adventurous practitioner would dare tamper with them. All other physicians are "fair game," and the pharmacist who balks or shows the least hesitation at such shenanigans quickly becomes *persona non grata* with his employer. After all, refills account for 40 to 60 percent of the typical pharmacy's business, and a consumer who has become a chronic user of an analgesic, sedative or tranquilizer is money in the bank, so to speak. I know a number of pharmacists who can tell what day of the week and what time of the month it is simply by taking note of which consumer is standing out front waiting for his Valium prescription to be refilled. Such consumers come back again and again for years on end, so long as no one gives them any static about their consumption.

Faced with this fact of life, the employee pharmacist is made aware that he is simply in no position whatever to control the injudicious, irrational use of prescription drugs—particularly since the physician generally goes along with this sort of haphazard, speak-easy refill policy. One of the first, and perhaps the most painful lessons the neophyte pharmacist learns is that any physician can generally bully any pharmacy owner into complying with anything that does not carry a high risk of evoking a confrontation with governmental regulatory agencies. After all, a relatively limitless supply of meprobamate or diazepam is an easy way out: it is the easiest way to keep the "hypochondriac" out of the physician's hair. The physician goes his own way; the pharmacy owner, because of his extreme dependence on the physician's good will, does his utmost to keep him happy; the employee pharmacist, who is in the best position to advise the consumer and monitor his use of prescription and nonprescription drugs, must hold his peace and help rake in the money as he struggles to survive.

Intent and blame are meaningless in such a context, but this uneasy alliance makes drug abusers of a great horde of consumers. How many is difficult to say, but I estimate—and I have heard higher estimates—that one of every three American consumers over the age of twenty-one abuses one or more prescription drugs sometime during their lifetime.

The Invisible Man Behind the Counter

As I have said, blame and intent are not important at this stage, but cause and impact are. The employee pharmacist is an economic peon and this is one cause that appears to be of overriding importance. The extent of the employee pharmacist's peonage is difficult to grasp unless his status and influence are objectively compared with the status and influence of the other professionals with whom he works. As the sociologists have indicated, the typical pharmacist comes from a lower-middle-class family; his father generally has only a high school education. In consequence, this typical pharmacist comes from a background which is unlikely to imbue him with either an innate sense of professional independence or the self-assured assertiveness that evolves from a generation or two of "comfortable" economic circumstances.

Furthermore, once the pharmacist has gotten through the educational process and obtained his license to practice, he is far from "having it made." At best, all he can hope for is a modest sort of economic security and a regular job that does not entail getting his hands excessively dirty. (I have held positions where I was expected to wash windows, dust, sweep and mop floors, police the area immediately surrounding the store, haul incoming freight to the stockroom and the like, but today a pharmacist can earn an employer more if he stays close behind the prescription counter.) In both absolute and relative terms, the economic rewards are puny. An experienced male pharmacist working for a chain outlet in most urban areas rarely earns over $20,000 per year, and this is pretty much the top of the salary range. At the other extreme, I have seen hospital pharmacists in recent years start at $9,000 per year and less. Falling somewhere between these two extremes, it is not uncommon for employee pharmacists in independent stores to peak out at between $13,000 and $14,000. It should be kept in mind that the pharmacist is a *salaried* employee: when business is brisk and he must work overtime, he seldom receives extra pay; by the same token, a pharmacist's day may start at 7:30 A.M. and end at 5:30 P.M., and he may be expected to work Saturday and Sunday. It is not uncommon for his work week to be 54 to 60 hours long. If he is paid for the extra hours, it is on a straight time basis.

After five or more years of professional education, the pharmacist thus finds himself in the same earning category as school teachers, plumbers and local truck drivers. On the other hand, he does not have the job security afforded by tenure, a union shop or, in many cases, the authority of the National Labor Relations Board. In any case he does not enjoy the extensive fringe benefits of a union contract. In balance, there are many worse ways to make a living. The work is relatively clean and safe, hernias and callouses are seldom a problem, there is little risk of black lung disease, and it is slightly easier on the nerves than being a Madison Avenue ad salesman. So long as one has no lofty ideals of professional service and no rigid standards of performance to be crushed or lost in the rush to fill fifty prescriptions an hour, it's a tolerable way of life. It does help to carry at all times what Dick Gregory once called a "Mississippi Survival Kit"—ten "Yessir Bosses" and a Shuffle.

Remember that out of the health care dollar, only $.09 goes for drugs (both prescription and nonprescription). Roughly $.19 goes to the physician, $.09 to the dentist, about $.51 to the hospital and nursing home, and $.15 for miscellaneous expenditures such as braces, prostheses, therapists, insurance, and the like. Since America's health care bill is now running around $118 billion per year (1975, latest available data) and climbing, the actual dollar amounts can be broken down as follows: physicians: $22.1 billion; drugs: $10.6 billion; dentists: $7.5 billion; nursing homes: $9 billion; hospitals: $51.1 billion; insurance (profits): $4.6 billion, and others: $13.6 billion. It is possible to break these figures down further (for the three categories important to this discussion) by converting them into terms of "cash flow per professional (or institutional—used for comparison) entity." When this is done we get a set of figures that looks like this:

each of 350,000 physicians controls $63,100
each of 8,000 hospitals controls $6,400,000
each of 150,000 pharmacists controls $70,000

All of these figures are, of course, averages. There is a wide range in actual values since some hospitals are known to take in over $20 million a year, certain physicians' incomes regularly exceed $300,000 a year, and a few pharmacists may earn as much as $40,000 a year, but *relative* cash flow can be used to illustrate an important point. Cash flow obviously bears only a distant relationship to individual income, but even here there are some surprises.

U.S. Department of Labor statistics indicate that the average earnings of an American physician stand at around $52,000 per year. (There are a great many different figures available—$42,000 to $85,000 per year—and one source warns that such data are not reliable. However, salaries listed by one medical employment agency ran the gamut from $32,000 for a prison physician to $85,000 plus fringe benefits for a partner in a group practice.) In contrast, average salary for a pharmacist is about $14,500. (The same source that warned about physician earnings listed $17,500 as earnings for a pharmacist, but surveyed only large chain stores in East Coast metropolitan areas.) Thus, the physician's earnings amount to about 80 percent of his cash flow, while the pharmacist's earnings represent about 20 percent of his cash flow.

The implication is this: while the physician is primarily selling his professional services, the pharmacist is primarily delivering a product, the acquisition costs of which tend to determine his charge. He is, then, functioning as a cog in the economic machinery. Furthermore, at least 90 percent of all prescriptions are written by physicians (dentists, podiatrists and veterinarians account for the rest) and an unknown percentage of over-the-counter drugs are purchased on the physician's recommendation. This means that perhaps $7 billion of the $10.6 billion that fuels and lubricates the pharmacy machine is spent at the direction of the physician (one physician-educator estimates that the physician directly controls 75 percent of *all health care expenditures,* or about $90 billion yearly). Typically, then, the machine is not individually owned or controlled, and the employee pharmacist's participation is two or three times removed from the decision-making facet.

Given his remoteness from the centers of both professional and economic authority, it is not too surprising that the American pharmacist becomes almost an "invisible man," not only to the physician and the hospital, but to the consumer and even to the governmental units charged with regulating health care. Just *how* invisible he can be is sometimes not evident even to the pharmacist himself, but the following incident is a more than adequate illustration.

As I mentioned in Chapter 3, those drugs which fall into the category known as Class II are so classified because they have a high potential for abuse and as such are more strictly regulated. There are two sets of regulations, state and federal, and though state regulations tend to be fashioned to mirror federal regulations, the state regulations may be stricter. In such cases, the stricter regulation applies, and in Illinois, where I happen to live, for many years the state has required the use of a special triplicate prescription form to order certain of these drugs (a control device which, I am sad to say, only a few states use). When the federal government enacted PL 91-513, it included many drugs that were formerly only very loosely controlled, and in passing conforming legislation the state made exemptions for the use of the triplicate form with regard to certain of the Class II drugs. Consequently, Illinois pharmacists have been allowed to dispense such potentially addicting drugs as amobarbital, pentobarbital and secobarbital on the authority of any hastily scrawled prescription which bears a reasonable facsimile of the signature of a licensed practitioner. Conversely, other drugs in Class II, such as certain of the opiates, have always required use of the special triplicate form.

In the fall of 1975, however, rumors began to circulate among Illinois pharmacists: *all* Class IIs will soon require triplicate forms; all Class IIs but methylphenidate and phenmetrazine will require triplicate forms; the change has already been made; the change will take place the first of the year; there won't be any change until after March and probably not then because the state medical association doesn't like it. Since I was not working behind a pharmacy counter at the time, I paid these rumors scant attention; pharmacists, like cuckolds, are always the last to know. It was something of a shock, then, when, eight months later (it was June 2, 1976, to be exact) I received a phone call from a colleague who wanted to know about "this business with the triplicate form on the Class IIs." He had been told that the requirement had been in effect since February and covered all Class II drugs but methylphenidate and phenmetrazine. He added that he had filled a few prescriptions for the drugs that were supposed to be covered, but that none of them had been written on the triplicate form. I told him that I knew nothing about the matter, but that I would check it out.

Word travels fast in the ghetto of the medical world. The next morning my phone started ringing off the hook—every pharmacist for miles around had heard that I was somehow involved. Each caller had a bit of information and a lot of questions. Before 10 A.M. I had enough conflicting stories to fill a couple of pages. The manager of one chain outlet was unruffled by it all: "Oh yes, we've required the triplicate for those drugs since last October." From one of his employee pharmacists, however, I got a different story: "That's a lot of malarky. I haven't seen a prescription for one of those come in on a triplicate form yet." A regional representative of the state pharmaceutical association claimed that the association had published a tear-sheet in its journal which detailed the new regulations. He told me that the sheet was dated January 1, 1976, and left me with the impression that it had been in the January issue of the journal as he said, "Those idiots must not read their mail—it went out to 2,100 pharmacists and nearly 4,000 stores." I learned later that the tear sheet was, indeed, dated January 1, 1976, but that it was contained in the *May* issue of the journal—some association members didn't receive their copies until mid-June. The kinkiest bit of this charade was that another pharmacist claimed that he had buttonholed this same association representative a week or so earlier and had been able to get no information out of him regarding the change—"I'm as much in the dark as you." (Note: only about 2,000 of the 9,000-plus pharmacists in the state belong to the state association.)

My next step was to double-check this highly unofficial information, so I went to the state officials who would ordinarily be directly involved with such changes. To my utter amazement, I found that no one denied that (1) the change *had* been made and (2) dissemination of this information had been hopelessly bungled. According to the Department of Registration and Education (which licenses pharmacists, physicians and a great many other "occupations"), the state's Dangerous Drug Commission had "acted—without public hearings—on October 9, 1975 (effective date: August 16, 1975[!]) to require triplicate forms for all Class II drugs but methylphenidate and phenmetrazine; they just passed a rule and forgot to tell anyone about it."

This is the sort of snafu one comes to expect when dealing with regulatory bureaucracies, but years of experience led me to believe that I still did not have the whole story. When I reached the public relations officer of the Dangerous Drug Commission itself, I discovered that my suspicions were well founded because she gave me a somewhat different version of the story. She, too, admitted that there had been a severe communications problem, that yes, the Commission had acted on October 9, 1975 (the effective date of November 9, 1975 had been confused somewhere along the line with August 16, 1971, which was the effective date of the Illinois Controlled Substances Act) and no, they had *not* reclassified any drugs, but merely removed exceptions which had been allowed when the Act was originally implemented. She went on to explain that the action had not been publicized because it was estimated that some 800,000 individuals would have had to be informed of the change—between us it was agreed that this might have cost upwards of a million dollars.

At this point the comedy of the triplicate form becomes exceedingly germane to the issue of the pharmacist's identity and professional visibility. Presumably the commission's estimate of 800,000 people who would have to be informed would include pharmacists, podiatrists, physicians, nurses, veterinarians, state, county and local law enforcement agencies, hospital and nursing home administrators, and officials within the state licensing and regulatory bureaucracy. Going one step further, I discovered that for some strange reason the Illinois Bureau of Investigation, most (if not all), county sheriffs, and the state police *had* been informed of the new regulation. Law enforcement agencies seem to have been given the word somewhere along the line that pharmacists who were found not to be in compliance should be issued a warning. Likewise, the bulk of the state's physicians had been informed of the change through their state association. (This did nothing to help implementation of the regulation, however, because the association had decided to oppose the change and physicians were simply not using the official forms. As late as March 1976, the state medical association appeared, without success, before an advisory commission in an attempt to forestall implementation, and further moves apparently are being contemplated because such rules "interfere with the practice of medicine.")

Why didn't anyone think of informing the state's 9,000 pharmacists? If every pharmacist had been suitably informed of the rules change, it would have been unnecessary to worry about the other 791,000 people who are ostensibly involved. Since those 9,000 pharmacists are required (in theory, at least) to review and approve every prescription filled in the state of Illinois, they *should* represent an easily controllable, effective "valve" for regulating such dispensing practices—they are the only people, as far as I can determine, who would suffer any legal penalties! A state-controlled computer contains the names and last known addresses of all pharmacists registered in the state, and at license renewal time it prints adhesive labels by the thousands containing this information. Since every pharmacist received a notice of renewal from the state in January 1976, it would have been simplicity itself to insert notices of the change. The valve would have been closed, the regulation implemented, and the cost would have been no more than a few hundred extra dollars.

Why didn't the individuals who are paid handsomely for the jobs they do think to do this? It might be just another example of the Peter Principle, but there are probably several answers to this question which have nothing directly to do with the problem at hand. Suffice it to say, however, that when I suggested such a solution to the Dangerous Drug Commission, the reply was an astonished, "My God, I never thought of *that*!" Not only is the pharmacist the only health care professional who is in a logistic position to instantly implement such regulations, but he *alone,* of all those involved, stands to suffer legal consequences for failing to know and follow the rules. Still, no one thought to inform him. The inescapable conclusion is that the pharmacist is the "invisible man" among health care professionals; the health care hierarchy has come to overlook him so thoroughly that it is no wonder that the pharmacist himself has difficulty "maintaining ego-autonomy." Since no one acknowledges his existence except, perhaps, at license renewal time, it is only to be expected that he sometimes doubts it himself—I think, but am I?

Professionalism: Arrogance and Insulation

This current invisibility of the pharmacist raises some important questions—questions that many of my colleagues, physicians, and state and federal governments have gone far out of their respective ways to avoid—that are fundamental aspects of health care, if health care is to be delivered in any sort of rational system. These questions are not just important to consumers, they are vital! It is relevant to ask if there is a spirit of professionalism among pharmacists as there is, say, among physicians or lawyers, and, at the same time, to consider whether or not the rise of such a professional ethos (hypothetical or real) might have significant repercussions in the way pharmacy is practiced. Beyond this, quite naturally, is the meat of the matter: is a professional ethos in the best interests of the consumer—what problems does increased professionalism pose in the area of rational, consumer-oriented health care?

This is a real Pandora's Box, but what does it mean to be professional, or perhaps more to the point, to be *a* professional? The two standard examples which come to most people's minds are the lawyer and the physician. What is a professional? Well, to many individuals, he's somebody who behaves like a lawyer or physician. This is all very well, except that in the last couple of generations everyone seems to have wanted to become "professional." Definitions have frequently been stretched to the camel-swallowing stage as everyone from architects and archivists to yardmen and zoo keepers has hired copy writers, founded associations and organizations of various sorts, and otherwise entered the struggle for clean fingernails, a monthly paycheck and a splendid sounding title. Although I didn't think it humorous, I recall one trash collector who placed (in the spirit of fun, I'm sure) the initials "D.G." after his name on the truck. Who knows, it may be that in awarding himself a degree of Doctor of Garbage this man made one of the most appropriate social comments of our time—"doctor" was originally used to designate a teacher.

Clearly there is an unreasoned feeling among most people as to what is and what is not professional behavior—even if it only extends to the observation that lawyers and physicians do not openly advertise their services on billboards at the edge of town. Just as clearly, this sort of intuitive classification will not serve the purpose when it becomes necessary to separate fiction from reality. In an attempt to achieve greater precision in this area, social scientists have for some years used questionnaires designed to sort out the prevailing attitudes among members of various occupations. One widely used test for the measurement of professionalism is known as "Hall's Professionalism Scale." This instrument was recently adapted by David W. Schack, working at the University of Iowa College of Pharmacy, in an attempt to test its validity as a measure of professionalism among pharmacists.

As adapted by Schack, the Hall Scale is intended to assess six "attitudinal attributes" of the would-be professional. The "ideal professional," as viewed by the social scientist:

(1) sees his professional organization as a major referent
(2) believes in public service
(3) believes in self-regulation
(4) has a sense of calling
(5) believes in autonomy for his profession
(6) believes in maintaining competence (Schack's contribution)

In his effort to devise an appropriate instrument to measure the subjects' attitudes in each of these areas, Hall devised a questionnaire containing statements to which the subject registers his response, ranging from "strongly agree" to "strongly disagree." Schack's addition of the sixth category displays considerable insight and, in my estimation, makes a very significant contribution, for, as we shall see, continuing competence is an embarrassing area for most health care professionals. Schack then revised and pretested the statements before administering the questionnaire to 800 pharmacists selected at random from the membership list of a professional organization.

By looking at some of the statements in Schack's questionnaire, it is a relatively simple matter to draw a mental image of the social scientist's concept of an ideal sort of professional:

(3) "My pharmacy colleagues and I should be the only ones who determine and set standards for our practice."

(35) "The public should be allowed input into the development of standards for professional competence which guide my practice."

The pharmacist who approaches the social scientist's ideal of professionalism can be expected to strongly agree with statement 3, thereby indicating his belief in the importance of self-regulation for his profession. At the same time, he would tend to strongly disagree with statement 35, thereby asserting his belief that his profession should be autonomous.

Since the primary purpose of Schack's study was to develop and, in a manner of speaking, standardize the questionnaire itself rather than to actually assess the overall degree of professionalism among pharmacists, his conclusions necessarily deal with limited aspects of the matter. One observation, however, warrants attention: those pharmacists who handled the heaviest work loads tended to score lower on the professionalism scale. It might be that these people are not good pharmacists to start with, or it might be inferred that one person can't fill 150 prescriptions a day or service a 200-bed hospital and give full attention to the task, but I shy away from such easy explanations. It is far more likely that those individuals who filled out and returned Schack's questionnaire are not your run-of-the-mill practitioners; they are in all probability not a representative sample—Schack himself questions this. I hope, as you, the consumer, should, that these individuals who took the time to fill out the questionnaire are those who have profound doubts about the quality of health care our present system is capable of delivering.

One thing that we can definitely infer from Schack's study is that *if* pharmacists were to score highly at the professional end of the scale, *then* they could be expected to act more like such model professionals as lawyers and physicians. If this were indeed the case, then the prospect of the professionalization of pharmacists raises some fundamental questions about the future development of the American health care delivery system. Put simply, it is not at all certain that the American consumer ought to *want* his health care technicians to exhibit certain of the "attitudinal attributes" implicit in a high degree of professionalism. At the same time, a close reading of all Schack's statements (see appendix) makes it quite clear that certain professional traits will have to go by the board before a health care system can be devised which is truly responsive to consumer needs. Let us then consider the attributes of professionalism as they apply to the pharmacist and weigh them in the light of the needs, successes and failures of our present health care system.

(1) *Sees his professional organization as a major referent.* I have known pharmacists to break down in hysterics when confronted with this attribute. The reason? Considering the concessions physicians have reaped through the efforts of the American Medical Association, most pharmacists see *their* national associations as emasculated scarecrows. Perhaps one out of three pharmacists belongs to a national professional organization and there are many reasons, but in general it is very much the same sort of problem we face with pharmaceutical educators—the organizations are out of touch with their constituancies. A great many pharmaceutical educators never have and probably never will work as employee pharmacists, and though the problem with the American Pharmaceutical Association is not as extensive as it is in education, it is of the same sort. Those pharmacists who are members of the APhA largely ignore it. A few months ago I had occasion to want to read an article that had appeared in the *Journal of the American Pharmaceutical Association* and, since I am not a member, I called several colleagues who are. To my request for the loan of the issue of the *Journal,* the first fifteen *all* replied, "Oh, I don't even bother to read the thing. I throw it out with the other 'junk' mail."

It appears to me, however, that in recent years the APhA has begun to move slowly towards the mainstream of the typical practitioner's thinking, and one reason for this is the competition offered by the American Society of Hospital Pharmacists. Until rather recently, hospital pharmacists had no independent organization but were affiliated with the APhA. The ASHP was founded to fill this need and has always been one of the few organizations which provide meaningful services to the pharmacist. Although, as its name suggests, it is not community pharmacist oriented, a number of them subscribe to its journal simply because it is about the only way to keep in touch with the current state of the art. I estimate that perhaps as many as half the hospital pharmacists in the United States are members of ASHP and the *American Journal of Hospital Pharmacy* is probably read by as many as 75 percent of our hospital pharmacists. Since its split with the APhA a few years ago, the Society has consistently increased in membership each year. However, there are only slightly more than a third as many pharmacists in America as there are physicians, so the absolute membership figures of the pharmacy organizations are depressingly low, and always will be even if they perform Herculean feats of recruitment.

(2) *Believes in public service.* This is an ambiguous area for any professional, largely because no one has ever managed to unravel all the consequences of Alexander Pope's famous bit of sophistry, "Self interest and social are the same." In a very real sense, one could visualize a belief in public service as a motivation for a garbage collector or a president of a steel company—after all, if either failed to do his job, society would suffer. In a way, we seem to expect a dedication to public service on the part of professionals because most professionals earn rather large incomes. In other words, they should be good to society because society is good to them. The monkey wrench in this machine is that the pharmacist is *not* all that highly rewarded. In addition to this, a pharmacist is not paid a penny more if he provides twice or four times the professional service that another pharmacist does. He may develop a following of consumers who prefer his services, but as an employee pharmacist any reward that does accrue generally comes only if his employer fears that he may move to a competitor's store and take the satisfied consumers with him.

(3) *Believes in self-regulation.* Here there seems to be a head-on collision between professionalism and consumerism. Self-regulation, extended to its extreme, would simply be a condition where there are no rules or laws governing the professional's behavior except those which he and his colleagues promulgate. Very clearly, even such traditionally self-regulated professions as law and medicine do not approach this "ideal." Medical schools are accredited by states, the physician is examined and licensed by government agencies before he can practice on his own, and he is expected to conform with certain record-keeping requirements. Pharmacists are under the same and greater constraints simply because the more extensive records they are expected to keep are more visible and open to inspection. Consistent non-compliance can provoke the state into revoking an individual's license to practice, and though this is not done as often as it should be among pharmacists, it almost never happens to a physician.

The ideal of self-regulation is, then, essentially to remove the policing of a profession from the hands of government and place it in the hands of those to be regulated. The assumption is that individuals are capable of self-regulation where such regulation may have to take the form of disciplining a member of the fraternity in response to the demands of individuals who are *not* members of the fraternity—outsiders. This assumption runs contrary to almost the entire experience of our civilization. The fact is that state pharmacy boards are made up of pharmacists and state medical boards are made up of physicians—by their actions our professionals even now give proof to the fallacy of self-regulation as an adequate control mechanism.

As a sort of devil's advocate test, let's look at the situation in another way: professional self-regulation affords members of that profession a comfortable degree of insulation from the complaints of the consumer. In some areas of certain states where consumer advocacy programs have been developed, state and federal regulatory agencies have found it expedient to do more than simply gather data, hold hearings, and issue reports. A consumer in such a locale whose TV set goes up in smoke as a result of an inept repair job finds a ready ally in the consumer protection division, generally run by his state's attorney general. The offending repairman usually has the option of presenting his side of the story, but in the majority of such cases he finds it far more expedient—and better for business—to make good on the bungled job with dispatch. It is to his advantage to satisfy the consumer rather than face a possible fine or suspension of his license to do business.

On the other hand, the consumer who is convinced that he has been had by a physician—or any other health care provider—is unlikely to obtain satisfaction from state or county professional associations even when it is obvious that the professional is at fault. The people assigned to investigate and, perhaps, mediate such complaints have every reason to be lenient toward the professional involved—after all, but for the grace of God, there go they. Small wonder that consumer frustration with the medical profession is being more and more frequently expressed in the form of malpractice suits. Still, there are many consumers (this was the case with Esther Sudell's family) who do not sue because no amount of money will bring a dead person back to life.

Empirically, self-regulation is a definite attribute of professionalism; this is not in question. What *is* in question is whether or not self-regulation, as it is now practiced, works to the advantage—

either immediate or ultimate—of the consumer. There are some who believe that our present system operates to the *disadvantage* of both the professional and the consumer.

(4) *Has a sense of "calling."* I strongly suspect that the way in which most pharmacists responded to the statements intended to assess their sense of "calling" is a reflection of the sort of day they had just had on the job. Romantic TV program depictions notwithstanding, no professional, be he pharmacist, physician, lawyer or whatever, lives in a world of constant action, excitement, confrontation and physical or intellectual intervention in which he heroically resolves even the majority of problems laid at his door. Few of anyone's problems are amenable to quick, easy solutions. The physician may spend weeks arriving at a proper diagnosis for a single difficult case—one from which he can derive a measure of satisfaction—but in thc meantime there are insurance examinations to be made, hypochondriacs to be dealt with, minor cuts and scrapes to be looked after, information to be compiled, and patient records to be transcribed. For the attorney, there are endless legal briefs and legal opinions to be studied in the hope of finding just one precedent he may cite, many dreary hours representing drunk drivers in a sleazy courtroom, wills to be drawn or amended, boundary disputes to be resolved and, for some, divorce settlements to be negotiated. The pharmacist's chores I have already described except to say that very few of the consumers he deals with will be in a gracious frame of mind when they walk away with a bottle of liquid or vial of tablets, which they probably didn't want to have to purchase but were afraid not to.

For most professionals there *are* nodes of excitement and satisfaction which are popularly thought to make up for the dreary aspects of the rest of the job, but I'm a little unsure of those people who claim to have a great many exciting, rewarding days on the job. Oh, I have experienced them, but they are rare. Most of them are the result of getting something accomplished outside of "official channels," or saying no when everyone else wanted to hear yes. All but a few of the exciting times I can recall from my years as a pharmacist revolve about incidents I would just as soon forget . . . a Christmas Day spent on the telephone, bullying my way up the ladder of officials of a patent medicine company in an effort to get them to release a "secret formula" so a local physician could treat a friend's three-year-old who had gulped down a bottle of their laxative tablets purchased at a supermarket . . . an epic scene in an emergency room with a furious physician (and two terrified nurses), he jumping and snapping like a rabid terrier, trying to get from me a vial of medication which I had little doubt would be fatal to the patient upon whom he intended to use it . . . A sense of calling may help a professional over the rough spots, but there is damned little in the profession of pharmacy—as presently practiced, at least—that offers the pharmacist any hope of experiencing this sort of spiritual uplift more than a few times in his career.

(5) *Believes in autonomy for his profession.* This is another attribute of professionalism which must, at best, be labeled as ambiguous. This is not to imply that most pharmacists would not feel a sudden sense of relief if they had the autonomy which the typical lawyer or physician now enjoys. To be able to set his own working hours (within reason), tell certain of his consumers/patients about the rational uses and needs for drugs that they receive on the basis of shaky diagnostics or even shakier "anecdotal recitations" culled from *JAMA,* tell the store owner that three sizes and three colors of phenobarbital will be stocked instead of 100, to announce to physicians that illegible, improperly written or irrational prescriptions simply will not be tolerated (your patients will be sent to a more competent physician)—this would indeed soothe the soul, but it is a beautiful dream and no more.

The problem is this: such "professional autonomy" would probably result in far better prescribing practices, would probably lower inventory costs and possibly prescription prices, and in general make the pharmacist a more effective consumer safety device—but, given the rest of our present health care system and the economic chains which bind the community pharmacist to his employer's profit margin, there is no way such autonomy could be achieved.

Even if we were to suppose it to be possible, we have a situation here that is unique among professional interactions. Several professions exercise sweeping powers as a result of their autonomy, but in no case does the autonomy of one profession overlap the autonomy of another, as would be the case if both pharmacists and physicians exercised complete autonomy with regard to prescribing. It is for this reason that the assumption of autonomy by a group of professionals is seldom questioned by other professionals or consumers. An architect and a lawyer involved, as often happens, in an urban shopping center development can each exercise sweeping professional autonomy and still avoid a confrontation: the lawyer knows it would be foolish for him to try to flaunt the laws of mechanics, and the architect will likewise refrain from tampering with the laws of the state. There are gray areas where one professional may well request an opinion of the other—zoning restrictions and building codes are two examples that come to mind. A pharmacist and a physician involved in the treatment of a patient are not so fortunate, however. The present health care system has evolved in such a way that the physician deals in an area about which he is ill informed and in which the pharmacist is in a far better position to know what is going on. At the same time the pharmacist is forced to work blind because he is not privy to the clinical information so painstakingly collected by the physician.

There are two obvious solutions possible for this autonomy conflict. One is to simply eliminate the autonomy of the pharmacist entirely, making him into a sort of technical storeroom clerk who does nothing but dispense drugs on command—something which machines have already been designed to do faster and cheaper than human hands. In this direction we are looking at the possible elimination of the pharmacist altogether. This has been the general tendency of our health care system for quite some time now and is largely responsible for the lackadaisical ineptitude which most physicians display as they use drugs in their practices today. The other alternative is to curtail the physician's autonomy at the most logical point, namely, at the point where diagnosis has been established and the ends (but not the means) of treatment have been decided. This is essentially the alternative and the promise of clinical pharmacy.

(6) *Believes in maintaining continuing competence.* This is the attribute of professionalism which was added by Schack to the usual list of five which appears above. Both in the idealistic and practical sense, this attribute ought to be one of the highest priorities for every professional. In actual practice, however, this attribute tends, not to distinguish the professional from the unprofessional, but to separate the highly competent from the mediocre and incompetent. In other words, it takes a considerable amount of effort and intelligence to be aware of the limitations of one's knowledge and to be sensitive to the colossal amount of new material which appears on the technical horizon each year. The competent professional—no matter whether he is a lawyer, pharmacist, physician, or TV repairman—is the one who has adequately learned the fundamentals of his area of knowledge and, because he ex-

pends the effort, is able to carry on his own education in order to stay abreast of developments in his field.

For years, physicians have made a fetish of seminars, lectures, and refresher courses. A glossy little brochure arrives in the mail in the dead of winter announcing: "The faculty of the University of Transylvania Medical School, in conjunction with Filpott Laboratories, is happy to announce the 13th annual symposium on myocardial infarction. To be held at the Flamboyant Arms on Waikiki Beach, February 1-6. . . ." It's just too good to resist: seven warm, wonderful, fun-filled days in Hawaii; it comes off the income tax; there are even seminars in tatting and tours to historic points of interest to keep the wives happy; and, ho-hum, another little certificate (that coincidentally looks like a diploma) to frame and hang in the new examining room. On February first, 300 physicians, who have dutifully registered for the symposium, troop into the hotel's grand auditorium for the first lecture. The lights are dimmed, a ten-minute welcoming speech introduces the eminent guest lecturer, and the lights go out for a series of color slides. The first ten minutes of the lecture are drowned out by shuffling feet and creaking seats, then a deathly silence falls. Half an hour later, 270 winter-weary physicians are queuing up for caddies at the hotel golf course, settling down at the bar with old acquaintances, or joining their wives at the beach.

In recent years, pharmacists have shown a bit of new-found professional mettle by initiating similar sorts of programs. Of course, everything is a bit less posh, and a few more stay for the lectures, because the participants are rather impoverished when compared to the physicians. The overall effect, however, is about the same.

Also in recent years, colleges of pharmacy, pharmaceutical manufacturers, professional associations, and some other loose-knit organizations have begun to offer correspondence courses to refresh pharmacists' knowledge in certain areas. While a few such courses are of excellent quality, many are nearly useless. In 1974 I had reason to become involved in a committee effort to review and evaluate the courses then available. We established a rating scale that took into account both quality and length of courses so that the longest and best course could rank higher than the same quality course that took less time. We had what appeared to be a normal distribution until we removed the time factor. To our chagrin we discovered a few courses in the high range, some at midrange and many, far too many, that ranged from 9 to 25 on a scale of 100. Until that time, I strongly favored mandatory participation in such programs as a condition for renewal of licenses, but since then I have taken a closer look at the sorts of activities certain states allow as credit towards mandatory continuing education requirements. The only thing such requirements have accomplished is to foster the proliferation of the sort of course that we would have rated very low on our scale—in fact some of these courses are so useless that they would fall off the bottom of our scale if our worst earlier evaluation were used as a standard.

Mandatory continuing education is a fraud and, as it stands, an expensive one. The only possible way it can become otherwise is to require hard evidence of his competence from each practitioner. This is the only way in which continuing education can be assessed for its impact on the professional. The debate now, among those who care, is between some form of peer review and standard examinations. I maintain that some sort of incentive is fundamental, some system by which the most competent are openly rewarded. The important point that every consumer needs to be aware of is that, as matters stand now, once a health care practitioner is licensed, he is licensed for life. His competence is not monitored and he is not, in any way, restricted as to what dangerous—for consumers—procedures he may perform. It is a sick joke among health care professionals—but one with a serious point—that, unless you have literally been caught in the act of killing a patient, your license is safe. A practitioner can become senile, "eccentric," or he may never have read a single word that relates to improving competence since leaving his professional school, and he will still be licensed to practice.

In sum, there is good reason to doubt that increased professionalism can come to the practice of pharmacy as it presently exists. At the same time there is the larger question of whether or not professionalism, as defined by our social scientists, is *appropriate* in the delivery of health care—is it not probable that it works to the detriment of the health care consumer? In practice should it not be a truism that health care practitioners are dedicated to excellence in their practices and keenly aware of the need to maintain their competence? For the sort of professionalism I've described to work equally to the benefit of consumers and professionals, a health care practitioner should be a well-rounded individual whose attributes are a balance of the six listed by Schack. Instead, the attributes of autonomy and self-regulation are the two which seem to receive the greatest emphasis. This has long been the case among physicians and, I fear, will soon be seen developing among pharmacists and others as we play the game of follow-the-leader. These two attributes are precisely the ones which tend to lead to a professional arrogance which in turn is very likely to blind the practitioner to his own shortcomings. Furthermore, self-regulation and autonomy tend to automatically oppose the development of effective legal controls on professional practices.

So, the question is perhaps not, "Should pharmacists become more professional?" but rather, "What professional realignments are needed within the health care system as a whole?" It might be possible that the American pharmacist could simply maintain his present status as a more or less invisible non-person, but to do so all but eliminates any possibility of his being able to utilize a vast body of available expertise to benefit the consumer. As long as this expertise is not utilized, there exists a technical vacuum in the health care delivery system, because the typical physician has neither the time, the expertise, nor the inclination to fully and effectively monitor drug therapy. I can't begin to count the number of times I have heard a physician complain, when confronted with a new or different drug, "Oh, Dear Lord. I haven't time to keep up with my specialty. How can I possibly handle all these new drugs?" The simplest answer to the physician's "prayer" is that *that is what pharmacists are for.*

INSTITUTIONALISM: A TRIPLE-LOCKED DOOR

Surprisingly (since we are facing a problem which affects not only the pharmacist's ego-autonomy, but also the health and well-being of a great number of American consumers), there have been only a few solutions proposed for remedying the pharmacist's non-person peonage. There is, and has been for some time, a small but persistent pressure from a minority within the ranks of pharmacy, advocating professionalization. As I have indicated already, such a course is not only of dubious value to both practitioners and consumers, but it is effectively blocked as a result of economic exigencies arising from the conditions under which most pharmacists work. As a result, it is occasionally fashionable to suggest solutions to the problem which involve elimination of the economic device—the drugstore—which appears to be the stumbling block to professional development. Somewhat surprisingly, these suggestions most often originate with, and are quite popular among, pharmacy educators. This, despite the fact that surveys indicate that eight out of ten pharmacy students see ownership of a drugstore as an eventual goal. (Of course, nowhere near 80 percent of American pharmacists end up as store owners, but the abysmal failure of pharmacy educators to come to terms with the expressed aims and interests of their students is not a healthy sign.)

This sort of solution amounts to the more or less complete institutionalization of pharmacy. More or less complete, because the different plans call for varying degrees of separation of the practice of pharmacy from the free enterprise system. I have not yet seen anything that goes beyond the "bare bones" outline stage, and the reason, I suspect, lies in the fact that the majority of pharmacists oppose the idea of institutionalizing pharmacy. This is one of the most profound philosophical divisions in pharmacy and every proposal I have seen contains major flaws. Though I am loathe to say so, there may be no solution that excludes governmental intervention, and what I fear more than anything else is an excess of governmental control, for reasons which ought to be clear to anyone who has ever had to deal with a pompous bureaucrat, a threatening form letter, an endless waiting line. It seems likely that neither health care providers nor consumers will be well served by the "forced busing" of pharmacists from the traditional drugstore setting to the institutional setting. It is conceivable that in the long run the best solution to creeping institutionalism will involve forbidding hospital pharmacies to fill outpatient prescriptions except in certain emergencies. For the moment, at least, I prefer to keep an open mind on the matter and explain some of the proposed plans generally.

In the most extreme case of institutionalism, prescriptions would be filled only at pharmacies operated by established institutions such as hospitals and, possibly, certain group practice clinics. Exactly what this would mean depends on the particular city one chooses to consider, but let me illustrate what would happen in one city of about 150,000. There are four hospitals and two group practices, but this would not mean that this city would have six dispensing locations, because one of the group practices is part of one of the hospitals. Unfortunately, in a stretch of about one mile, four of the projected dispensing sites are located within three blocks of a main arterial east-west street. The fifth site is located less than a mile farther west and for about a third of the city's population it would be the closest dispensing site; however, it is the smallest and most poorly equipped of the five. The result here, as elsewhere, could well be that a patient would have to travel across town in one direction to see a physician, then go back across town in another direction to get a prescription filled. Aside from the obvious dangers to the patient if he happens to be seriously ill, the inconvenience would almost certainly lead to a reduction in the use of health care services—especially by the poor and elderly—in a country where we already under-utilize a great many of the available services. Clearly, this is not one of the sorts of situations (as with open-heart surgery suites) where centralizing would bring overall savings. The fact is that not one of these projected dispensing centers is designed to handle the prospective load of prescriptions, as doubtless is the case with most other similar sites. We are looking at the prospect of each of the sites having to fill from 1,000 to 2,500 prescriptions a day. At peak periods there could well be hundreds of people waiting to have prescriptions filled at each location.

Once we leave the cities the situation becomes even more acute, since there are thousands of rural centers in the United States which possess no health care institutions of any kind—many do not even have drugstores and many more are without physicians. In these areas, the hole-in-the-wall drugstore at the back of a combination general store and post office may be the only place for thirty miles or more where a prescription can be filled. Alternatively, physicians in rural communities frequently dispense drugs directly to their patients and, as bad as such practices often are, they would be eliminated if pharmacy were totally institutionalized. Not only would this entail considerable hardship and inconvenience, but the inaccessability of drugs would almost certainly encourage physicians to move closer to urban areas. This would add insult to injury for consumers in areas where there is already a grotesque imbalance of available health care.

The solution usually offered to these sorts of problems is to permit the continuation of prevailing practice in thinly-populated areas, while requiring institutionalization in areas of denser population. This would, of course, entail endless haggling over census figures, periodic redistricting, and the problem of adjusting to local conditions (living ten miles from a pharmacy in Vermont can easily be as troublesome as living fifty miles from one in Nebraska).

Even if these problems could be equitably resolved, the institutionalization of services, in our culture anyway, seems invariably to entail an unacceptable degree of depersonalization and dehumanization. I still have nightmares about one brief encounter I had at a "trend-setting" institution in a city of over 300,000 population:

> There were 1,000 beds for inpatients, extensive outpatient facilities, emergency treatment, x-ray, inhalation therapy, physiotherapy, psychological and psychiatric therapy, pharmacy and more. The hospital was as well equipped as any hospital could be and was affiliated with a medical school and two colleges of pharmacy. It looked like an ideal place for a pharmacist to practice, and it appeared that I had a very good chance at one of the positions they had open. All I had to do was go to the personnel office, show my credentials and fill out the application.
>
> After I had finished looking through the pharmacy—it was a beauty, no expense had been spared—I was given detailed instructions on how to reach the personnel office and was let out, *through a triple-locked steel security door*. Before I had traveled more than a few yards, I was stopped by an *armed* guard who was so surly that I took down his name and badge number so I could report him. I headed for an elevator, but before I got there I was stopped twice again; both of these characters were as bellicose as the first guard had been and they, too, were armed.
>
> Before I could ride the elevator I was told to "get the hell back to wherever you came from and get a damned pass!" On the way back, I mistakenly wandered into what was labeled as "Patient Waiting Area" where I found about fifty people milling around a window with large steel bars and a wire grill, over which hung a sign indicating that prescriptions would be processed "by the numbers." A pharmacist, standing back out of reach, was telling a guy on crutches that if he didn't like the drugs he had just been given, he'd have to go argue with his physician—"I haven't time to fool around with the likes of you, so buzz off!"
>
> With this, I turned on my heel and headed for the elevator where I told the obnoxious guard that all I wanted was to shake off the dust of this "zoo" and get out. To my surprise he let me aboard with the observation: "Who the hell don't!"

There may be some magic formula for preventing this sort of animalism from dominating institutionalized services, but our nation's experience with Social Security, welfare, and the state employment services leads me to believe that we have not yet found it. Nor, quite obviously, have we found an answer to the matter of institutionalizing pharmacy in the example just discussed.

Other less stringent forms of institutionalization have been suggested, but none of them succeeds in resolving the economic bind in which the pharmacist currently finds himself. The fact is that few people appear to give the matter of economics much consideration in this regard. The seemingly insurmountable problem lies in providing a system in which the pharmacist's income—and by extension, the profit margin of the enterprise of which he is a part—is independent of whether or not he fills prescriptions. In effect, how do we pay for his professional services? So far the most promising proposal seems to be to establish clinical pharmacy practice at the community level. You may recall the experimental unit in Iowa of which I spoke earlier and ask why institutionalization of pharmacy could not start at that level. Not all the details of this project are available, but the clinical pharmacist did fill prescriptions as part of his duties, and a rough calculation from a time-and-motion study done on the project indicates that he took over *eight minutes* to fill each prescription—if this pharmacist did *nothing* but fill prescriptions, he would manage 60 in an eight-hour day. The problem is that one physician can easily generate that many prescriptions in a day and, nationwide, we have nearly three physicians for every pharmacist.

The Community Clinical Pharmacist

It appears that establishment of clinical pharmacy practice at the community level is at least a portion of the answer, although the logistics are shaky. The community clinical pharmacist, like his counterpart in the hospital, would have to be essentially a consultant on the selection, use and monitoring of drugs—he would not fill prescriptions, although he might employ or collaborate with a technician who did. The clinical pharmacist would charge a fee for his services that would be paid by the consumer (or perhaps by a third party), very much in the way a physician is now paid. Assuming that the prescription-filling end of the practice were set up either as a break-even proposition or as a separate entity, the clinical pharmacist would be in a relatively autonomous position when it came to advising a consumer on the limitations of a course of treatment or refusing to use questionable drugs.

At the same time there are severe limitations on what can be expected from the community practice of clinical pharmacy under present circumstances. For one thing there is the limited appeal, in the consumer's mind, of the sort of services that can be afforded. There is also the matter of prices. To a consuming public already confused by claims and counterclaims, given data they are hardly equipped to understand and, in some instances, deliberately misled, we are now suddenly talking about another professional whose services will add to the cost of health care. Most consumers are pleased by some of the lower prices to be found in the mass merchandising stores, but as I indicated earlier, those prices seldom reflect the difference between what the typical independent store pays for the drugs and the prices the large chain pays. Even if a clinical pharmacist were to set up shop in a low overhead neighborhood and have his technician dispense those drugs at cost, the mass merchandiser is in a position to undercut his prices. The consumer would simply look at the professional fee, add it to the prescription cost, and ask why the need for the clinical pharmacist.

Even if a clinical pharmacist were to arrive in a town, open an office, and find plenty of consumers eager to take advantage of his services, there are complications. The first and most important part of a visit to such a clinician is the taking of a drug history: he must know what drugs the consumer takes or has taken, what foods may be eaten that might affect the actions of certain drugs, height, weight and a great many other things, even the consumer's ethnic origins. Such a complex procedure requires skill and time, from twenty to thirty minutes. As a result, every new client would require, say, twenty minutes, and at this rate the clinician can take only about twenty histories a day. At later stages the average time spent with a client might drop to ten minutes, but even at this rate we're talking about only forty clients a day. Clearly, we're involved in a situation where sheer numbers alone, whether it be clients or clinicians, are just too much.

Beyond this, yet, there is the matter of physician acceptance—without this the clinical pharmacist is lost. The clinical pharmacist cannot perform properly unless he has access to the results of clinical tests: he must know the state of the consumer's liver and kidneys, whether they are functioning at full efficiency, and a great many other things, the tests for which can be ordered only by the physician. To be effective, he must be in a position to consult with the physician as an equal. Thus, if the physicians do not cooperate he is stymied.

The inescapable conclusion is that although community clinical pharmacy offers much the same promise as its equivalent in the hospital, it is an idea whose time has not yet come. As is the case with the clinical pharmacist in the hospital, there simply are not enough trained people to go around, and there is evidence to indicate that the vast majority of community pharmacists, and a substantial portion of hospital pharmacists, either could not or would not assume the clinical role if they were given the opportunity.

In 1974, I conducted a survey among a sample of highly motivated pharmacists from central Illinois. Virtually every pharmacist agreed that consumers would receive safer and more effective drug therapy if the therapy was not only monitored, but even *chosen* by the pharmacist, rather than by the physician. Yet, of this group of pharmacists a significant percentage indicated that they would be reluctant to assume such a clinical role if the opportunity were presented. Likewise, in 1974, researchers reported on a 100 pharmacy survey: "Only 5 percent of the pharmacists surveyed gave the minimal pharmaceutical service of a properly prepared prescription *with counseling* as generously defined by this paper." * (Emphasis added.) The indications are that most community pharmacists are involved in such a struggle to stay afloat that they are either unwilling or unable to assume any role beyond their present technical one. This in turn indicates that under *present circumstances* the establishment of clinical pharmacy in the community must await the training of substantial numbers of clinical pharmacy specialists, or—and this is not too likely—the retraining of our more able current practitioners.

Clinical pharmacy will probably not have any extensive impact on the quality of health care until the status of the clinical pharmacist is defined by law. Such legislation will have to strip the physician of the prescribing function and hand it over to the clinical pharmacist. If this were done, we would then be dividing the medical functions at a logical and workable point. How eager American physicians would be to accept such a redivision may safely be left to the reader's imagination.

It may seem fanciful, but the role of education is important to

* Rowles, Keller and Gavin, *DICP,* May 1974.

what consumers can expect of the future. Schools of pharmacy have been asking themselves what changes will need to be made for the 1990s and the year 2000. The sad fact is that for such schools to be dealing with this in an appropriate way today, they should have been asking *everyone* these questions ten years back. It takes five years to turn out a pharmacist—one with a Pharm.D. degree takes longer—and it takes at least five years, but more likely ten, for a pharmacist to become "settled in," and another ten for him to become influential in his profession. In effect, then, the pharmacist who graduated *in 1975* is the influential practitioner of the 1990s. In view of this lag, I would have to say that community clinical pharmacy probably cannot come about by evolutionary mechanisms much before the end of the first quarter of the twenty-first century. No, I do not advocate some sort of revolution, unless legislation can be considered revolutionary. However, there will be no such legislation without strong pressure by consumers. Neither physicians nor the majority of pharmacists have sufficient interest in making such changes.

In the meantime, the consumer is left with the prospect of making an economic sacrifice to utilize the services of a clinical pharmacist—in the unlikely event that one is available to him. The clinical pharmacist *can* tell you important things about the drugs you take—what they can and cannot do, exactly how they should be used, what side effects are likely and what to do about them. Of course there are, scattered throughout the country, thousands of other pharmacists who are capable of doing the same thing, if they dared. What neither group can offer you is a true collaborative relationship with your physician—and this is what is *essential* if we are to see any major improvement in the quality of care delivered by the American health care system.

7 *Profits, Proliferation* AND THE INFORMATION GAP

Money, profits, promotional budgets, special price lists, research, good manufacturing practices, generics, brand names, bioavailibility, and a great many other topics have been the subjects of congressional investigations which, to a limited degree, have spilled out to become subjects of books, magazine articles, and newspaper features. The American pharmaceutical manufacturers have gotten a pretty bad press in the last decade or so; there's no denying this and even the manufacturers themselves seem to be acutely aware of what their public thinks about them. How else can the elegant and persistent public relations campaigns conducted by the Pharmaceutical Manufacturers Association (PMA) be explained?

The typical American consumer is already so drug-conscious, drug-zealous and drug-careless that there would appear to be little need to stimulate the market. What has happened is that the American people have become certain—as the result of an extensive series of investigations, both private and public, which hardly need be detailed here—that they have been, and are being, exploited by the drug manufacturers to an extent that would bring envious sighs from a nineteenth century industrial robber baron. (It is an unnatural, ambiguous situation for me, but in all fairness I am compelled to observe that, as we shall see in this chapter, the American pharmaceutical manufacturer is being as badly used in many sectors as he has been guilty of using consumers.)

For everyone concerned it is most unfortunate, but this is not merely an "impression" or an "image problem"—it goes far beyond the sort of thing that can be expected to respond to a high-powered P.R. blitz. The cold, hard facts are against it. Note: the average net profit margin of *Fortune* magazine's "top 500" U.S. corporations amounts to a mere 4.5 percent of sales; the net profit margins of the 20 largest American pharmaceutical manufacturers range from a rock bottom low of 4.6 percent to an unbelievable high of 33.5 percent. Over a twelve-year span, 1962–1973, one pharmaceutical company showed a mean net profit of a mere 6.4 percent while another showed a mean net profit of 20 percent. During the same period, these 20 pharmaceutical manufacturers, combined, averaged from 10.1 to 13.7 percent net profit while the list of 500 U.S. manufacturers averaged between 3.8 and 5.6 percent.

On a more specific level, the incredible revelations of price gouging go on and on:

- The British government orders one large American manufacturer to reduce its price and refund overcharges on a popular tranquilizer it sold to that government in the years 1966–72. This drug and two others, according to Dr. T.D. Rucker of Ohio State University College of Pharmacy, "carried a wholesale price to [American] community pharmacists where less than 5 percent of the list represented direct costs of production."
- In 1969, the drug erythromycin is produced by Mylan Laboratories and the unprocessed chemical is sold to such large manufacturers as Smith-Kline, Pfizer, Parke-Davis, Squibb, and Upjohn, who process it into tablets and sell it for anywhere from $10.15 to $15.87 per hundred. One small company, Sherry Pharmaceuticals, buys the same raw materials from Mylan and processes it into tablets which it sells for $5.70 per hundred.

The record is so blatant that the question in the minds of consumers and legislators alike is not *whether* we shall control such outrageous price discrepancies, but only what means we shall use to do so. Will it be antitrust suits, repeal of "antisubstitution" laws, or simply the relentless, intolerable glare of publicity that finally slays the dragon? As we speak of slaying the dragon, it is worth noting that eleven of the top nineteen pharmaceutical manufacturers in the U.S. had become so diversified by 1970 that ethical (prescription) drugs accounted for less than half of their sales. As such diversification takes place, overall corporate profits tend to decrease, and this masks the true rate of return on ethical drug products—corporate financial reports can be very deceptive in this respect.

Beginning with the investigations of the late Senator Kefauver in the 1950s, the American pharmaceutical manufacturers have been so thoroughly painted as the villains of the health care system that there is real danger that we may lose our perspective as we consider the failures of our drug delivery system. Certainly there is very little excuse, morally or ethically, for the manner in which American drug manufacturers manipulate price and sales policies. On the other hand, two facts must be considered which substantially alter our perspective on the activities of the manufacturer: (1) overall, prescription drugs account for only a small fraction of the health care dollar, and (2) the drug manufacturers under scrutiny have only been able to get away with such economic savagery (along with needless proliferation of drugs and dosage forms) because there is an ethical vacuum in the practice of medicine in America.

Perhaps the most pointed question that could be asked here is "How serious is this situation in terms of nationwide health care spending?" Everyone appears to have a different estimate, but, for the sake of argument, let us assume that unnecessary expenses arising from excess profits and discriminatory pricing policies run between $2 billion and $3 billion annually—that's about half of the nation's expenditure for prescription drugs. In absolute terms, this is a lot of money, but on a per capita basis it is chicken feed. There are, after all, some 220 million of us in America to share the load, so the cost comes out to somewhere between $9.10 and $13.65 per person annually. Conversely, of course, the fact that this amount isn't likely to bankrupt many of us provides no moral justification whatever for the practices which lead to such an overcharge. It is merely to say that, given the most stringent imagineable controls on the pharmaceutical industry's profit-taking propensity, coupled with mandatory generic prescribing, about the best the typical consumer can expect for these efforts is enough savings to pay for a fairly decent restaurant meal at the end of the year.

It has a salutory effect on the tendency to hyperbolize if we recall that, of the entire health care dollar, only $.09 is spent for drugs *of all kinds*. About $.06, or a little less, goes for prescription drugs, so there is actually very little fat to be pared, even by the most drastic procedures. This is not to say that we ought not to attempt to achieve greater control of the virtually unregulated economic antics of a significant facet of our drug industry. As a matter of fact, this is a moot point at this stage because, as a nation, we have already extensively committed ourselves to a course of greater governmental regulation in this area.

To those whose primary concern is the improvement of health care delivery through improved management of drug usage, however, economic considerations of this sort are of secondary importance. Dollar savings are almost meaningless unless there is a concomitant improvement in the quality of health care. In a sense, then, the important question is not, what will the economic overhaul of the drug industry do for our pocketbooks, but rather, what, if anything, will it do to improve our health care delivery system?

Name Brands and "Bathtub" Pharmaceuticals

The first line of defense for the major, name brand pharmaceutical manufacturer is to raise the spector of a disintegrating health care delivery system as a result of his being deprived of what a number of leading economists have labeled exorbitant profits (profits which, during an eleven-year period ending in 1970, exceeded the corresponding net return of all manufacturing in this country by 66 percent). Drawing on a word palette dripping with gory chiaroscuro, the ad writers paint pictures of shoddy, fly-by-night laboratories, known in the trade as "bathtub" or "schlock" operations, popping up like mushrooms throughout the land; packing crate factories in the backs of dirty warehouses where substandard raw drugs, probably produced from stolen technologies, become contaminated with rat and roach droppings as they are stamped out into crude tablets which will then be hawked to unsuspecting pharmacists and physicians who will eventually dispense them to unknowing consumers at nearly the same price as the "real thing." Make no mistake, the name brand manufacturer lives in mortal fear of generic prescribing and the generic manufacturer, in spite of the fact that most name brand manufacturers also have lines of generic drugs which they peddle, and the quality of their offerings is *not* significantly better than that of the other generic manufacturers.

Essentially, the situation is this: the original discoverer of a new drug can obtain a patent on it. This effectively gives him a seventeen-year monopoly during which he has the exclusive rights to make and sell the drug. (He can of course license others during this time, but even so, by adjusting his license fees, he can control the price of the drug.) As with any other patent, the idea is to reward the innovator, or, at the very least, to allow him to recover the costs of research and development. Beyond this, however, there is only a very superficial similarity between a drug patent and a patent on, say, a new type of magnetic tape system. For instance, when the Phillips Co. of Holland developed the tape cassette a few years ago, they were quick to license virtually everyone who wanted to produce cassettes or cassette recorders. The reasoning? Simple. Overall expansion of the market is good for everyone involved. Furthermore, failure to license competitors would have meant that, instead of one tape cassette system, there would soon be two or three dozen systems competing for recognition and a share of the market—and it is always possible that a better system might come along and wipe out any edge Phillips had. So, in place of several mutually incompatible systems of about equal value, each capable of achieving only a small share of the market at the expense of very costly promotion, Phillips assured its primacy and the costs to consumers were greatly reduced. What might have happened with the tape cassette is approximately what *does* happen on a regular basis in the field of prescription drugs.

Let us say that company A perfects a drug which is effective against each stage of the plasmodium of malaria (few drugs are effective against more than one stage, so this would be a remarkable find). As soon as an NDA (new drug application) with proof of safety and efficacy can be rammed through the FDA, company A puts the drug on the market, assures its rights to be the sole producer for seventeen years by obtaining a patent, and proceeds to charge every penny the market will bear.

In the meantime, plenty of midnight oil is being burned in the laboratories of company B and dozens of others. The technology of the new drug is, of course, a matter of public record—at least enough of it is—since this information is fundamental to obtaining a patent. Therefore, the scientists at all these other companies are hard at work on the drug's molecular structure, trying to manipulate it into something just different enough to be patentable, but similar enough to have more or less the same pharmacological effect. Perhaps a given company will succeed, perhaps not, but the odds are that, by the time the patent on company A's drug is halfway to expiration, and maybe much sooner, at least two or three of these "molecular manipulations" will have been marketed and extensively promoted. Occasionally, molecular manipulation does yield a new and markedly superior drug, but more often than not the result is like that in our hypothetical example of what might have happened had the tape cassette been held as a monopoly: the field becomes cluttered with several similar products, no one of which is demonstrably superior to the others, and all of which are inordinately expensive because the promotion and development costs (among other things) are multiplied by the number of "different" products involved. It is difficult, at best, to convince a consumer of a product's advantage when no clear advantage exists; under these circumstances, a non-technician, who is commonly called a copy writer, is prompted to "manufacture" advantages.

A cassette is obviously not the same sort of problem as a drug for many reasons. If there were several different types of cassettes that were supposed to be interchangeable and a consumer bought one only to find it did not work properly in his equipment, he would seldom have any trouble making an exchange for one that did work. As I indicated in Chapter 4, however, drugs cannot be legally returned once they have left the pharmacy. Too, equipment manufacturers generally label their products as being compatible with certain accessories and incompatible with others, but as you can imagine there simply is no way this can adequately apply to drugs.

Carbenicillin is a semi-synthetic penicillin that resulted from efforts at molecular manipulation starting back in the late 1950s. One detail man explained that it resulted directly from an effort to circumvent the patents on ampicillin which, incidentally, illustrates what can happen when a drug becomes available to a great many manufacturers, thereby giving their researchers the basic processes to manipulate. Whether or not the patents have expired on a drug, if it is licensed to several companies and one of them chances to find better, cheaper ways of production, he has an advantage. The licensing fees charged to all companies must be uniform to avoid anti-trust problems, but the company that can produce at lower costs can drop his prices to gain an edge over his competition. In effect, this does not hurt the patent holder and may actually help him. Naturally it doesn't harm the consumer as prices fall. (With antibiotics, the FDA certifies each batch, and other drugs are covered by a provision that changes in manufacturing procedures must be reported to and approved by the FDA.) Since the name brand manufacturer who holds the patent can depend on a measure of "name identification" (some name brand generic producers can do this also), it does not prevent him from continuing to sell (at high prices) and promote (vigorously) his own brands of such drugs. For instance, until quite recently, ampicillin (perhaps the second most prescribed drug in the U.S.) was available primarily under brand names, and the average cost for this drug ran nearly $.35 per tablet or capsule. More recently, ampicillin has become available as a generic tablet from a number of smaller pharmaceutical manufacturers—at an average cost of a little less than $.10 per tablet.

In view of all the controversy that has raged, it is appropriate to ask who the generic manufacturer is and what he does. In most cases, the generic manufacturer is a small concern, compared to the name brand giants. He does not generally maintain extensive research facilities, nor does he generally engage in direct promotion to pharmacists and physicians. As in the case of Sherry Pharmaceuticals and their erythromycin tablets, the generic manufacturer may well buy his raw materials from the same sources as the name brand manufacturer. No matter who produces the drugs, they are subject to FDA scrutiny, but there is some evidence that the smaller producers are more closely watched. Overall, American generic manufacturers have a *slightly* (but statistically insignificant) better safety record (fewer of their shipments are seized and condemned by the FDA) than do the name brand manufacturers. It may be simply that the name brand manufacturer is more likely to be dealing with new drugs produced by relatively new and untried procedures, but this fact would seem to indicate that the characterization of the generic manufacturer as a back-alley packing crate operation simply is not true.

What is unquestionably true is that the drugs turned out by the generic manufacturer are almost always cheaper than the same drugs as produced by the name brand manufacturer. And the difference is generally anything but slight: it frequently amounts to as much as 50 percent or more. Because of the magnitude of these price differences, there is a perpetual war over the question of "generic prescribing," with the consumer organizations, some legislators, and the generic manufacturers on one side, and the name brand manufacturers on the other. As a result of pressure from the name brand faction, via the PMA, many states (forty-four at last count) have passed "antisubstitution" laws which make it illegal for the pharmacist to use generic (or even other brand name products) where a prescription is written for a particular brand name of a drug. On the other side of the balance, most state and local governments now insist that public aid prescriptions be written and/or filled generically whenever possible.

There is no question whatever that if prescriptions were routinely filled with generic rather than brand named drugs, the savings for the consumer would be substantial. What is not so clear is, first, what impact such a course would have on the overall structure of the American health care delivery system, and, second, whether generic prescribing and filling is likely to be implemented by our present system.

We can begin by dismissing, out of hand, the usual argument that generic prescribing or dispensing will result in the consumer receiving inferior drugs. In the late 1950s, when evidence of name brand overcharges first began to emerge, there *was* some truth to the contention that certain generic drugs were of poorer quality. I was personally responsible for the destruction of several lots of such drugs from several manufacturers, and because of this, like many of my colleagues, I came to depend on the brand name manufacturers for quality drugs. Today, however, this simply is not the case. Twenty-five years have made a great deal of difference in the level of quality control, and without question much of this has come about because of pressure from the brand name manufacturers. Being "little guys" with no significant political influence, the generic manufacturers have been strictly policed by the FDA. To survive, a generic manufacturer had to measure up, so the fly-by-night operations of the 1950s and early 1960s have gone by the board. The current crop of generic manufacturers has largely come into prominence, if not existence, in the last decade—under the pressure of rigorous licensing requirements.

Prescription Pricing: AWP x 2 = $

When we leave the area of basic drug safety, however, generic prescribing becomes much more complicated. For one thing, it does not necessarily save the consumer any money if the physician writes the generic name of a drug on the prescription, because in that case the pharmacist is perfectly free to fill the prescription using either the brand name or the generic drug. Let us say that the prescription calls for 500 milligram capsules (often physicians do not designate either tablets or capsules) of the antibiotic ampicillin. The pharmacist might fill it with capsules from Bristol-Myers (Polycillin) which have a wholesale cost of about $.29 each. Or he might use a generic ampicillin from Interstate Drug Exchange, at a wholesale cost of about \$.09 each. A look at pricing methods will tell you why he is most apt to choose the brand name drug.

There are many different methods a pharmacist may use to determine the price he'll charge, and except for a few rare instances (or a few rare birds behind the counter) the cost of materials is the first consideration. The actual acquisition cost is not the figure the pharmacist will use to calculate prices, incidentally, but the average wholesale price (AWP) of the smallest container available (most often 100s in the case of tablets and capsules). For the sake of illustration, I'll use two common pricing formulas often encountered: Prescription Price = AWP + 25% + \$2.00 Professional Fee; and Prescription Price = AWP x 2. In either case it is easy to see that the pharmacy profits more from the sale of the more expensive name brand drug. For a prescription calling for 30 capsules the breakdown would be as follows:

	Name brand		Generic brand
drug cost	\$.29@ x 30 = \$ 8.70		\$.09@ x 30 = \$2.70
25% markup	\$ 2.18		\$ .68
Prof. fee	\$ 2.00		\$2.00
Total:			
first method	\$12.88		\$5.38
second method (AWPx2)	\$17.40		\$5.40

By using the generic drug the pharmacy would "lose" \$7.50 by the first pricing method and \$12.00 by the second. It should be clear from my discussion in Chapter 6 what the employee pharmacist is expected to do. The economic pressure is in the direction of filling all but public aid prescriptions with name brand drugs. (In some pharmacies I have seen "discounts" given to "senior citizens," in which case the generic drug may be used, but the price is figured on the AWP of the brand name drug and the "discount" taken from this price.)

From the examples given here, it is also clear that if the consumer is to be treated fairly, the most equitable pricing schedule must depend on the use of a professional fee rather than a percentage markup. One objection to the use of a professional fee is that it would make the price of very inexpensive drugs inordinately high. For instance, suppose a physician wrote a prescription for 100 tablets of 0.6 mg (approx. 1/100 grain) atropine, for a patient with a "nervous stomach." These tablets can be bought from generic houses for about \$1.85 a thousand, which makes the cost of 100 tablets about \$.20 or 1/10th of the \$2.00 professional fee used in the illustration. All other arguments aside, however—and there are many, both pro and con—the pharmacy's costs are the same when it comes to filling a prescription regardless of whether the drug costs \$.20 or \$20.00.

A different sort of problem in pricing arises from the fictional nature of the Average Wholesale Price. The AWP, as it is called, does *not* represent the price a pharmacy actually pays for a drug. It is the highest price any wholesale customer would pay for a particular quantity of the drug, and in reality few pharmacies—except small independent stores—actually pay this price. Returning to the ampicillin prescription considered earlier, the AWP is \$30.97 for the name brand in bottles of 100, and in the neighborhood of \$47.40 for the generic in bottles of *500*. This works out to nearly \$.31 apiece for the brand name product and \$.095 for the generic. However, if the prescription were filled at a large chain pharmacy, it is unlikely that the name brand ampicillin cost the store more than \$.14 or \$.15 a capsule because of quantity discounts. On the other hand, the generic ampicillin probably did cost very close to \$.09 per capsule, since the generic manufacturer's costs are a fairly accurate reflection of production and shipping costs and a decent profit margin. Thus, in filling the prescription with the name brand drug, the chain store would realize an additional \$.16 (or so) profit per capsule. What actually happens is that the chain store makes an adjustment in its cost such that it sells the product at what appears to be a discount and still keeps half or more of this "hidden" profit. At the same time, there is likely to be little or no hidden profit in the price of the generic drug. The result: even if the chain store charged only a professional fee plus the "altered" AWP, it would still be far more profitable for them to dispense the name brand drug.

What all this means with respect to the question of generic filling of prescriptions (as opposed to generic prescribing, per se) is that, under our present "drugstore" system, it is unlikely to be done so long as there is any available alternative. In the event that our drugstores were replaced by economically insulated dispensing pharmacies controlled by the professional decisions of clinical pharmacists, we could probably expect prescriptions to be generically filled in almost all instances. However, so long as physicians continue to prescribe by brand names (and most states continue to enforce antisubstitution laws), generic filling can only account for a small fraction of all prescriptions. This brings us to the questions of "brand name identification" and "company name identification." How do major pharmaceutical companies manage to get their names, and the names of their products, before the professional public so thoroughly and effectively? The reasons for this lie at least partly in the arcane economics of extreme mass production.

Product Identification: Selling for Less at a Profit

From time to time, consumers and even some of my colleagues ask me to put the matter of generic prescribing into a tight little package and come up with a one- or two-sentence solution. I would hope that after the lengths to which I have gone in an effort to present a *very general* picture of prescribing, dispensing, and the roles of the interacting individuals and businesses, it is clear that there *is* no simple answer. I say this with the realization that I haven't really dealt with some facets of the situation at all. One wrench that often ends up in the works is the fact that, while the generic manufacturer is selling ampicillin to everybody at the "fair" price of $.09 per capsule, some brand name manufacturers are selling their $.30 capsules to the federal government for $.03 apiece.

In a society which was brought to its present state by mass production, it appears that a great many people still do not understand how a company might benefit by selling a huge number of a single item to a governmental unit at production cost plus delivery cost—essentially making no profit. This is an extremely complicated area, on the fringe between economics and black magic, but as I understand the situation, a manufacturer can actually hold the price of his product down by such seemingly irrational practices. For instance, it is a fact of life that the more raw material a manufacturer buys, the smaller his costs—there is a point commonly referred to as a break-even point. All overhead costs, including research, development, wages, rent, material and the like, tend to remain more or less constant at certain levels of production. The more of the product that is produced, until the next level is reached, the greater the producer's profit. When he reaches the next plateau and must expand his facilities, then a new break-even point is established. Because of the law of diminishing returns, there eventually seems to be a point beyond which no further economies appear to influence this situation. In any case, if a company, finding itself close to a next higher break-even point, expands production, it can sell a large portion of its production (the expanded portion) at or close to cost.

Providing it keeps the sales level it had before, the company can expand its profits and, if costs are reduced sufficiently, it may even be able to reduce the price to consumers of its nominal production sold at a profit. A company, then, might be selling half of its total production at little or no profit and still be making more money than before. The philosophy may, in some respects, be sound, but I can see instances where it appears irrational, out of proportion, and works to the detriment of the consumer. (I prefer to ignore the possibility of a single, large government-controlled industry producing each commodity as being the ultimate in efficiency because of the experiences of other nations, notably the U.S.S.R.)

The practice of selling drugs to the government at or near cost has other benefits that apply particularly to brand name manufacturers. If Jones Laboratories discovers and patents an antibiotic for which it obtains protection for the name, "Alphacin," it typically seeks to obtain brand name identification in the minds of consumers. After a year or so, it has "settled in" and has a fair share of the antibiotic market, comes to a break-even point and decides to expand production. Before expanding, the company offers its Alphacin to the government at a very low price which is consistent with the new production costs. Once it is established that a market is there, the company expands and tailors production to meet the new market. Above and beyond the reduced production costs, the company, even though it is selling its product to the government under its generic name of "alphamycin," finds increased demand for its entire line of products, and for Alphacin in particular. What has happened is that government studies make mention of alphamycin, pharmacists and physicians all over the country are exposed to the name of the company, as well as the drug alphamycin. Studies of the drug which might never have been possible otherwise are done in VA hospitals, and the attendant, free publicity causes an increased demand. This phenomenon is known as brand and company identification. At one time this was the best way for a consumer to be sure of quality (in drug products), but today it is almost meaningless.

Nevertheless, the top American pharmaceutical houses are where they are because they did manage to establish a high degree of product and company identification. I have seen rather consistent estimates that indicate that $.25 of every dollar of sales of American brand name pharmaceutical manufacturers is used to influence prescribers and dispensers to use certain brand names. In this we enter an ethically ambiguous zone in which the principal conflict is between the supposedly scientific process by which drug therapy decisions are made, and the pressures of drug promotion, which are largely shaped by commercial and economic motives. In this arena we encounter the pressures which pharmaceutical manufacturers place on physicians in the form of voluminous advertising and frequent personal contact. The detail man and the pseudoscientific house organ (a promotional gimmick which is an advertising brochure disguised as an honest scientific journal) are very often the first and only sources of information a physician may consult to make a decision to use a drug. Two questions quickly come to mind: how complete and accurate is the information presented in this manner, and how competent is the typical physician to objectively evaluate such information?

The Detail Man and a Full-page Glossy

The fact is that drugs are not actually "sold" to the ultimate consumer, but to an intermediary who actually selects the product: the physician. Whether or not this is a single or multifaceted problem is inconsequential: the effect is the same. The manufacturer of the "me too" molecularly manipulated drug sets in motion a promotional scheme for his product, and all too often over-eager marketing people stretch insignificant data into "dramatic advantages." What is worse is that negative information is played down or ignored completely, and the health care professional gets a false impression of the drug's potential. In the case of Mr. and Mrs. Miles, detailed at the beginning of Chapter 5, the physician's decision to use carbenicillin to prevent the possible development of a pseudomonas infection was influenced by a slick job of promoting on the part of one company's detail man. This is the way the physician tells it:

> My God, it looked good, the way that guy described it. By the time he used the word "prophylaxis," I was chock full of terminologies that I had never had the opportunity to study. He'd talk about T½, average serum concentration, mean blood levels, expotential blood level data, cumulative urinary excretion profiles,

elimination constants, and then, when he really had me confused, he pulled out a graph that seemed to clear it all up. He was telling me how great the drug was for urinary tract infections, almost as though that was an extra benefit. Well, this graph looked good with its line running steeply to the top and leveling off. "This is cumulative urinary excretion," he explained, "and as you might expect in a first order, single compartment model, the blood and plasma concentrations will be reciprocals."

You know, it wasn't until after this business with the Mileses when I sat down with the hospital pharmacist that I really understood what this bum had done to me. He hadn't lied, but I don't know how he could have come closer. What surprised me most of all was to discover that the manufacturer actually had put all the information anyone really needed to clarify the matter right there on the package insert. When the pharmacist took two sheets of graph paper and actually plotted the mean blood levels before my eyes, I knew I'd been taken in. That pretty graph the detail man showed me was actually a picture of the drug going *out* of the patient's body—certainly, there is a sort of reciprocal relationship between the concentration of this drug in the plasma and urine, but this guy fudged. When the mean blood levels are plotted on a semi-log graph, the line drops almost straight down and even without any calculations, it's plain that half of the drug is out of the patient's blood in less than an hour. The situation with the tablets is even worse, because very soon after the tablets are swallowed, the kidneys are removing the drug almost as fast as it is absorbed. Sure, it's fine for urinary tract infections if the organism is sensitive, but I needed a good blood level, and there's just no way to get that with the tablets. When I saw the blood levels that were recommended for inhibiting pseudomonas, I could see that this drug couldn't be used effectively for prophylaxis in this instance at all.

This drug detail man did a masterful job of concealing some facts and putting others in a good light. The cumulative urinary excretion graph, with its nice soaring line, has a positive look to it—unless the "consumer" (physician) is sufficiently well grounded in biopharmaceutics to realize that such a curve means that the drug does not stay in the blood for more than a few minutes. Likewise, the emphasis on carbenicillin's efficacy in treating urinary tract infections, while true, is misleading—the drug should be reserved for situations where no other drug is appropriate. The older sulfa drugs are as effective in most cases, more effective in a few, and *far* cheaper in any case.

Years ago the drug detail man, who visits physicians with sales pitch, literature, samples, and a sort of gossipy camaraderie, usually held a degree in the biological sciences. He might be a zoology or biochemistry major who hadn't been able to get into medical school or, and this was frequently the case, a pharmacist who found it more interesting (and profitable) to go into sales than to spend sixty or more hours a week behind a prescription counter. Today this is no longer true: the detail man now is a "marketing specialist" who generally holds a degree in business administration, accounting, or advertising. So far as "business" is concerned this change appears to be all to the good; I have heard district sales representatives claim as much as a 50 percent increase in sales as a result.

I find it sad, but this appears to be a pattern that has long been evident in other areas. It seems to be generally accepted that an automobile salesman need know nothing more about his product than what he can learn from company sales materials. Likewise, few TV salesmen know anything at all about electronics beyond being able to locate the on-off switch and roughly adjust the "up-front" controls.

Aside from the obvious explanation that an automobile mechanic or a TV serviceman is probably going to prefer to ply his trade instead of selling the wares, there is at least one other reason for employing non-technical personnel in sales positions: most consumers appear not to be interested in what makes things work, but are interested in which button to push. In most cases the consumer lacks the necessary expertise to appreciate the fine points of design and engineering. An automobile salesman with a background in automotive engineering would almost certainly have a tendency to get out of the consumer's depth, to offend a prospect by telling him more than he wants to know about things he does not understand. (As frustrating as this can be, I have, from time to time, been saved from making terrible mistakes by salespeople who knew their wares and who, after a furtive glance around to see who might be watching or listening, responded to my questions with honest answers.)

Unhappily, this phenomenon seems to be a major factor in the drug companies' shift to the use of non-technical personnel for drug detailing. If an arm-chair mechanic who thinks he knows all there is to know about cars is suddenly made to see, by a knowledgeable salesman, that he really doesn't know the difference between a lean-burn engine and a stratified-charge engine, he is apt to get quite hot under the collar. How much more disconcerted a physician is likely to be if a detail man who knows biochemistry leads him in over his head—and then leaves him there! The detail man whose prime area of expertise is sales or advertising is, almost literally, incapable of committing such a faux pas because his programming precludes it. He knows and is guided by the first principle of salesmanship: always build the prospect's ego, never risk deflating it. Furthermore, a good salesman finds out the trend of his prospect's desires, then takes advantage of this knowledge to show how his company's product is compatible with the prospect's preconceptions: "Dr. Blank, I know that in your practice you treat a lot of bladder infections, and you know how stubborn they can be. Now our new antibiotic, Betacin, is just the thing for infected bladders. . . ." The last thing a busy physician wants is to be bothered with a detailed explanation (no matter *how* much he may need it) of a drug's pharmacology—don't tell me how it works, tell me what it's good for.

There is, of course, no way to verify it statistically, but among pharmacists it is accepted that at least half of all prescriptions are written "anecdotally." The original anecdotal prescription may have been Jonathan Doe telling Simon Roe to carry a horsechestnut in his trousers pocket to relieve his rheumatism. In the wider sense, anecdotal prescribing is based on: "So-and-so says that such-and-such is good for this-or-that." The "so-and-so" may be a physician colleague, a drug detail man, an advertisement, or the abstract of an article in *JAMA (Journal of the American Medical Association).* Whatever the source, the physician who prescribes such-and-such does so without a thorough understanding of what the drug can and cannot do under the circumstances of any particular case. He has not gone through the (sometimes arduous) process of accommodating an understanding of the drug's pharmacological activities with an understanding of the physiological and pathological mechanisms of the underlying disease state.

By-passing this fundamental process, as the physician does when he prescribes anecdotally, leads to such useless and, consequently, irrational therapy as giving penicillin for malaria (plasmodia are not affected in the least), treating victims of mononucleosis with steroids (the drug masks dangerous symptoms without altering the course of the disease), or treating simple anxiety states with major tranquilizers (bizarre, psychotic behavior may appear in people who are otherwise essentially normal; and a severe, irreversible toxicity known as tardive dyskinesia, which often worsens when the drug is withdrawn, may occur in as many as 10 percent of certain groups of patients).

The drug detail man—and the pharmaceutical company he represents—are fully aware of the physician's penchant for anecdotal prescribing, and they know the reasons behind it: time and training. The typical physician is "overworked," in the sense that he has more patients than he could handle if he were to devote to each one as much time and attention as he ought to. And the medical profession regularly issues, for popular consumption, hand-wringing statements about the situation. The principle seems to be that the physician deserves to be overpaid because he is "overworked." What is omitted in such pronouncements is that the typical physician is "overworked" because the medical establishment has successfully restricted the output of America's medical schools for the last sixty years. On the other hand, since he is his own boss, the typical American physician manages not to be overworked in the usual sense by simply reducing the time and intellectual attention he gives to each patient. One of the most effective methods for reducing the necessary intellectual attention is to prescribe anecdotally. He's got a stiff neck and sore shoulder muscles? Parafon Forte is supposed to be good for that.

Pharmaceutical advertising tends to follow this sort of pattern as well, although the implications are often subtle and sufficiently well hidden to allow the copy to clear the "ethics committees" of the medical journals in which it appears. The anecdotal approach is especially prominent in those areas where the physician's training is least competent to provide him with guidance in determining a course of therapy. With monotonous regularity, ads appear in a format of this sort: full-page color photograph of the finest technical quality, taken over the shoulder of a white-coated male, presumed to be a physician. Facing him from the opposite side of a desk is an archetypal middle-aged housewife, brows tensely knit, biting her lip, clutching and wringing her handkerchief. The caption reads: "What Can You Do For Her?" There follows a block of smaller print (not so small it can't easily be read, of course): "There she sits in your office, a bundle of nerves, a history of migraine or cluster headaches, insomnia, tension—symptoms for which you can find no apparent cause. What can you do for her?"

The answer is provided in the next line which is set in a slightly larger type size: "Give Her ________." Fill in the blank, it may be an ad for a minor tranquilizer, a sedative, a mood elevator, or some combination of these. Off to the side, in a smaller type size is a "busy" compilation of facts, disclaimers, warnings and a bit of pharmacology. The physician is intended to assume that all the information in this "busy" box supports, in some scientific way, the exhortation to "Give Her ________," and that he may read this material if he wishes, but that he really need not.

The only real "science" involved has nothing whatever to do with the product, but with motivating some innocent to prescribe a chemical which cures nothing. In such cases the typical physician hasn't the faintest idea where to start treatment, regardless of the patient's sex. The patient is probably leading a dog's life and it might take an hour of patience and a sympathetic ear to determine the breed of dog; but this simply will not do—there are six other patients in various stages of undress in as many examining rooms, and sixteen more, at last count, in the waiting room. Note: the typical consumer spends two-and-a-half minutes with a physician at a typical office call. The physician knows that if he is to stay on schedule, he can allow no patient more than six minutes, and this unattractive person has already hemmed and hawed away four-and-a-half minutes of his precious time. He knows that treating this patient properly would be a long, drawn out process and, in the long run, likely be unsuccessful for lack of a supportive environment. Remembering the last ad for an antidepressant-phenothiazine combination to cross his desk, the physician grabs, as for a straw, his prescription pad and starts to write. With the prescription he delivers a brief litany of virtues, about thirty years too late to be of much use: "These will make you feel better. Get plenty of sleep, eat a balanced diet, get as much fresh air and exercise as possible, and make an appointment for next month on the way out."

Case dismissed, temporarily at least: our physician has successfully avoided a confrontation with the limitations of his knowledge, he has put off an unsatisfying patient, and he will be on time for supper—thanks to pharmaceutical company X and its glossy ad. If questioned about this sort of prescribing and the advertising which fosters it, the manufacturer is likely to respond, "We are simply meeting the physician's needs. He is our customer, because he is the one who selects the medication. You can't stay in business if you don't provide what your customers want and need." Shades of Nuremberg: I was only following orders.

What is lost here is that the aim of treatment is to meet the needs of the *patient,* not the physician. It is the patient, not the physician, who consumes the drug and takes the consequences. However noble his intentions, the physician, by virtue of both his work load and his spotty training in pharmacology, is in a poor position to be the prime evaluator of promotional material. This is so for the simple reason that such material is designed to play on his weaknesses as a practitioner. He cannot assess the material because it requires knowledge he never possessed or uses so infrequently that it is of no value to him.

In the case of the physician who prescribed the ineffective doses of carbenicillin for Mr. and Mrs. Miles, it is a safe bet that somewhere along the line he was exposed to the concept of a reciprocal. On the other hand it's about a 50–50 proposition that he might have gotten through medical school without being required to study any mathematics beyond elementary algebra.* In his everyday practice he rarely had occasion to study data presented in graphic form. Consequently, when the detail man showed him the graph of cumulative urinary excretion and then used the word "reciprocal," his mind did not automatically invert the graph to get a rough picture of what would happen to the blood level of the drug—precisely the kind of information he would need to evaluate any drug of the sort, whether it was for active treatment or prophylaxis.

This is not to suggest that the typical physician is either a fool or a pushover. Wiser heads have been befuddled by simpler tactics.

* Having said this, I thought it might be interesting to know the pharmacist's exposure to mathematics. I was chagrined at first to discover that he had failed two algebra courses at one university, transferred to another school where he failed algebra again, dropped out of school for a period of three years, then returned to the first school and took a simple arithmetic course twice before passing it. When I spoke to him, he was working on a fairly complicated statistical problem, and I wondered how he managed some of the more or less sophisticated mathematical procedures, so I asked. His answer was the biggest surprise of all and relates significantly to the overall problem: "I saw very soon after I graduated that I would have to learn to handle the math if I intended to be any sort of pharmacist, so I just went out and found people who would take the time to explain these things to me. Anybody who is really interested can find other people and books to explain such things. Interest, I think, is what it takes."

What it does suggest is that the physician is perhaps not the person who should be placed in the position of having to evaluate, screen, and possibly reject promotional material which largely sidesteps the significant pharmacological issues pertinent to the rational use and monitoring of a particular drug. One ever-present and much-debated potential solution is, of course, to eliminate promotion of prescription drugs altogether. Aside from the uncertain economic repercussions of such a move, there is a good chance that eliminating promotion would simply mean that, instead of receiving defective information about drugs, the physician would receive almost none at all. It is a consummation devoutly to be wished that the physician would obtain his information directly from sources in the professional literature. Considering the physician's "overworked" condition and his sparse training in the basic principles and language of pharmacology, it is wishful to think that more than a very small percentage of practitioners will take this course either willingly or diligently.

Universal Clinical Pharmacy

It makes a great deal more sense to place the responsibility for evaluating drug information in the hands of someone who has the time and training to do a satisfactory job. Time to become familiar with the primary literature of drug research and testing on a continuing basis. Training in pharmacology that will enable him to cut through the extraneous, unimportant information presented by economically interested parties. Perhaps even expertise so formidable that no manufacturer would dare present him with anything less than the unvarnished facts, data that at this time is all but impossible to obtain. From the record, it should be clear that this individual is not going to be the typical physician—although it is true that a few highly competent physicians manage to do this today (usually at the expense of working themselves into early graves or extensively limiting the number of patients they care for). Nor does the typical pharmacist stand much chance of filling this role. Although most pharmacists in practice today received adequate pharmacological grounding in pharmacy school, only a few appear to have made the effort to maintain their professional competence in the face of the pressure to fill a hundred or more prescriptions a day (and in the face of the jibes of their peer group).

It is entirely possible that physicians could be adequately trained to handle the tasks set out, but this would require adding another two years to the present medical school curriculum, and it would cost us between 40,000 and 60,000 physician graduates—for two successive years there would be no graduating classes. Nor would this solve the problem of what to do with the 320,000 physicians now practicing. This is obviously nonproductive and, in the long run, quite probably counterproductive—nine years to become a physician? With considerable trepidation, I suggest that the universal practice of clinical pharmacy would largely solve the problem.

To digress: the trepidation I feel while suggesting clinical pharmacy as a solution is multi-faceted, but, in general, it stems from two main points: (1) we are dealing with an ad hoc situation for which there is no real precedent, hence very little practical experience, and (2) my experiences with the hierarchy of my profession have left me with an abiding mistrust, or lack of confidence, in its overall ability to cope with a problem of this magnitude.* Combining the two, I must say that my overriding concern is that the clinical pharmacist will simply become another arrogant, physician-like specialist who, at the same time he performs a valuable service, will tend to complicate the consumer's access to care.

More essential than anything else, I see such a practice as a vehicle for a collaboration among consumers, pharmacists, nurses, physicians, and any other group that will contribute to an appropriate, holistic health care delivery system. And it might very well be that sweeping, unprecedented changes, such as making professionals subject to consumer review, will be discovered to be the only way to make the system work. I do not believe that more than a small handful of the present pharmacy hierarchy could possibly cope with such a situation, but I do believe that such a confrontation is an inevitable consequence of establishing universal clinical pharmacy practice.

Keeping these reservations and conditions in mind, placing the

---

* The leadership level of the hierarchy of pharmacy is primarily made up of educators; as I have indicated, both in this book and in the literature of pharmacy, it is my belief that contemporary education and contemporary pharmacy educators are generally lacking in both quality and appropriateness. It is a fact that more pharmacy educators practice clinical pharmacy (as it is now constituted) or hospital pharmacy than practice community pharmacy, even though any appropriate practice of universal clinical pharmacy will require a thorough familiarity with *every* aspect of current institutional and community practice and a blending of the best attributes of each.

responsibility of drug selection in the hands of the clinical pharmacist would largely solve the problem of economic pressures on prescribing. We may as well face the fact that the complexities of modern drug therapy long ago outstripped the ability of the physician practitioner to comprehend and apply. One price we may have to pay for the continued use and expansion of the technology of modern drug therapy may well be the need to establish a new class of professionals to deal with the evaluation and application of current drug information. There is already a special interest group known as "Drug Information Specialists" being formed as an adjunct of the American Society of Hospital Pharmacists. These individuals do not spend their days filling prescriptions, but evaluating drugs and therapy, primarily in response to questions generated by pharmacists and physicians. It is possible that one such person with access to a computer could act as a double-check for clinical pharmacists in a large area, say several counties, or he (she) might generate the prescriptions and monitor their use. There are many possible variations.

To the question "What will this cost the American health care consumer?" there is no appropriate answer, but, effectively, it should add *nothing* to the cost of health care. As explained earlier, it seems fair to assume that the universal practice of clinical pharmacy would result in virtually all prescriptions being filled with the most economical drug available. Not only would this result in a direct savings of between $1 billion and $2 billion a year, but it would also tend to bring the prices of name brand drugs to more competitive levels and stimulate greater competition throughout the industry that could result in even further savings. Finally—and there is some indication that this has already happened in a few hospitals—close monitoring of therapy would probably cause a reduction in prescription volume as irrational prescribing practices and "ad lib" dispensing were eliminated.

Let us say that such an innovative system could lop $3.5 billion annually from the nation's prescription drug bill. If anything, this is a conservative estimate since the irrational use of over-the-counter drugs can be expected to be reduced by, perhaps, an equal dollar amount. Let us say further that a clinical pharmacist is to earn today's equivalent of $30,000 a year. This is a princely sum by present pharmacy standards, but little enough for an individual with an educational investment and professional responsibilities at least as great as those of the physician. (It may be no more than wishful dreaming, but the physician's malpractice situation should also be alleviated and his insurance rates lowered, while the clinical pharmacist should not see any great rise in his.) Given this figure, the $3.5 billion saved on prescription costs would pay the salaries of nearly 117,000 clinical pharmacists *at no increase in the current health care bill!*

This number of clinical pharmacists might not be adequate to serve the needs of the current American population, but it would be a good start, and additional savings should accrue in other parts of the system as a result. For instance, no one is quite sure of the percentage of hospitalizations that are brought about as a result of adverse drug reactions, interactions, misprescribing, and overdoses, but few estimates run under 5 percent and some are as high as 18 percent. I hesitate to suggest that such mishaps would dramatically disappear were clinical pharmacy instituted, but for each 1 percent of reduction in this area, the savings could pay the salaries of an additional 20,000 clinical pharmacists—again at no increase in the nation's overall health care bill.

Finally, it should be noted that, in areas besides direct drug costs, we can expect some relief in future years. The nation's private health insurers have already gone on record in opposition to the continued upward spiral of hospital costs, which in 1975 accounted for $.43 of each health care dollar. The era of mindless proliferation of hospital facilities seems to be drawing to a close, and in consequence the future seems to hold some promise of reducing this, the largest single bite out of the health care dollar.

Beyond the economic extrapolations—which seem to indicate that here, for once, is a meaningful reform which will not require us to shell out any more than we are now—we must not forget that we are talking about a major improvement in our health care system. The evidence is strong and compelling that we will not be able to significantly improve the level of drug-related health care available to most Americans until we succeed in overhauling our present, antiquated prescription system. Beyond this, instituting the universal practice of clinical pharmacy may well turn out to be the only way to permanently relieve the pressures of commercialism which presently beset the practice of medicine, i.e.: the aggressive pharmaceutical manufacturer vs. the prescription-dependent community pharmacy and the all-too-vulnerable physician.

It is all too easy to do as many critics of American medicine have done and lay the entire blame for the prescription mess at the door of the major pharmaceutical manufacturers. If only the greedy monsters could be restrained, we could then return to lofty professionalism, Olympian restraint in the practice of medicine . . . and so it goes. What this approach fails to take into account, among other things, is that the practice of medicine today is a wide-open field for economic exploitation: we could not have designed a worse system for its ability to resist commercial pressure. Furthermore, there probably is a legitimate place for the right sort of drug promotion, because certain sorts of information *should* enter the system by way of those who actually produce the drugs. Eliminating all drug promotion would be a classic case of throwing the baby out with the bath water.

The philosopher Fritjof Bergman once noted that "Philosophy has no greater force than preference. If you want more force than that, then you do not want philosophy, you want a police state." This statement ought to have a sobering effect on those who are eager to attempt cures by way of drastic legal intervention. It seems a far safer course, so long as we continue to desire and strive for a free society, to work toward changes in the philosophy and structure of our institutions. The result of such changes ought to be—as in the case of the establishment of clinical pharmacy—to harness and provide natural checks upon the dominant forces which characterize our society, in this case, the commercial spirit and the free enterprise system.

One physician-educator on hearing of the clinical pharmacy proposal, sarcastically asked if the clinical pharmacists would also do the post mortems; to this my answer is, "Absolutely not, Doctor, that's the way it is now. The clinical pharmacist will strive all the harder to be right in everything if he knows that skeptics like you are looking for his mistakes. You are the consumer's best guarantee, provided you are checking someone else's work and not your own." What I am advocating by suggesting the establishment of universal clinical pharmacy is the introduction of reasonable checks and balances into a system where none now exist. It is the old question of *quis custodiet ipsos custodes?*—who shall keep watch over the guardians? And although the ultimate solution to this problem in the area of medicine must involve consumer participation, it is also essential to make the system of drug delivery self-limiting—something which it is not today.

It seems unlikely at this point that we will ever be able to eliminate human greed, or the pliability it introduces into the human moral sense. What we *can* do is to structure our social institutions in such a way that the individuals involved are insulated from the effects of greed *in that portion of their existence which concerns the performance of their professional duties.* We do not really care, for instance, if a judge makes a fast buck on the side by speculating in antique coins, but we would never tolerate a system in which, in lieu of a salary, he was allowed to pocket the fines he assessed. (Something of this sort did happen early in our history and the record speaks for itself.) In very much the same way, it seems only prudent to make our health care system as thoroughly proof as possible against the commercial pressures that beset it. There seems to be no better or safer way to do this than by removing the pressure from both the physician and the dispensing pharmacist and placing it upon the clinical pharmacist. He, too, is only human, but he is in a far better position, by virtue of both training and function, to remain professionally immune to commercial pressure and serve the interests of the pharmaceutical manufacturer's true customer—you, the patient, the health care consumer.

8 A Consumer's Survival Manual

Nothing will ever be attempted if all possible objections must first be overcome.

Samuel Johnson

I am convinced that the most difficult thing one man can undertake, outside of trying to be right in everything he does, is to explain his area of expertise in simple language. I've tried to do it more times than I care to recall and I have seen others struggle with the problem; with a single exception they were no more successful than I have been. The man who did manage the job was a really exceptional person—but just how often is anyone called upon to explain the construction of an outhouse these days?

On the surface this last may seem to be a joke, but if we look closely there is a serious lesson to be learned. The building of an outhouse is a matter of using tools and techniques that are familiar to most people. This is not to say that construction of an outhouse is either easy or simple, but that there are few mysteries and little jargon involved. In short, there is little that needs to be explained. The previous chapters have not been attempts to explain the *entire* health care delivery system, simply because, as Dr. Johnson's statement suggests, all possible objections cannot be overcome. The jargon alone is too much.

In these last chapters we seek to provide answers to two phases of the question: how do you, the patient/consumer, survive your interactions with the health care system? Chapter 9 will be devoted to the future, to consideration of how, over the next generation or so, we can attempt to set our badly disoriented health care house in order. Following the fiat "First, do no harm," the present chapter is a survival manual for your present-day, routine encounters with the two professionals who deliver most of your health care—the physician and the pharmacist.

There is one point to be made at the outset: if you want to be the immediate captain of your soul and master of your own fate in matters of health care, you must go to medical, osteopathic or dental school, graduate, then pass your licensing exams. It's the only sure way and in an ideal situation every family would have a member who had done something like this. Barring this, the next best thing is to aim at being an active partner in the delivery of health care—regardless of who lays out the actual cash, it is you, the consumer, who pays the bill—and the penalty. There is no rational reason why, if you want to, you should not be a partner in your own care. You must bear in mind, however, that there are many different sorts of partnerships, and out of simple self-interest you want to enter into the one that serves you best—an equal, sharing collaboration in which your health is the first consideration.

A note of caution: you are going to meet resistance. At first you will lose more encounters than you will win, but if you persist, you will eventually win most of them and, best of all, so will your professional partners. Unfortunately, they don't know this yet, so be patient with them. It will pay dividends.

To get an idea of how far you will have to go in establishing a health-care partnership with your physician and pharmacist, tune-in for a moment on an imaginary dialogue. Dr. Headman has just finished a physical examination of Mrs. Mousse, a forty-three-year-old housewife:

Dr. Headman: Now then, Mrs. Mousse, we've got to get that blood pressure down. I'm going to have you take one of these white tablets [*hastily writing as he speaks*] four times a day and one of these pink tablets [*turning to a second prescription blank*] every morning after breakfast. Oh, yes, here is a diet plan [*tears off a sheet from a pad provided by a drug manufacturer*]. Now, [*he leaves his seat behind his desk, walks to the door and opens it*] I want you to make an appointment with the receptionist for next month on the way out.

Mrs. Mousse: I will, thank you, Doctor.

[*one hour later at Simon Counter's neighborhood pharmacy*]

Mrs. Mousse: I'd like these prescriptions filled, please.

Simon Counter: Certainly, ma'am. They'll be ready in about ten minutes.

[*four minutes later*]

Simon Counter: Here we are, Mrs. Mousse, that will be $11.95, please. Will that be cash or charge?

Mrs. Mousse: Good heavens, [*handing Simon a $20 bill*] what are those things anyway?

Simon Counter: I'm sorry ma'am, but Dr. Headman didn't say to label 'em, so I can't say. Perhaps you could ask him.

Mrs. Mousse: Oh well, as long as they do what they're supposed to. . . .

Simon Counter: Yes ma'am. . . .

The first impression anyone overhearing these imaginary (but typical) dialogues receives has to be that a great many words are passed between individuals, but little is actually said—people talk without communicating. This is the consumer's greatest difficulty when it comes to obtaining health care: extracting, with all its painful implications, information from the professionals. The only facts that emerge with any clarity from the Headman-Mousse-Counter conversations are dosage and price. This amounts to one "bit" per professional. Of these two, the more important fact, the dosage, remains an ephemeral oral communication.

Obviously, a great deal of very important information is missing in this encounter—important to Mrs. Mousse. You might well ask, as I have heard some of my colleagues do: "How important? After all, this is a forty-three-year-old, obese, slightly neurotic, hypertensive housewife whose kids are nearly grown; she's spent the last twenty years going to seed—indulging herself. The chances she'll follow a treatment regimen are statistically insignificant. . . ." Admittedly true, but our legal system is based on the proposition that she is neither more nor less important than any other person. As for the matter of following treatment regimens, I am convinced that in at least 90 percent of the cases where a consumer fails to follow directions, the professional "team" is to blame and not the consumer. As an object lesson, let's go back through Mrs. Mousse's encounter and examine the implications of what was said.

". . . we've got to get that blood pressure down." That "we" hints at some sort of partnership, but when all is said and done, Mrs. Mousse is cast adrift to do whatever it is that must be done. When she kept her appointment with Headman because of moderate concern over recurring dizzy spells, she was, in effect, hiring a technician to render an opinion (what is wrong with the equipment?). This is a situation that can hardly be differentiated from consulting a TV serviceman when the living color becomes livid green, or a mechanic when a fabulous four-speed transmission becomes a tremulous three-speed. In every case our first question deals with "what's wrong?" The technicians all want symptoms upon which they can base a diagnosis, and they depend on the consumer to supply them. Once some sort of diagnosis is established, all but the health care technicians offer the options of repair, discard, or trade-in on new equipment. (I am fully aware that in posing the "How important?" question earlier, there could be the implication that health care technicians *do* on occasion offer the discard option. The only comment I care to offer is that I reject this as an option unless there is no other—and sometimes not even then.)

In effect, then, the differences are a matter of degree; most of us are more attached to our bodies than to all the machines in our sphere of consciousness. This comparative concern ought to make us *more* rather than *less* cautious about accepting advice from the relevant technician (in this instance, the physician). We hire the physician, he renders an opinion for a fee, and it is left to us to understand and follow his recommendations as we will.

Before we re-examine the Mousse-Headman-Counter encounter in more detail, let's assume that the individuals involved are typical professionals and consumers located in a community of about 50,000 inhabitants. The reasoning behind these assumptions is that probably 75 percent of all health care in the United States is delivered under similar or poorer circumstances. Before Mrs. Mousse made an appointment to see Dr. Headman, she probably had several episodes of dizziness, possibly ringing in her ears and an occasional blinding headache, or she may only have felt vaguely unwell. Hypertension, which is Mrs. Mousse's problem, may never make itself known as a set of clear symptoms until severe damage has been done. There are an estimated 10 million people in the United States with high blood pressure (or hypertension) who aren't aware of it. With these facts in mind, let us re-run the dialogue, but with Mrs. Mousse doing her best to get out of Dr. Headman the information she will need if she is to really assist in the treatment of her condition:

Dr. Headman: Now then, Mrs. Mousse, we've got to get that blood pressure down . . .

Mrs. Mousse: Just a moment. The way you say that sounds serious.

Dr. Headman: Well, your pressure is up.

Mrs. Mousse: Can you give me some idea?

Dr. Headman: Yes. It's 210/140, but we're getting off the track. I'm—

Mrs. Mousse: Is that dangerous?

Dr. Headman: Well 210/160 would be more dangerous, but . . .

Mrs. Mousse: I see. What would be about right for a person of my, er, circumstances?

Dr. Headman: [*pause*] Well, there isn't really a "normal" blood pressure exactly. . . .

Mrs. Mousse: Well, if my pressure happened to be 190/140, would that still be too high?

Dr. Headman: Yes. But that isn't the important thing, we've got to—

Mrs. Mousse: What about 170/120? Is that too high?

Dr. Headman: It should be treated and that's what . . .

Mrs. Mousse: Suppose my pressure was 150/100? Would you want to treat me then?

Dr. Headman: Ah, well, that could be borderline.

Mrs. Mousse: So my blood pressure isn't just "up," it's pretty high?

Dr. Headman: Yes. Now can we . . .

Mrs. Mousse: Just how dangerous is blood pressure that's "pretty high?"

Dr. Headman: Mrs. Mousse, I don't like to discuss these things because I don't like to have my patients frightened. But since you have asked, blood pressure that high could cut twenty or thirty years off a normal lifespan—if it is not treated. There is no organ in the body that is immune to the effects of hypertension; sooner or later something gives way. But there is one thing in your favor: I don't find any evidence of real damage—yet.

Mrs. Mousse may be a bit frightened by the information she has extracted from her physician at this stage, but she has two of the most important pieces of information she needs. First, she knows that her blood pressure is dangerously high, and second, she has a fair idea of the risks involved in allowing her condition to continue unabated. She knows that at age forty-three she can expect to live another thirty or so years, but Headman has indicated that at least twenty, and possibly more, of those years of life expectancy are in the balance. This will certainly affect any decision she makes with regard to Dr. Headman's treatment program. If she is willing to take the risks, that is her business. If it concerns anyone but herself, it concerns her family, friends, and insurance company more than it concerns her physician.

The information Mrs. Mousse has at this point, while important, is not enough, so she will have to ask more questions:

Mrs. Mousse: You say there's no evidence of damage, but why is my blood pressure so high?

Dr. Headman: Well . . . [*taking note of her tar-stained fingers*] smoking is one thing that contributes to the problem. Of course, being, er, over-weight [*glancing at the height and weight recorded on her chart*] doesn't help, and anxiety and drinking may add to the situation. It's a complex of many possible things.

Mrs. Mousse now knows, even before Dr. Headman hands her the diet sheet, that she is going to have to become *involved* in the solution to her problem. The four packs of cigarettes a day, between-meal snacks, rich desserts, double martinis, weekend six packs, and a miscellany of other excesses of which she is vaguely aware will have to be balanced against the probability of premature death. Though Mrs. Mousse isn't, strictly speaking, a hedonist —she probably wouldn't know what the word means—at this moment she realizes that a more Spartan lifestyle is what Dr. Headman is suggesting as part of her therapeutic regimen.

Dr. Headman: This sheet outlines a fairly well balanced diet that will furnish in the neighborhood of 1000 calories, and I'm going to prescribe some tablets. . . .

Mrs. Mousse: What are these tablets?

Dr. Headman: Just a little something to help lower your blood pressure.

Mrs. Mousse: Yes. But what are they?

Dr. Headman: Oh! [*Chuckles nervously*] They'll help relax you . . . [*sees her surprised look*] they're a minor tranquilizer.

Mrs. Mousse: [*suspiciously*] I thought the trouble was with my blood pressure, not my nerves.

Dr. Headman: Well, we find that nervousness or anxiety tends to play a part; it tends to drive blood pressure up.

Mrs. Mousse: [*snapping*] What makes you think I'm nervous or anxious about anything? [*She recalls, unhappily, the look in her husband's eyes as he describes the pretty young receptionist at his office; the snide remarks she has overheard about her daughter and the older men she "picks up" at the bowling alley; the dog and cat that leave stains on her expensive, new rug; the pesky neighbor who . . .*]

Dr. Headman: Strictly speaking, I don't know that you are, but I've found that nearly all of my hypertensive patients have a moderate degree of anxiety. Most of them don't recognize it, but the minor tranquilizer seems to help. Now, I'll write a prescription for another tablet that I want you to take after breakfast every morning for . . .

Mrs. Mousse: What is *this* tablet? What does *it* do?

Dr. Headman: This is a diuretic, which also helps to lower blood pressure.

Mrs. Mousse: But I already take a diuretic—water pills—that I buy at the grocery store. What's so different about these you are prescribing? Won't the ones I get at the grocery lower my blood pressure—I mean this is confusing—why are yours any better?

Dr. Headman: Well, I have no idea what drug is involved there, so it's hard to say, but I don't think you can buy any drug at the grocery store that would do much for your blood pressure.

Mrs. Mousse: Then you don't want me to take them anymore?

Dr. Headman: Yes. I think that's best.

Mrs. Mousse: Well, what are the names of the drugs you're prescribing? It seems like a good idea for me to know what I'm taking since I can't tell you what is in the pill I get at the grocery.

Dr. Headman: I'll instruct the pharmacist to put the names on the labels.

Mrs. Mousse: Would you have him put the directions on the label so I'll know how to take them? I always seem to forget doses or get them confused.

Dr. Headman: Certainly. Perhaps you could take those tablets you got at the grocery with you and ask the pharmacist if he can tell you what they are.

Clearly, the encounter between Mrs. Mousse and Dr. Headman has taken a great deal longer than the original brief exchange. However, this time Mrs. Mousse participated—she did not simply deliver her one line, "I will, thank you, Doctor," after Headman rushed through his quick three-line delivery. The point is that Mrs. Mousse drew her physician out, ignored his apparent wish to keep things moving, and goaded him into providing at least a minimal amount of information that she felt necessary. Had she not been *forced* to extract the information, the interview could have been much shorter—possibly even more productive. Regardless of how it came about, what happened in the second illustration is important because Mrs. Mousse is now at least partially a partner in her own treatment. She may not completely eliminate the excess Headman pointed to, at least not right away, but she is in a better, more open frame of mind. When she returns to Headman's office for a follow-up appointment a month hence, the chances are that her blood pressure won't have changed greatly (although, in a significant number of cases, a month of treatment is enough to bring a patient's pressure to more on the order of 170/125), but if any positive change happened with Mrs. Mousse and it turned out that she had reduced her cigarette consumption by a pack a day, passed up a martini or two, and walked away from a rich dessert once or twice, a verbal pat on the back would leave her receptive to almost any serious therapeutic suggestion—possibly even completely eliminating cigarettes.

Physicians who treat their patients in the same vein as Headman did in the first dialogue seldom learn of the personal problems that so frequently play a large role in how their patients progress—they frequently get the impression that their patients are "fighting" them. There are many people who believe that as often as not the drug component of treating essential hypertension is perhaps slightly less important than adjusting the lifestyle.

When Your Physician Prescribes

The second, more extended dialogue comes a good deal closer to the ideal of educating the consumer and disclosing the physician's motivations and treatment rationale. From this latter hypothetical encounter we can formulate some general guidelines for interacting with the physician with regard to his examination and drug therapy:

(1) Ascertain, to your satisfaction, *what the physician is attempting to achieve* with his course of treatment. It usually helps for the consumer to have some idea as to what the diagnosis is. Do not accept generalizations such as the tired, old "to help you get better." Above all, do not be afraid to ask a "stupid" question—you can't help him if you don't know what he's trying to accomplish. Is he trying to reduce inflammation, wipe out an infective organism, relieve pain, control spasms, or what?

(2) Don't stop with the name of the drug he's using; *find out what class* it belongs to—antibiotic, analgesic, anti-inflammatory, antispasmodic, etc.

(3) If you don't understand what the class name means, *press for an explanation.* How far you will have to go will vary, but keep in mind that any physician who fails to tell you, in language you can understand, what you want to know about your treatment has two big strikes against him in a malpractice situation—he might overlook that even with the large number of suits now in the courts.

(4) Find out if there are *alternatives to his treatment.* What will be the likely result if you don't want to undergo surgery? Is there a safer drug? Do you really need drugs at all? By this I don't mean that you should demand a detailed explanation of *all* possible courses he might take or every drug he might use, but your questions should aim at being certain that he is adopting as conservative a course of treatment as possible. Try to assure him that you do not wish to pressure him into prescribing *anything,* and that if your condition doesn't clearly indicate to him the need for some sort of intervention, you will be happy to follow a course of non-intervention. Some very competent physicians have gone on record as saying that less than 10 percent of the patients they see require *either* drugs or surgery.

(5) Ask your physician *what to expect from the drugs* he orders. You particularly want to know about side effects. Ask what the most common side effects are, which ones might be dangerous and which are merely annoying. Ask under what

circumstances you should stop taking the medication and report the effects to him.

(6) Advise your physician of *all other drugs you are taking* or may have to take during the time you will be taking the drugs he prescribes. If he hedges or does not appear to know what interactions might occur, go slowly. As you get to know him better, he may feel enough at ease to look up the information as you sit facing him, but it may take years to develop a rapport of this sort. I know many—far too many—physicians who are more afraid that you will learn they don't know everything than they are of injuring you and facing a malpractice suit. In the meantime, this is where your pharmacist is important. He generally knows more about the drug or is in a better position to get the answers you need. In any case, few pharmacists are afraid to have you see them using a reference book.

(7) If you have a *chronic condition* (asthma, diabetes, allergies, heart trouble, glaucoma, hypertension, a diseased or missing organ, etc.) do not assume that your physician remembers this fact; name the condition and ask if there is an incompatability. Here, again, your pharmacist can be of help.

(8) Be sure your physician includes *full instructions* for taking whatever drug he prescribes as he writes the prescription. Tell him you don't like prescription labels reading "Take as directed," because you forget what to do with them.

(9) *If a prescription label is indefinite* ("one or two, three or four times daily as needed") find out when you should take two at a time instead of one and under what circumstances you should take them four times a day instead of three.

(10) *In the case of antimicrobial drugs,* ask if there is enough in the prescription to finish off the organism in question. If you are apt to need refills, you should know under what conditions to have the prescription refilled.

(11) Demand that your prescriptions have the name and dose size of the *important active ingredients* on the label. This is not simply a convenience; in case of an overdose, reaction or interaction, such information could well be life-saving.

(12) Inform your physician of *any other treatments or drugs* you may be receiving from another practitioner. Later you can call the other practitioner and inform him of the treat-

ment and drugs recommended by his colleague. As a cross-check you can ask him about the possibility of reactions or interactions between the two sets of treatments. If there are possible, but unlikely, problems, ask him what symptoms you should be concerned about. In many smaller communities, and even in some of the larger ones, the physicians exchange information among themselves regarding patients they have in common. Where this happens you have a built-in safeguard, but you can never be sure that this is being done, so it is in your best interest to do the job yourself—besides doing yourself a service, you may be doing the practitioner a favor.

(13) Always insist that you be given a *written prescription.* In this way you reduce the possibility of error, and you can take the prescription to whatever pharmacist you choose. There are a few physicians still in practice who dispense drugs in the office and in this case I personally insist on a written prescription. I have never seen one of these individuals, known in the trade as "dispensers," who adequately labeled or packaged the drugs he dispensed, and there is always the tendency to use "off-brand" drugs. I have known several physicians who began dispensing in their offices with the best of intentions. For a time they did an excellent job, but invariably their methods became slipshod in spite of the best of motivations. One other way a written prescription protects you is that it is a written record of what medication was ordered for you. Unfortunately, there are physicians whose concept of record-keeping is difficult to rationalize. Even some who write prescriptions fail to enter the details of the medication on your office record, but the pharmacist is required to keep records by law—you are far more certain that the whole story of what drugs you are given is maintained in the pharmacist's files.

None of these rules, nor any other set of rules, can guarantee that you are going to receive either better or safer drug-related care from your physician. Putting them into practice, however, *will* have at least two salubrious effects. The first, and in my mind the more important, is simply that you put your physician on notice that he is being watched. No matter how bumbling you feel about the job, you are telling him that you will not routinely accept everything he tells you, so he had better stop and think before he prescribes or advises you.

The second effect of such strategies is that, indirectly, you test your physician's competence. (It is worth considering too that, as incredible as it may sound, *you* will become more competent.) The principle is this: very few highly competent physicians will object to being questioned by a consumer. (I almost said "intelligently questioned," but everyone seems to have a different view of intelligence. I recall a situation when I was a first-year pharmacy student that illustrates this very well: an eminent physiologist gave a guest lecture which I found exciting, but parts of it were over my head and I was left puzzled by one point. After the lecture, I approached the lecturer to ask for clarification. The exact words I used are not important, but I conveyed the impression I knew my question was "stupid." The lecturer smiled and after a short pause replied, "Young man, there is no question that is too 'stupid' to ask, although there are a few people who are too stupid to ask questions." I felt ten feet tall as he not only answered my question, but also explained why it was important.) You will be pleasantly surprised to find that a great many physicians are genuinely excited by your curiosity and welcome the opportunity to impart some of their knowledge to a willing listener. On the other hand, physicians of marginal competence are much more likely to react badly to questioning. They become annoyed at being asked about things they can't explain. Some—and I speak from many years of experience—are actually frightened by even the simplest question, regardless of who asks it.

If your physician starts to bluster and sputter or uses words you can't understand and he won't explain, it's a fairly sure sign that you had better look elsewhere for your health care. These are not positive signs of incompetence, but under these circumstances there's not much chance of a productive partnership being developed. Spending the price of an office call on three or four physicians is probably the best way to find a competent, compatible practitioner, and in the long run it may be the cheapest.

One parting word of advice: if the only chance you have to question your physician is in the examining room, get dressed quickly and position yourself between him and the door; the average physician is a master escape artist and once he has gotten away from you, your chances of finding him in the labyrinth of his office complex are nearly nonexistent. Avoid this sort of interview at all costs—a half-dressed (or, depending how you look at it, a half-naked) state leaves you at a distinct disadvantage. The sort of physician you want will, upon being questioned at length, suggest his private office for a conference. If at first he doesn't take the hint, keep him cornered until you have accomplished your purpose. An office call generally costs the same whether it lasts 2 1/2 minutes (which research indicates is typical) or 12 1/2 minutes, and you can ask a lot of questions in the extra ten minutes.

If your physician complains that he is busy and can't spend so much time with you, *do not feel guilty*. In the first place you are paying him anywhere from $1 to $5 a minute, and in the second place it is the medical profession itself which is responsible for the shortage of competent physicians. It is your tax dollar that subsidized his education and the hospital he uses so freely. You have done more than your fair share. Too, it is the American physician who insists that American health care is the best in the world and you are merely helping him to live up to his own high standards.

Face to Face with the Invisible Man

Taking on a belligerent physician in an effort to extract better health care from the existing system is often a spirited sport. Under the right circumstances it can assume all the drama and stylized conflict of a first-class bull fight (pun intended). Similar dealings with a pharmacist, however, often lead to nothing more than the frustration of trying to crack the Great Stone Face. As I have indicated elsewhere in this book, our present health care system makes it difficult, if not impossible, for the American pharmacist to use more than a very small fraction of his expertise for the benefit of the consumer. If he is an employee pharmacist, as the vast majority of pharmacists are, then he stands to lose his job if he does anything that appears to discourage the filling of a prescription. Even if he owns or (more often) is buying a store, he is unlikely to turn away a faulty prescription, because to do so means a personal economic loss. The physician gets his fee regardless of whether he prescribes half a dozen drugs or simply tells you to go home and rest, drink plenty of fluids, and take two aspirin every four hours. The pharmacist does not have this sort of professional freedom. Finally, the pharmacist lives in the very real fear that he may offend a physician by criticising—no matter how justly—one of his prescriptions.

In spite of these problems, however, there are certain things you can do in this area that can improve the quality of your drug-related health care:

(1) *Choose a pharmacist with at least as much care as you choose a physician.* You want someone who keeps a drug profile, not just a tax-reporting record or a record that is simply designed to help him keep track of your prescription numbers in case you forget or lose them. Chapter 9 will go into greater detail in this regard, but at the very least you want someone who writes down and keeps track of even the over-the-counter cold preparations you take and has a record that he reviews every time he fills a prescription for you, listing your allergies, chronic conditions and the like. He should even record such things as the fact that you have trouble swallowing tablets but not capsules. What you want is someone who takes sincere interest in your health, and, generally speaking, you will *not* find an individual of this sort at the nearest supermarket drugstore.

(2) Once you have selected a pharmacist, *do all of your prescription business with him* and, if at all possible, all of your over-the-counter drug business. Let him know that he is getting all of your business and that he will continue to get it. This will help soften his hard economic shell; when the time comes that he must make a professional judgment that sends you away with an unfilled prescription or that causes you not to buy an expensive therapeutic vitamin preparation, knowing that you will be back makes it easier for him to do so. He can forego a short-term profit and base his judgment on what's best for you if he knows you are a "regular" customer. Once you have established a rapport, he can advise you of ways that save you money, time, and effort. He will do this because satisfied customers bring in new customers, and the more he sells, the more profit he makes.

(3) *Determine your pharmacist's busy periods and try to avoid them.* Generally, these times are two hours in the morning, about an hour after the store opens; an hour and a half after lunch, about 2:30 to 4 P.M.; and perhaps an hour between 5 and 6. A sort of rule of thumb is that the pharmacist is busy from about half an hour after the local physicians begin office hours in the afternoon until about 5 P.M. In

spurts he will be receiving prescriptions and refills during this period at the rate of some fifty prescriptions per pharmacist per hour. It is difficult, under such circumstances, to get the sort of attention you want, so if it is at all possible, avoid these time periods. If the store is open in the evening and on Sunday, these may be the best times for you. If you have prescriptions to be refilled, call the pharmacy the day before, give the prescription numbers, and tell them you will call for them the next day (during a slack period, of course).

(4) *If you should happen to obtain drugs at a hospital* or some place other than at "your" pharmacy, you will want this recorded on your drug profile. You may even want to discuss them with your pharmacist. It may seem a trifle to you, but as things stand today and are likely to remain for years to come, there probably is no drug that humans ingest that does not have the potential to cause problems either alone or when combined with certain other drugs or foods.

(5) Until you have established a "working relationship" with your pharmacist, ask to *be sure that he is aware of your allergies, chronic conditions and the possibility of interactions with other drugs* listed on your profile. After a while the pharmacist or pharmacists in the store will automatically check these things, and it may become part of their repertory to bring the profile sheet and the filled prescriptions to you at the counter to go over them with you. You may even have the experience of having a pharmacist you haven't seen in the store before go through the routine without your having to ask.

(6) As with your physician, *you should never be afraid to ask questions.* If there is any aspect of a prescription you don't understand, you can use the same technique on your pharmacist you used on your physician. Many of the pointers regarding the physician also apply to the pharmacist, and it could require extracting information in the same manner Mrs. Mousse used on Dr. Headman.

Keeping Watch over the Guardians

What will these efforts get you, in terms of improved health care? Because of the current structure of our health care system, it must be said that the improvement, though significant, will be quite small compared to what it ought to be. Perhaps the most important benefit is that, should you suffer a drug-induced condition, a complete drug history is available to the physician who happens to treat you. Furthermore, if you periodically remind your regular physician that your pharmacist keeps a complete and ongoing record of the drugs you take, it tends to make your physician more cautious about his prescribing. Despite the fact that the physician can be quite confident that the pharmacist will never contradict his therapy, he can never be absolutely certain.

It would be reassuring and pleasantly satisfying to be able to say that the American consumer could, by exercising his economic prerogatives, assure himself of high quality drug-related health care. Unfortunately, this would be both a dangerous deception and a bare-faced lie. As I have tried to outline above, about all you can do with your physician is to shake him up so he does the best job he is capable of when it comes to prescribing. Because of the grave limitations of his education and his attitude regarding drugs, his best will probably not be good enough. On the other hand, about the best you can expect from your pharmacist is to get him to keep better records of what the physicians are doing to you—records which will probably not be readily accessible in time of crisis. In order to obtain even this dubious service you will almost certainly have to pay the economic penalty of patronizing a smaller, non-mass-merchandising pharmacy. On top of all this, the times when you encounter your physician and pharmacist are generally the times when you feel least like fighting for your rights—namely, when you are sick.

Keep in mind one thing as you work on your health care partnership: you may not be able to find competent professionals. After all, I have indicated that a mere 10 percent of all health care professionals can be considered highly competent (about 32,000 physicians and 13,000 pharmacists), 35 to 40 percent are passably competent (about 125,000 physicians and 40,000 pharmacists), while perhaps as many as 55 percent are so therapeutically adventurous or inept that they constitute a hazard (about 175,000 physicians and 72,000 pharmacists). Because of the many oligarchies within the health care system, your chances of obtaining the services of competent professionals are even further diminished.

I went so far as to examine a dozen or so books, some adult education courses, and the offerings of several junior colleges in the faint hope I could recommend a sort of do-it-yourself approach, but it was of no use. The state of Illinois, for instance, requires that some sort of drug education course be provided in public schools, yet I found nothing of value there beyond the development of a primitive course or two.

Clearly, there is only a limited amount that can be achieved by way of consumer protection in the health care arena as long as our system continues to operate as it does presently. Any significant change will probably have to await reforms of the sort outlined in the next chapter.

9 What is To Be Done?

In dealing with the steps the consumer can take right now to improve the health care he receives, I have tried to make it clear that such steps barely scratch the surface of the problem. Before there can be a significant improvement in American health care, we will have to have major changes in the health care system. I am not a practicing Utopian: I do not wish to raise false hopes for the reform of a system which may well be beyond hope of reform. Nevertheless, in this chapter I present for consideration several areas of change which could be imposed on the American health care system.

System reforms can be classified as either *procedural* or *structural,* in other words, changes in the way the present system does things, or changes in the system itself so that it will subsequently do things differently. I have three reasons for presenting two sets of reforms: first, procedural reforms tend to be immediate—the sort of changes that can be implemented more or less at once—while structural reforms are more useful as long-term remedies; second, it is not at all clear which of these sets of reforms will ultimately provide the greatest benefits to health care consumers (it is even possible that the two sets of reforms are incompatible); and third, I do not wish to fall into the trap of dictating, from a professional podium, what is "good for" the consumer. It seems to me that, although there is little question that immediate procedural changes would save consumers time, money, and even life itself, still the ultimate liberation of the consumer will be to make him as independent as possible of the professional health care hierarchies. In the massive development of health care technology and institutions, we have lost sight of the basic and obvious fact that *health care is a private affair between the individual's mind and body.* Structural reforms that tend to restore this private relationship will not only help free the consumer from the economic burden of supporting a vast and monolithic professional edifice, but will also help to restore a measure of precious individual freedom.

Procedural Reform

"FEE FOR SERVICE"

The problem with procedural reform of a traditional institution, such as health care, is not that there is any difficulty in determining what needs to be changed, or even in working out changes that would achieve the desired goals. Rather, the problem is that the *structural* interconnections within traditional institutions are so complex that a procedural change in one part of the system may suddenly exaggerate undesirable factors in another part. By way of illustration, let us consider the "reform" represented by Medicare-Medicaid, and by most schemes thus far proposed for a system of national health care insurance. The "evil" which is to be reformed by such measures is the practice of rendering "fee for service." What "fee for service" means is that, instead of being on a fixed salary, the physician is paid for each individual service he performs. Thus a person who must use a large number of medical services ends up paying more than a person who uses fewer services. In strict free-enterprise thinking, this is considered "fair," just as it is "fair" that a person who abuses his automobile ends up paying for more repair services than the careful driver. The problem is that care of the human body is not very much like automobile repair; despite the overriding cash nexus of our society, we still hesitate to suggest that (to paraphrase the old spiritual) "the rich should live and the poor should die." In this respect, medical care should be likened to fire or police protection, both of which were long ago taken off a strict "fee for service" basis. We are horrified when a city fire department refuses to respond to a call in an unincorporated suburb because the owner has not paid his annual fire protection fee.

In the delivery of health care it is almost a truism that those who need the most services—the poor and the elderly—are those least able to pay the fees. Hence it was to be expected that social welfare programs such as Medicare and Medicaid would be evolved to help soften the blow to these groups of patients. The actual result of such programs is a matter of public record: routine, massive overcharging by every category of health care provider, unnecessary prescribing and extra office visits, obvious overuse of health care services with no measurable improvement in the actual level of care received by needy patients.

The abuses of Medicare-Medicaid need not be further detailed here to make the point that these programs, being merely *procedural* changes, simply compound—and underwrite at public expense—certain abuses that have always existed in our health care system. In outlining reforms that might be applied to the drug-delivery aspect of the system, it will be my aim to avoid changes like Medicare-Medicaid, "reforms" which merely dress up existing barbarities and make them acceptable to the contemporary social conscience. It is interesting to note that, for all the AMA's hysteria over "creeping socialism," organized medicine today placidly accepts Medicare-Medicaid. The physician has discovered that such programs make it possible to collect fees from patients whom he would previously have felt obligated to treat as an act of charity.

At the outset of this discussion, let me be the first to point out that the procedural reforms I will suggest are unlikely to profit anyone but the health care consumer. Consequently, resistance on the part of physicians, hospitals and most pharmacists is to be expected. On the other hand, I think it is virtually impossible to deny that these reforms would result in improved health care, if only by correcting certain abuses now present. This instinctive resistance on the part of health care professionals is simply one more reason to believe that control of health care policy should largely be shifted into the hands of the health care consumer himself.

THE PRESCRIPTION SYSTEM

When we look at the way in which prescription drugs are chosen, delivered and monitored, what could be done to reduce the chaos in the present system? Earlier in this book we have had occasion to mention the triplicate forms required in some states for narcotic prescriptions. If such forms were required for *all* prescriptions, there would be a massive reduction both in prescription mistakes and in prescription fraud.

This is a reform which I have advocated for over twenty-five years. Yet whenever I have broached the subject to health care professionals, the response has been not actual resistance but pure apathy. Most health care professionals are so little interested in such safeguards for consumers that they can't even muster the energy to attack or refute the idea.

This is how such a triplicate prescription system would work: When a physician filled out a triplicate prescription form, one copy would remain in his files for future reference. (A physician who sees forty patients a day is unlikely to recall at the end of the day what he prescribed for his 9:45 A.M. patient, and many physicians do not regularly enter complete prescription information in patient records.) The second copy of the form would go to the pharmacist who filled the prescription. (The presence of a copy in the physician's file would make it dangerous for the pharmacist to alter the prescription, say to make it refillable when it was not, or to dispense 100 tablets instead of 10.) Finally, a copy of the prescription would go with the patient for his own records, and for the use of any emergency room physician faced with treating the patient for an overdose, interaction or reaction to the drug.

If four additional provisions were incorporated into this reform, control of prescribing would be about as complete as we can expect it to be, if the other aspects of health care are left as they now stand:

• Telephone prescribing should be completely eliminated—it saves the patient very little time or trouble and it is completely uncontrollable.

• It should be legally required that *every single* piece of information be filled in on the blank by the physician—otherwise the patient would be sent tramping back to have the physician complete the job.

• Nurses, secretaries and other office personnel must be forbidden to write in the physician's signature to any prescription, no matter how "routine."

• Refilling of prescriptions should be completely eliminated—like a check, a prescription should be "cashed in" only once.

If these additional controls were actually imposed on prescribing practices, the reaction from physicians and pharmacists alike would be swift and violent. Uniformly and predictably the charge would be that such changes would "encumber and impede" the practice of medicine. Ironically, this charge is true—it would make the current variety of speak-easy prescribing almost impossible to practice. It would take a physician a minute more to fill in a triplicate prescription form, instead of the ten seconds now required to scribble on a prescription blank. Likewise, the physician could not simply write a tranquilizer or sedative prescription for a troublesome patient, check the "refill" box, and be rid of said patient for years at a crack. In effect, the inconvenience would require physicians to stop practicing prescription-writing and start practicing medicine. What is actually implied by the charge that thorough controls on prescribing would "encumber" the practice of medicine is that the current practice situation is characterized by overprescribing, incomplete diagnosis, and a tendency to "process" patients on an automatic, assembly-line basis.

Most pharmacists as well would be annoyed by such controls, but for purely economic reasons. Overall prescription volume would fall off and pharmacies would lose the lucrative refill business, which is today often conducted without the physician's knowledge or consent. Because of the reduced volume of prescriptions, pharmacy practice might have to be altered so that pharmacists were paid on some basis other than the volume of prescriptions they fill. In fact, the triplicate form might lead to an increase in the practice of clinical pharmacy at the community level.

If the system of prescription-filling were truly set up to serve the consumer, there would be no shortage of things for the pharmacist to do. For a start, it should be part of his legal responsibility to collect information for a standard drug history on each consumer, and to enter in it each prescription filled for that consumer. Thus, each pharmacy would keep not only a file of prescriptions, but a file of patients. Without resorting to a national computer network linking all physicians and all pharmacies, there is of course still no way to stop a consumer from visiting several physicians and having the resulting prescriptions filled at several pharmacies. It might be appropriate, however, to require the patient to sign his completed drug history, attesting to its truth and completeness much as he now does when filing his federal income tax return.

In addition to these duties, the pharmacist would take on the responsibility of authorizing refills for prescriptions for drugs that must be taken continuously, such as phenobarbital for epilepsy. It would also be left to his judgment whether to allow telephone prescribing in special cases (it would be the physician's responsibility to have the written prescription delivered to the pharmacy immediately after calling it in). If universal clinical pharmacy were established, *all* prescribing would be done by the pharmacist in any case.

FEDERAL LICENSING

Many objections which are raised to attempted reforms of American health care center around the questions of "states' rights" in setting legal standards for the medical professions. The argument generally runs something like this: "With fifty sovereign states we have fifty different sets of licensing requirements, fifty different sets of rules for prescription filling. If one state tightens its controls, it will simply result in an exodus of medical practitioners—and even patients—to neighboring states." The obvious counter to this line of thinking is that we must simply consider federal licensing and rule-making in the practice of medicine, nursing, pharmacy, etc.

Such suggestions raise gasps of horror from legislators, state officials, medical professionals, and even some consumer advocates. However, a quick look at the realities of the situation should set everyone's mind at ease. For one thing, "home rule" in medical care is an illusion anyway. Health care education, hospital facilities, and much direct patient care is subsidized, standardized, and regulated by the ebb and flow of federal money; every year the Department of Health, Education and Welfare disburses more money for health care than do all American consumers put together. Nor is money the only means of federal control. At present, classifications and minimum controls for narcotics are established by federal legislation and then implemented accordingly by the states. And most individual states are not so jealous of their rights that they do not freely reciprocate one another's medical licenses. If federal licensure were enacted tomorrow, no one would notice the slightest adverse effect—no one, that is, except a few thousand superfluous bureaucrats in the state licensing agencies. (As a matter of fact, much of the existing licensing machinery would be retained to service the federal licensure.)

Several major benefits to consumers could result from uniform federal licensure of medical professionals. For one thing, it would finally be possible to gradually raise standards, not only for initial licensure but also for proof of continuing competence. Under the present system of state licenses, the problem is not that the requirements are not uniform, but that they are uniformly too low. No one state can, for instance, require that all physicians desiring re-licensure take an additional two-year course in pharmacology (or diagnostic logic, or whatever the majority seem to be lacking). The result *would* be a massive exodus of physicians to other states. Consequently, any "upgrading" which a state requires tends to be so slight as to be nearly meaningless, perhaps only one or two non-credit correspondence courses a year.

As we have already seen, not only are state requirements for continuing education very scanty, but there are no means of checking on the quality or appropriateness of the courses offered to medical professionals on a non-credit, correspondence basis. Under a system of federal licensure, it would be a relatively straightforward matter to establish standards for such courses and require that they be taken regularly by all health care professionals. Nor would it be very difficult (or very expensive) to administer periodic re-licensure examinations to all health care practitioners, thus ensuring that the practitioners have not only taken the courses, but that the courses have "taken" on the practitioners.

There are two basic assumptions behind this sort of continuing education and continuing examination: (1) not all practitioners (in any field) are equally competent, and (2) proof of competence at the beginning of one's professional career is no proof at a future date, since the field of knowledge is constantly changing. The "pass-fail" aspect of re-licensure examinations would help to determine continued competence and, by employing the actual, relative scores achieved by the practitioner, could be used to separate the professional sheep from the goats. This is not a new idea, but it has largely been abandoned in the face of the demand for professional autonomy. In nineteenth century America, for instance, school teachers often had to demonstrate their competence through *annual* examinations for re-licensure. And the proof was relative as well as absolute: a teacher who had previously found that he could earn a Class II certificate might find that, when more experienced or better-educated candidates moved into the school district, he might be dropped to a Class III certificate, or he might be given no certificate at all.

The usual argument for discontinuing such competitive examinations is that the improvement in the education of would-be professionals makes such checking unnecessary. In the first place, anyone who has had the slightest experience with two or more institutions of higher learning knows that this is simply not so. Education is surely the most wildly variable commodity "produced" by our technological society. And furthermore, a large portion of the physician's education is obtained outside medical school, through the completely uncontrolled and unstandardized process of internship and residency. One assumption behind professionalism is that professionals will pursue such experiential education with sufficient dilligence to render all of them at least minimally competent. This is contrary not only to the observed facts but to a rule of thumb in education which states that the rich get richer and the poor get poorer. In other words, those who do best at the early stages of the educational process progress at a continuously accelerating rate, while those at the bottom of the scale gradually fall behind. Thus, educational processes tend to accentuate rather than reduce individual differences, and the longer the process, the greater the spread. In other words, the highly competent physicians and pharmacists (especially of the clinical variety) are the ones who continue to work like dogs at their education, while the marginal incompetents display at best a stodgy indifference and at the worst a lackadaisical arrogance which is imaginable only among the "professional" classes.

One swift cure for this state of affairs might be to issue graded licenses to health care professionals, with certain privileges and procedures being restricted to the higher levels of licenses. Thus a Grade C physician might be forbidden to practice surgery, or to act as a consultant to another physician, while a Grade A pharmacist might have certain clinical privileges, such as consulting with physicians, or prescribing on the basis of physicians' clinical records. At present we have a situation where any physician who knows enough to hold the scalpel by the handle end can bill himself as a surgeon and any pharmacist who can feed enough blarney to the hospital administrator can take on the job of clinical pharmacist. In nursing, the situation is even more chaotic, an unintelligible scramble of two- and four-year graduates, RN's, LPN's, NA's and NP's, and what not else. A national system of graded licensure and continued re-examination would not only help sort out the current crop of nursing practitioners, but would also be a powerful incentive to the nursing schools of America to set their disorganized house in order.

So far as the practice of pharmacy is specifically concerned, graded federal licenses would help to separate the clinical and dispensing functions in pharmacy and, coincidentally, provide us with a pool of clinical pharmacists from within the existing ranks. By means of uniform examinations it would be possible to determine which pharmacists now practicing have the knowledge and skills to handle the clinical end of pharmacy. My guess is that we might find that we have as many as 15,000 pharmacists in this category right now. We would probably also find that another 15,000 practicing pharmacists are so nearly incompetent that they are a danger to public health if they are allowed to do anything beyond the file-clerk level. Between these two extremes we would probably find the remaining 120,000 or so current pharmacists. They are probably adequate to the tasks presently imposed on them, but—and this is extremely important—given the incentive of progressing to a higher class license, perhaps as many as 30,000 to 50,000 of them could successfully pursue the studies necessary to join the clinical ranks.

This is perhaps the greatest benefit to be derived from graded federal licensure, and not only in pharmacy, but in medicine and nursing as well—the visible, public incentive for the practitioner to improve his level of competence. At present there are few incentives to such improvement and most (such as "Board Certification" for physicians in certain specialties) are meaningless to the general public. In pharmacy and nursing there are currently *no incentives whatever* to improve competence. In all of the health care professions the rule now is that as long as you keep your license, you are "in business." How "successful" you are is determined by how many patients you service, not by how competently you treat them. Under a system of graded licensure we would not only have a fighting chance of knowing who is competent and who isn't, but we would almost certainly see a definite improvement in the competence of thousands of middle-level practitioners who have always had the latent ability to pull themselves up, but have never had the necessary incentive to do so.

Structural Reform: To Inform Their Discretion

When we leave the area of procedural manipulations that could readily be performed upon our existing health care system, we enter a foggy zone of futurology and social engineering where methods are largely untried and results uncertain. This is not to say that there is any real difficulty in projecting the direction in which we must move: the problems of modern health care are largely philosophical and it is not difficult to experiment with various deductive formulas, substituting various assumptions about health care and seeing what sort of results they give us. In the main, I think that such projections must move us in the direction of *deprofessionalizing* health care.

The first assumption about modern health care which I would like to question is that it is a technological agreement whereby the patient places himself under the care of technological specialists and agrees to submit to their will. A prior assumption in that health care is a subject which only an intellectual elite can master. It therefore follows that taking health care out of the exclusive province of the professional and placing it in the hands of the people themselves, requires a re-education of the health care consumer.

Such a change would result in the *democratization of health care,* and the success of any democracy depends on the readiness of the *demos,* the people, to accept the responsibilities of self-government. There would of course be an immense outcry from the health care professionals. This is only to be expected since oligarchic groups achieve their own identity primarily by mistrusting the abilities of the masses.

In response to the oligarchic tendencies of early American federalism, Thomas Jefferson asserted: "I know no safe depository of the ultimate powers of the society but the people themselves; and if we think them not enlightened enough to exercise their control with a wholesome discretion, the remedy is not to take it from them, but to inform their discretion." The constant theme of organized medicine is that ordinary mortals would be incapable of exercising "control with a wholesome discretion," when in fact the ordinary mortals have never had a chance to try.

It goes without saying that the present level of consumer education in matters of health care is pretty abysmal:

- At a PTA meeting thirty-five parents take a fourth-grade health and hygiene quiz: only one parent passes.
- A college sophomore asks her roommate to show her where her stomach is located. The roommate brings home a dogfish from zoology lab to demonstrate. The first girl is aghast when she sees the fish's internal organs: "But that's just a fish. I don't have tubes and things inside me . . . do I?"

The layman's ignorance of his own anatomy is simply one small part of the continuing crisis of education in the modern world. It is a fact that in almost every area the American consumer is ignorant of the nature of that which he consumes. In part this ignorance can be laid to the door of education, but it is also an inevitable result of technological proliferation. The backyard mechanic who once blithely (and successfully) tuned his '49 Plymouth with nothing but a wrench and a screwdriver, now finds to his dismay that his '76 model is untunable without the help of an oscilloscope and an air/fuel ratio meter. Likewise, it used to be commonplace for a consumer to remove the back of a non-playing radio and replace an offending tube. Like as not, the radio played again; but today the owner of the latest solid state marvel is confronted by a plain-block-lettered sign on the back panel which proclaims: "Refer servicing to competent technical personnel. No tubes or other user-serviceable components inside."

In health care, the gap between consumer knowledge and the state of the technical art is far more severe than in almost any other area of goods or services. To some extent, one could make a case for the idea that there has been a constant gap since the time of the ancient Babylonians, but the social implications have become seriously compounded in the modern age. In a sense, it mattered very little a century ago whether or not the patient understood what the physician was doing to him. The physician didn't understand either, and there were strict and close-set limits on what he could do to the patient. He could of course poison him with drugs or infect him through surgery, but such procedures were self-limiting: before Faustian levels could be achieved, the patient became food for worms.

With the explosion of modern medical technologies, the "natural" limits of what the patient could survive have gradually been pushed back, or eliminated altogether: He can't breathe? Put him on a respirator. His heart won't go? Plug him into a pacemaker. His joints won't move? Take them out and put in plastic and metallic replacements. In current practice there are few reasons for the physician to take responsibility for inserting common sense limits into his treatment regimen: in the direction of proliferation lies medical glory.

Instead, it is the *patient* who is faced with having to decide what he will and will not allow to be done to his body. And, although the patient is often in a legal position to put a stop to a course of treatment, he rarely comprehends what is being done to him, and thus rarely objects, except in a generalized way and out of the physician's earshot. To his wife he may say, "Dr. Schmitt wants another bunch of x-rays. I don't know what he wants more for, he's already got about twenty of my stomach. . . ." It may be that there is a perfectly good reason for the new x-rays, such as a need to study a suspicious spot from a different angle, or it may be that Dr. Schmitt hasn't the foggiest notion of a diagnosis and is grasping at straws, or it could mean that the x-ray technician lost the previous batch of film. One thing it definitely means is that the poor consumer hasn't the slightest idea what is happening to him and consequently cannot act as a check on the physician's actions.

With the extensive body orientation of our culture, one would think that knowledge of the body would be a major concern of our educational system. However, at the same time that we are Celtic/Anglo-Saxon body worshippers, we are also Roman state worshippers, Greek mind worshippers and Hebrew spirit worshippers. We have never quite gotten all of our cultural threads together. Furthermore, it tends to remain true, as George Bernard Shaw observed, that "He who can, does; he who cannot, teaches." The result is that most education below the college level (and a good deal beyond) remains purely descriptive. Thus, although few students escape from high school without being exposed to a health course, and many take a general biology course as well, knowledge of body processes, especially an understanding of the relation of structure and function in the body, is often lacking.

Health care professionals universally prefer to ascribe the public's ignorance of medical matters to the complexity of the subject. Along with Dr. Thomas Szasz and a few other radical educators, I prefer to believe that this is a myth generated by the health care establishment and that this myth has had a pervasive and stifling effect on health education for the layman. Szasz has commented, for instance, that he is convinced that both anatomy and physiology of a fairly advanced sort could be taught to twelve- and thirteen-year-olds. I would go further: by age three or four most children will spend hours poring over anatomy charts, and a three-year-old will cheerfully memorize lists of terms that would cost a medical student a week of all-night study sessions. The tremendous popularity of toys such as the Visible Man, the Visible Woman and the Visible Heart should tell us something. Unless we accept that children are both eager and capable of learning about their bodies in great detail, it is impossible to explain why, in our machine-mad culture, these plastic anatomic models should be more popular than the Visible V-8 and the Visible Wankel Engine! It is pretty clear that the health care professions have sold us a bill of goods when it comes to health education for the masses, but it is equally clear that it could take us a generation or two of concerted effort to come up with a populace which would be capable of making most of its own health care decisions.

It is, to use the hoary textbook apology, beyond the scope of this book to present anything approaching a full discussion of the future of health education in America. It can be said, however, that a major aim of such education must be to end the isolation in which most health care information is today generated, disseminated and consigned to oblivion.

The Future of Health Care Professionalism

The almost universal information vacuum, when it comes to bringing such "hard core" material to the medical consumer, brings us to a (necessarily brief) consideration of the future of health care professionalism in America. It should be clear from my discussion of pharmacy professionalism in Chapter 6 that there is a basic conflict between the goals of professionalization and the needs of the consumer. The credo of professionalism assumes that the professional (as defined by other professionals) is capable of self-regulation and can be trusted to supervise his own continuing competence. I contend that there is little evidence to suggest that this actually happens, much to suggest that professionalization tends primarily to ossify the status quo, and, furthermore, that there is an inherent contradiction between the practice of self-regulation and autonomy.

What this all suggests is that, before we can see a significant shift in the direction of consumer-oriented health care, we will probably have to make certain changes in our definition of professionalism. One central fact must be kept in mind: professionalism as we now know it depends upon vesting the powers of regulation in the hands of the regulated. Conversely, as soon as the powers of regulation are shifted to the hands of those who are affected by the actions of the regulated, we have utterly transmogrified the profession in question. In this sense, governmental regulation of professions is at best a stopgap measure. For years it has been a standing joke among consumer advocates that the majority of the members of the Federal Communications Commission seem to be former radio and television executives, while an inordinate proportion of top radio and television executives seem to be former FCC commissioners. The more highly technical the field to be regulated, the more likely this is to be true. In consequence, we may have this sort of prospect to look forward to in governmental regulation of the health care professions, unless we make quite certain that such regulatory agencies are dominated by persons whose primary interest lies in being *consumers* rather than *generators* of health care. This is the direction in which we are already moving in other areas of regulation, and there is some reason to believe that we could incorporate this orientation into a federal medical agency, provided there is sufficient consumer pressure to do so.

At some point in the evolution and refinement of our social institutions we must come to a point where there will no longer be a distinction between "government control" and "consumer control." This, after all, is what we mean, in the economic sector, by government of the people. What most Americans seem to yearn for most is health care that is personable, friendly, sincere, easily accessible, cheap, effective and safe—in short, virtually everything that present American health care is not. Governmental control that was responsive to the desires of the people would be at pains to provide this sort of care. On the other hand, present "regulation" seems primarily to benefit the regulated, resulting in health care that is cold, impersonal, machinelike, threatening, inordinately expensive, far less safe and effective than it should be, and utterly inaccessible to millions of Americans. It is high time we openly and sincerely asked the question: For whose benefit does regulation of health care exist, the consumer or the health care professional?

A further reform of professionalism that would ultimately benefit the consumer would be to break down the present rigid distinctions between the health care professions. This change could be brought about by altering the educational process which produces those professionals. Our present hodgepodge of medical schools, nursing schools, and pharmacy schools could be merged into a system of "schools of health science." In such schools, all persons desiring to enter *any* health care profession would begin their education together, and during alternate years, work together side by side in the field. After reaching a level equivalent to the present bachelor's degree, they would then branch out into course work and training in their chosen fields—but still on the same campus and in close social and intellectual proximity to one another. Thus we could reduce or eliminate both the haughty isolation in which physicians are today reared and the second- (or third-) class citizenship to which nurses and pharmacists are assigned.

To the patient, this sort of "co-professional" atmosphere would mean a vastly increased chance of receiving truly collaborative health care. The physician would be aware (since he had studied in the same classes with them) that the nurse and the pharmacist were fully capable of catching his careless errors. And for the same reason, the nurse and the pharmacist would be far more likely to assert themselves professionally on the patient's behalf. Finally, such unified education might well prevent that emergent professional, the clinical pharmacist, from turning into an arrogant and isolated pseudo-physician.

The Promise and Perils of Computerization

At the same time that we talk of remaking our health care professionals to more fully meet the needs of the consumer, we must be aware of both the promise and the perils involved in fulfilling the futurist's dream of a fully automated system. Compared to coordinating a spacecraft landing on the moon or Mars, setting up a data processing system to link and coordinate the entire American health care system would be child's play. All we need is a national computer network and a main data storage bank in which every consumer's entire medical history is stored. Each consumer would carry a coded card which the physician would insert into his desk-top computer terminal to tell the system where to file or retrieve clinical data. Likewise, the pharmacist would enter each prescription by the same means, and the computer would automatically compare the prescription to the patient's record to determine contraindications, or possible reactions or interactions.

Aside from the formidable problems of safeguarding the security of 220 million medical records kept in a single data bank (and total centralization is the only way to make such a system work), the computerization of health care raises certain philosophic problems to which there are no foreseeable solutions so long as we demand, as we should, that the system fill certain emotional and social needs. For one thing, when we inject machinery into human interactions, it is not always possible to predict the behavioral results. Machine advocates, for instance, usually theorize that providing a machine to do routine tasks will free the humans involved to do things that only humans can do. This does not often seem to be the case; instead, the machine operator is likely to use the machine's increased work output as a smokescreen behind which to withdraw from the scene of work to an extent that would not be possible if he were still doing all the work himself.

It is not difficult to visualize this effect as it would apply here, because much of the therapeutic effect of health care arises from the patient's personal interaction with the medical professionals. When someone takes our detailed history, and takes the time to consider therapy in relation to that history, then we become in our own eyes a being who is cared for, and therefore one who is far more likely to respond to treatment. Going a step further, I would assert that truly holistic health care is as much a philosophic as a technological act; we need to be able to place ourselves under the care of wise men and women, "doctors" (teachers) who will show us how our inevitable physical deterioration binds us firmly to the universal human condition.

What has gone wrong with modern health care is that it has evolved to a stage of machinelike impersonality without accruing the advantages of precision, interconnection and repeatability which belong to true machinery. Consequently, we have sacrificed much of the philosophic value of health care, while we have failed to reap more than a tiny fraction of the benefits to be expected from current technology. The task in any proposed reform is thus to restore the patient to the center of attention in the system, and at the same time to attempt to bring under control the staggering mechanical giant of modern health care technology.

The Impervious Wall

The reforms which I have presented in this chapter could all be implemented quite easily—in the sense that they could be mandated by law. What is not so clear, however, is whether implementing such reforms would result in *reform* of the health professions in question. This is so because the health care system is really quite different from, say, the trucking industry: even the most cloak-and-dagger commercial venture takes place in a fishbowl, compared to the most commonplace transactions between consumers and the health care establishment.

Consider, by way of analogy, a vast, even infinite, wall of impervious concrete. On one side of the wall, 220 million consumers are milling about, waiting for "service." On the other side of the wall are slightly less than a million health care providers. What are they doing? There is no way for you, the consumer, to know, because you are on the other side of the wall, and the only passage through this infinite wall is a single, narrow hole—just big enough to let through a clenched fist. From time to time, someone goes up to the hole with a demand clenched in his or her fist, thrust the fist through the hole, and leaves the demand on the other side of the wall. From time to time, a hand appears from the other side, deposits a reply, and withdraws. When this happens, a horde of consumers gather at the hole in the wall and a spokesman reads out the reply. Strangely the replies never seem to have anything to do with the demands. Somehow, in the mysterious darkness on the other side of the wall, everything that the consumers send through is "processed" and comes out as another "statement of policy."

When it comes to health care reform, more and more American consumers are losing patience with the endless, futile business of shoving notes through the hole in the wall. I share this impatience with a vengeance, and those who have the stomach to breach the wall by whatever means are invited to proceed to Chapter 10. Otherwise, stop here: the "remedies" in Chapter 9 are "safe," but as a health care professional I must also warn you that they are "probably ineffective."

10 *The Future*

At this point we reach an impasse: the hole in the infinite wall allows consumers to pass only a single handful of reform at a time. And, ironically, the more pieces of reform passed through, the more raw material provided for the shadowy figures on the other side to turn into shiny new versions of the same old pablum which they have been doling out for the last two millenia. It is high time someone took the step of tearing down the wall instead. It goes without saying that those on the inside—the health care providers—will never take this step. It is up to the outsiders—the health care consumers—to take sledge, pick, and shovel and get to work.

Can Consumers Become Informed?

For the existing walled-in health care establishment to be "regulated" by the active concern of the body of consumers probably requires critical powers which we, as a species, do not possess and are unlikely to acquire under any foreseeable circumstances.

Hidden deep in the back pages of my Sunday newspaper a few months ago was an Associated Press release, datelined New Orleans, proclaiming that a five-year study had found 20 percent of adult Americans to be illiterate: "They lack the skills and knowledge to achieve even moderate success in life." An additional 33 percent were subsequently discovered to "possess minimum skills, but need tremendous improvement for substantial advancement in modern life." In all likelihood, from one third to one half of all Americans over the age of eighteen years are able to make sense of the increasing amount of information available to them. When it comes to health care the picture is more dismal—I would guess that fewer than one out of every ten Americans avail themselves of the material that *is* at hand. It is an unfortunate fact of life that there are only a few such articles readily available, since nearly all of the good, comprehensive ones—the sort every consumer ought to have at his fingertips—are in the professional journals of either nursing, medicine, pharmacy or sociology:

> . . . analyses of patient records showed that some outpatients were receiving as many as 54 prescriptions over a 112-day period.
>
> *Med. Care* 9:383-395 (Sept. Oct.) 1971

> . . . Stanley Shor, a biostatistician formerly at the American Medical Association, reported on an analysis of papers dealing with drugs which were published by a number of prestigious medical journals. He found that the conclusions of only about one out of four of the papers were valid in terms of the design of the study, the type of analyses performed and the applicability of the statistical tests applied.
>
> *Drug Intell. Clin. Pharm.* 7:491 (Nov.) 1973 see:
> *J.A.M.A.* 195:145-150 (Mar. 18) 1966

> The time has come when it must be recognized nationally that a public health problem exists from the misuse of drugs.
>
> *Drug Intell. Clin. Pharm.* 4:203 (Aug.) 1970

> Specialized knowledge and experience are the elements qualifying physicians to select products for other people. To the extent that pharmacists equal or exceed physicians on this specialized knowledge and experience, this would seem to qualify pharmacists to assume the role of product selector.
>
> *Am. J. Hosp. Pharm.* 30:123 (Feb.) 1973

Of the journals cited, only one, the *Journal of the American Medical Association,* is commonly available even in the libraries of medical schools. (Six months ago, at the request of one of the librarians, I recommended *Drug Intelligence and Clinical Pharmacy,* the *American Journal of Hospital Pharmacy* and several other important journals to the School of Basic Medical Sciences at the University of Illinois; not one of them is yet in the stacks and it is unlikely that they ever will be.) Not one of these or similar publications is apt to be available in any public library, with the possible exception of those in the three or four largest cities in the country.

The point is this: such journals have documented, on a continuing basis, that *for decades* health care consumers have been ill-served by health care providers. Depending on what form of peer review is used, from 1.4 percent (group consensus) to 63.2 percent (individual reviewer explicit criteria) of the patients reviewed were considered to have received *adequate* care. A mere 5 percent of the pharmacists in a 100-pharmacy study appear to have given *proper* service. Only 13 to 33 percent (in two studies) of the antibiotics consumed by hospitalized patients were prescribed on the basis of any discernible *need.*

It is strongly tempting to stop at this point with the observation that our American educational system is a miserable failure and to imply that this alone is the basis for the equally miserable failure of our health care system. After all, on the basis of the survey just cited, 20 percent of our citizenry are literally incapable of coping with the problems of modern life, and an additional 33 percent are apparently merely able to hold their own. Nonetheless, this would be both unfair and short-sighted since educational deficiencies are only one facet of the overall problem. It must be emphasized again that the existence of a closed medical establishment—behind the wall—means that even the most gifted and critical consumer cannot be expected to obtain and use the information needed to cope with the health care system.

The situation has, however, led me to wonder if the typical consumer is really concerned about the system which delivers health care. Does he really want a rational, holistic health care system? After three decades of dealing with health care consumers, it is my impression that very few ever really wanted any more or less from their health care delivery system than it was actually delivering—until very recently. The reason for the change does not appear to be that Americans have suddenly become aware of the extensive damage the system is doing to their health, but, rather, what it is doing to their pocketbooks—the present system is now gobbling up 10 percent or more of their wealth! Don't get me wrong, there is no one who has a better right to take a cold-blooded, crassly commercial view of health care, but I would have preferred other focal points. Still, it is a start, although what it means is that apparently only the most blatant aspects of health care affect most consumers: again, we notice only what is passed through the wall; in this case it is the bill for services.

American Health Care: An Illegitimate Pseudo-science?

As I review the material I have presented thus far, I am convinced that it is vital that we not presume the guilt or innocence of any individual or group of individuals—it is a trap; placing blame at this late date is futile. It is a proposition very much like blaming the automobile for atmospheric pollution. A very strong case could, and by some has been made in this direction, but nearly a decade ago I learned that scientists had discovered smog in a tropical rain forest thousands of miles from any concentration of internal combustion engines. It is of more than secondary importance that we know what natural phenomena as well as unnatural, artificial circumstances are at work; otherwise we may either overestimate or underestimate the validity of any corrective measures we may take. Still, it is difficult to be certain of cause and effect since we are confronting a situation which is so complex that conjecture is frequently more meaningful than hard data.

One thing that makes an entity such as health care so difficult to pin down, study, analyze and reform is that, like Proteus, it has no distinct form. Health care is a hodgepodge of wild growth, taking its character from antecedents beyond the reach of human memory and recorded history. We cannot pinpoint its exact origins, therefore we cannot easily come to grips with its current nature. Like MacDuff it is "not of woman born" and, cloaked in mystery, it is a source of terror. It is literally "illegitimate"—does not proceed from law—and as such it cannot be dealt with in an orderly, logical and civilized way. In *An American in the Gulag,* Alexander Dolgun describes a similar sort of situation with regard to the NVD, the Soviet secret police:

> An illegitimate body that is really big and powerful is much more effective in its capacity to frighten people than a legitimate body. Because it is illegitimate, it answers only to the whims and appetites of its masters, and its masters are always shadowy, indistinct people or myths like Stalin, with infinite power and not answerable to any law or any system.

In our own recent history, we have only to think of the CIA, FBI or Senator Joe McCarthy. None of them was vested with much legitimate power, but all three managed to shake the American social fabric to its very roots by usurping large amounts of power that no one contested. There was a power vacuum and they moved in to occupy a strategic position of their own devising. This is precisely the same tactic health care professionals—particularly physicians—have used for centuries.

In the case of the health professions it is impossible to identify a legitimate base upon which the system of delivery can be said to rest. There is no such base because the practice of medicine antedates all recorded forms of government and law. It is true that there are now certain laws which *pertain* to the practice of medicine, but they exist only to place the stamp of legitimacy on the traditional structure and values of medical practice as well as government. Because the power of the medical profession does not rest on law, but on *custom,* there is no available pattern to follow in bringing medicine under legal control; there is no way to use the force of law to make medicine serve the ends of those who consume medical services and pay its bill.

Health care is claimed, by health care professionals and government, to be a scientific institution, but in reality is it? It may be scientific—and I am making no concessions in this regard—in as many as one out of ten cases. Based on nearly thirty years of observation, it is my belief that about 10 percent of *all* health care professionals are *really* competent and that perhaps 35 or 40 percent of the rest are defensibly able. Easily half of the health care professionals in the United States ought to have signs hung around their necks that are similar to those mandated for every package of cigarettes: "Warning: It has been determined that the care delivered by this individual may be dangerous to your health!" Health care *should* be a scientific institution, but there is scant evidence that it is:

> I wonder whether I am not more honest and even more humble about what I do than a practitioner who prescribes pills all day long thinking he is not doing experiments and that he is not taking risks with his patients' lives *without their explicit instructions.* (emphasis added)
>
> Dr. Walter Modell
> *Medical Tribune,* Nov. 28-29, pp. 7-17, 1964

> The only area in which the U.S. can boast of being first is the cost of health care.
>
> Dr. C.W. Blissett, Dean
> University of Oklahoma College of Pharmacy

American health care is more a socio-economic institution than a scientific one. It is also an iatrotheomorphic (iatro=physician; theo=divine; morph=form) oligarchy which is controlled and administered by people who do not wait in line with the common herd, who have no concept of the lot of the other 99.9+ percent of the population, and who *may* care about the others but give no indication that they do. In no other aspect of modern life can it be said with greater certainty that the typical consumer is a helpless pawn—a passive participant in the most expensive, all-encompassing institution yet devised, one which affects his life from before his first breath (usually) to his last. No government has ever held such iron-heeled, unbridled power.

Procedural Reform: A Mere Finger in the Dike?

What is to be done? Should we concentrate on procedural or structural changes? Should our health care system be restructured *in toto* or should it be procedurally overhauled in piecemeal fashion? It is unfortunate, but our health care delivery system has deteriorated beyond the point where we have the luxury of asking such questions. We face the stark reality of having no real choice.

In Chapters 6 and 7, I extensively discussed clinical pharmacy as one possible solution, in spite of personal ambivalence, and in doing so I constructed, in a rather loose sense, a model of procedural change and how it might affect the future of health care delivery; however, it is only one of a great many possible courses open. For instance, it has been possible for the past fifteen years to do without the pharmacist in his traditional dispensing role. There are machines which can dispense drugs at the command of a person who is either in the same room or at a remote location. By the same token, machines have been developed that surpass their human counterparts for accuracy when it comes to diagnosing human ailments. Then, there are machines in the clinical laboratory which automatically complete twelve tests on sixty samples an hour. It is conceivable to combine these three functions in a single machine so that a consumer might not need to bother with the laboratory technician, pharmacist, or physician. Properly programmed, such a machine would certainly appear to accomplish everything the institution of clinical pharmacy could and more. The question (and it lies close to the heart of every health care problem) is: who will run the machine? If the running of the machine is placed in the hands of the existing health care system, the only thing we can be sure of is that we will be billed for the use of the machine.

Suppose we impose the procedural change that I have advocated since before the "amphetamine epidemic" of the 1950s: every prescription would be written on a duplicating form of some sort and could not be refilled. At some point a decision will have to be made concerning the information required to make the prescription legitimate—consumer's name, address, telephone number, social security number, height, weight, sex, age, genetic background, fingerprints—perhaps his picture? Yes, it could become absurd, but this single, relatively simple, procedural alteration could require answers to a great many seemingly unrelated questions. A change of this sort could be more effective than universal clinical pharmacy in controlling irrational prescribing, but are consumers willing to submit to this sort of interrogation?

Clearly, the prescription is our *fundamental* control device in health care. As I indicated in my discussion of the Illinois Dangerous Drug Commission in Chapter 6, it would be quite easy for the state to control the flow of legal drugs. The fact that such control is not in fact exercised is simply another indicator of the "lawless" relationship between the health care professions and would-be government regulators. In the same chapter you should not forget the experiences of Ralph Bloomberg and the young pharmacist in Ed Ward's drugstore—there is no doubt in my mind that any consumer who seriously wishes to obtain a legal drug can do so, and he can do it without ever seeing a physician.

There is an intriguing possibility which, though it may seem farfetched, was proposed by a physician, Dr. Thomas Szasz of the State University of New York at Syracuse, a few years ago. Dr. Szasz contends that there should be *no* prescriptions. He believes that it is impossible, and probably immoral, to protect people from themselves. With this proposal Dr. Szasz apparently offers consumers almost complete individual freedom. It may seem strange for someone who has been a pharmacist for nearly thirty years even to acknowledge such a proposition, but Dr. Szasz has a point. In the first place, he qualifies his proposal by prohibiting the sale of drugs to minors; but the most important consideration of all has to do with educating consumers. Without drawing a detailed blueprint, Dr. Szasz would rely on self-control and, by inference, some sort of grass-roots educational mechanism. The fact of the matter is that there are several areas throughout the world where Dr. Szasz's proposal is now the normal condition—consumers may purchase any drugs they wish, the only limiting factors being price and availability. It is true that many people do manage to kill themselves as they self-medicate, but there is some evidence that they do no worse than if they were required to obtain prescriptions. As I have pointed out many times in this book, the prescription system does little to control the abuse of most drugs anyway. Furthermore, if consumers *realized* that they were in fact practicing self-medication, there is a good chance that many would be somewhat more cautious than they are now.

Who Will Tear Down the Wall?

Although I have discussed several potential, probably stopgap, solutions, there is only so much that can be accomplished by procedural changes. Medicare-Medicaid is as good an example as I know of the danger inherent in legislated procedural modification. Billed as a major innovation, this bureaucratic monstrosity has led to scandals which put Watergate and Teapot Dome to shame. Health care professionals in the state of Illinois alone are stealing from $1 million to $2 million a *day* from the programs!

Procedural changes appear to be only slightly better than no answer at all, because the health care system as you and I know it has no future! There is no way in which it can be justified either in terms of costs or improved health. American consumers are receiving poorer care and they are paying more for this deteriorated care. There is scant hope that the situation will improve before we have reached a breaking point. To those of you who have read this far in the expectation that I would produce a blueprint for some magical system, I offer only my most profound regrets. I have tried, as subtly as possible, from Chapter 1 on to tell you that if there is to be any effective *structural* remedy for our American health care delivery system, it cannot come from the providers because it *will* not. Reform of our health care system—if there is to be any change at all—will have to come from you, the consumer.

The question which is inevitably asked at this stage is: "All right, what should we do? What do you recommend?" Because I am not a typical consumer (for which I thank my lucky stars) but a member of one of the three professions which have been most instrumental in allowing health care to attain its present low state, I am not the person of whom consumers should expect cure-all proposals. I can serve consumers and my profession best by raising questions and pointing out successes and failures, not by proffering advice that cannot help but be professionally biased.

The first and most important question consumers must ask is: "Do I *really* want a health care professional to tell me how health care systems should work?" Had Thomas Edison's young assistant known it was impossible to work tungsten, we might not have the electric light bulb. . . .

A NOTE ON THE APPENDICES

In these three appendices I have collected a fair proportion of the "codes" and "shorthand" used by physicians in writing prescriptions, charts and clinical reports. If your physician is doing his job and living up to his title of Doctor (teacher), then he should be both willing and able to explain to you everything that he has discovered about your condition and everything he wants to do by way of treatment—and to explain it in language which you, as a layman, can understand. This is of course not often the case. Usually, you must meet the physician halfway, penetrating the jargon which he is unable to escape. With the aid of these appendices you may be able to determine to your own satisfaction what has really been said in your prescription or chart.

One word of caution: it is indicative of the way in which our health care establishment presently views consumers that, in many states, it is illegal for you to see your own medical chart.

APPENDIX A

Some Common Latin Abbreviations Used in Prescription Writing

Abbreviation	Approximation
aa, āā	of each
a. c.	before meals
ad	to
ad lib.	to please
alb.	white
ante	before
aq.	water
aq. ferv.	warm water
b.i.d.	twice daily
c, c̄	with
cap.	(let be) taken
caps.	capsule
coch. mag.	tablespoonful
coch. parv.	teaspoonful
comp.	compound
d.	day
da., det.	give
dil.	dilute
disp.	dispense
d.t.d.	dispense such doses
el.	elixir
e.m.p.	as prescribed
et	and
ex	from
ext.	extract (of)
f., ft.	make
fl.	fluid
Gm., gm.	gram
gr.	grain
gtt.	drop
hora	hour
h.s.	bedtime

Abbreviation	Approximation
m.	mix
mag.	large
m. dict.	as directed
m. p.	as directed
no.	number
non rep.	do not repeat
O	a pint
o.d.	right eye
o.l.	left eye
o.s.	left eye
o.u.	both eyes
p.c.	after meals
per	through
p.r.n.	as needed (according to circumstances)
pulv.	powder
q., q̄	every
q.d.	every (once a) day
q.i.d.	four times a day
q.o.d.	every other day
q.s.	quantity sufficient
R/	take or prescription
rep.	repeat
s., s̄	without
s.a.	according to the art
sat.	saturated
Sig:	label thus
s.o.s.	if required
sol.	solution

Abbreviation	Approximation	Abbreviation	Approximation
solv.	dissolve	t.i.d.	three times daily
ss., ss	one-half	tr.	tincture
stat.	now, at once	ung.	ointment
tab.	tablet	ut. dict.	as directed
tal., t.	such		

APPENDIX B

Some Common Abbreviations Used in Clinical Situations

This listing contains some of the abbreviations I have seen used on patient's charts; it is not complete and it is variable. Such abbreviations are unofficial and, as indicated, their meanings vary from place to place and from physician to physician—new meanings and new abbreviations are constantly being "invented."

Abbreviation	Approximation
@	each; at
ABS	at bedside
ab.	abort; abnormal
abd.	abdomen; abdominal; abduction
ABE	acute bacterial endocarditis
ABR	absolute bed rest
Ac., AC	acute
A/C	anchored catheter
A/G	ratio of albumin to globulin
ACTH	Adrenocorticotropic hormone
add.	adduction
adm.	admit; admission; administer
AFB	Acid fast bacillus
A. fib.	atrial fibrillation
AHF	antihemophilic factor
AK	above the knee
alb.	albumin
alc.	alcohol; alcoholic
ALS	amyotrophic lateral sclerosis
AMA	against medical advice
AMAP	as much as possible
amb.	ambulate; ambulatory; ambulance
amp.	amputation; ampule
amt.	amount
ANA	antinuclear antibody

Abbreviation	Approximation
AOAP	as often as possible
A/P, A&P	anterior to posterior; ausculation and percussion
AP	antepartum (before birth)
aq	water
ASAP	as soon as possible
ASHD	arteriosclerotic heart disease
ASO	antistreptolysin-O
AV	arteriovenous; atrioventricular
ax.	axillary
B	bacillus
BA, ba	barium
baso.	basophil
BBB	bundle branch block
BC	bone conduction
BCG	a tuberculosis vaccine
BE	barium enema
BK	below the knee
BM	bowel movement
BMR	basal metabolitic rate
BP	blood pressure
BPH	benign prostatic hypertrophy
BS	bedside, bowel sounds, breath sounds, before sleep
BT	bedtime
BTL	bilateral tubal ligation
BUN	blood urea nitrogen
BW	body weight
c̄ hold	withhold
CA	carcinoma, chronologic age
cath.	catheter
CBC	complete blood count
CBR	complete bed rest
CC	chief complaint; chronic complainer
ch.	child; chronic
CHF	chronic heart failure
ck.	check
CNS	central nervous system
c/o	complains of
CP	cerebral palsy; cleft palate; chronic pain
CRP	C-reactive protein

Abbreviation	Approximation
C & S	culture and sensitivity
C sect.	Caesarean section
CSF	cerebrospinal fluid
CV	cardiovascular; cell volume
CVA	cerebral vascular accident
CVP	central venous pressure
D & C	dilatation and curettage
dex.	right; dexterity
diff.	differential blood count (white cells)
dk.	dark
DOA	dead on arrival
DOE	dyspnea on exertion
DT	delerium tremens
DTR	deep tendon reflexes
Dx, DX	diagnosis
EBL	estimated blood loss
ECF	extended care facility
ECG, EKG	electrocardiogram
EEG	electroencephalogram
eos.	eosinophils
epith.	epithelial
ER	emergency room
EST	electroshock therapy
FBS	fasting blood sugar
F	Fahrenheit; female
Fe, fe	iron; female
FH	family history
FP	family planning
FUO	fever, undetermined origin
Fx	fracture
GB	gallbladder
GC	gonorrhea
GFR	glomerular filtration rate
GI	gastrointestinal
gm	gram
gr	grain
GSW	gunshot wound
GTT	glucose tolerance test
GU	genitourinary

Abbreviation	Approximation
Gyn	gynecology
h, hr	hour
H	hypodermic
Hb, Hbg	hemoglobin
HCT	hematocrit
HEENT	head, eyes, ears, nose and throat
HHD	hypertensive heart disease
H & N	head and neck
HO	house officer (resident or intern)
ht	heart; height
hwb	hot water bottle
Hx	history
ID	identification; initial dose; intradermal
I & D	incise and drain
IM	intramuscular
imp.	impression
inf.	infection
int.	internal
I.O.	intake and output
IV	intravenous; four
JVD	jugular venous distention
KUB	kidney, ureter, bladder
L, lt.	light; left; liter; low; long; fifty
LA	left atrium
lab	laboratory
lac.	laceration, milk, lactating
lap	laparotomy
lat	lateral
LBBB	left bundle branch block
LB	low back; left breast; pound
LDH	lactic dehydrogenase
LE	left eye; left ear; lupus erythematosis
LHF	left heart failure
LKS	liver, kidney, spleen
LLE	lower left extremity
LLL	left lower lobe
LLQ	left lower quadrant
LMD	local medical doctor
LMP	last menstrual period

Abbreviation	Approximation
LOA	left occiput anterior
LOP	left occiput posterior
LP	lumbar puncture
LSB	left sternal border
LUE	left upper extremity
LUQ	left upper quadrant
LVH	left ventricular hypertrophy
L & W	living and well
MA	mental age
MBD	minimal brain damage
mcg	microgram
MCL	mid-clavicular line
MD	muscular dystrophy; mental deficiency; a physician
med	medical; medicine; medication; medium
MH	marital history; menstrual history
MI	myocardial infarction; mitral insufficiency; mental institution
min	minimum; minim; minute
MR	mental retardation
MS	morphine sulfate; minimal support; multiple sclerosis
N	never; not; no; Negro; normal
NAD	no acute distress
NBM	nothing by mouth; no bowel movement; normal bowel movement
NC	neurological check
ND	not done; normal development; no doubt
neg	negative
NG	naso-gastric
NP	neuropsychiatric; not pregnant; no pain; no particular; newly presented; not present
NPN	nonprotein nitrogen
NPO	nothing by mouth
NS	normal saline; not seen; not sensitive
NSR	normal sinus rhythm; not seen regularly; nonspecific reaction
N & V	nausea and vomiting
O	oxygen; oral; eye; open; overt; obvious; often; other
OB	obstetric
OD	right eye; osteopathic physician; on duty

Abbreviation	Approximation
od	every day, etc.
OOB	out of bed
OP	out patient; operation
OPB	out patient basis
OR	operating room
P	pulse; pint; pound; patient; persist
PA	posterior/anterior; pulmonary artery; pernicious anemia; presents again
PE	physical examination
PEG	polyethylene glycol; pneumoencephalogram
PERLA	pupils equal, react to light and accommodation
PH	past history; poor health
PI	present illness
PID	pelvic inflammatory disease
PM	afternoon; evening; postmortem; physicam medicine; presents mainly; primary motivation
PMI	point of maximum intensity
PMSB	(politely) a chronic complainer; male child with no father (literally) poor miserable Son-of-a-Bitch
PMT	premenstrual tension
PND	postnasal drip; paroxysmal nocturnal dyspnea
PO	by mouth; phone order; postoperative
prep	prepare (for surgery, etc.)
PTA	prior to admission; pre-treatment anxiety
PVP	peripheral venous pressure
Px	physical examination
q, $\bar{q}$	every; each
R, r	regular; right; rectal; rate
Ra	rheumatoid arthritis; right atrium
RBBB	right bundle branch block
RBC	red blood count; red blood cell
RF	rheumatic fever; right foot; right femur; right frontal
RHD	rheumatic heart disease
RHF	right heart failure
RLE	right lower extremity
RLL	right lower lobe
RLQ	right lower quadrant
R/O	rule out

Abbreviation	Approximation
ROS	review of system(s)
RQ	respiratory quotient
RR	recovery room
RTC	return to clinic
RUE	right upper extremity
RUL	right upper lobe
RUQ	right upper quadrant
RV	right ventricle
Rx	therapy; prescribe; medication; take; treatment
s, $\bar{s}$	without
SA, S-A	sinoartial
SBE	subacute bacterial endocarditis
SBR	strict bed rest
SCB	strictly confined to bed
SC	subcutaneous
sep	separate; septum
S & H	speech and hearing
SH	social history; serum hepatitis
sib	sibling
sig	sign; signify; significant; signal
SLE	systemic lupus erythematosis
SOB	shortness of breath
sol	solution; solve
spec	specimen
S & S	signs and symptoms
SS	social service; social security; one-half; soap suds; saline solution
ST	speech therapy or therapist
STS	serum test for syphillis
sub-Q	subcutaneous
SVC	superior vena cava
T	temperature; time
T & A	tonsillectomy and adenoidectomy
TAH	total abdominal hysterectomy
TAT, tat	tattoo; tetanus antitoxin
TBNA	treated but not admitted
TBW	total body water
T & C	type and cross-match (blood)
TLC	tender loving care; thin layer chromatography

Abbreviation	Approximation
TO	telephone order
TPR	temperature, pulse and respiration
TT	bosomy female patients in some clinics and hospitals find themselves the center of attention—"consultations" they are called—because these two letters (they may be encircled or starred) appear at pre-arranged places in their charts
Tx	treatment; transmit; telephone; try
UA	urinalysis; uric acid; uncertain about; unknown aspects; unusual aspect
UE	upper extremities
UGI	upper gastrointestinal (tract or series)
URI	upper respiratory infection
UTI	urinary tract infection
V	five; various; volume; vagina; vomiting
VC	vena cava
VD	venereal disease
vit.	vital; vitamin
VO	verbal order
VP	venous pressure
VS	vital signs
w	with; white; widowed; will; would; where; why
WBC	white blood count
wd	well developed; would; word; without doubt
wf	white female
wm	white male
wn	well nourished
WNL	within normal limits
wt	weight
yo	years old

APPENDIX C

Latin and Greek Prefixes and Suffixes Commonly Used in Medical Terms

Suffixes		Suffixes	
-able, -ible	capable of	-ia	condition
-aceae	of the nature of	-iasis, -sis	condition, disease
-al	pertaining to	-iatric	physician
-algia	pain	-ic, -id	pertains to, like
-ase	an enzyme	-ism	condition
-asthenia	weakness	-itis	inflamed
-ate	like	-lateral	side
-blast	formative (cell)	-lemma	sheath
-cele	hernia, swelling	-lith	stone
-centesis	puncture	-logy	science, study of
-cide	kill, destroy	-lysis	reducing, dissolving
-classia	breaking	-malacia	softening
-clysis	injection	-mania	insanity, madness
-cutaneous	skin	-mentia	mind
-cle	small	-mere	part
-cyte	cell	-metry	measure
-cytoma	cellular neoplasm	-mycin	fungus
-derm	skin	-nomy	law
-dynia	pain	-nosis	disease
-ectasis	dilation	-odont	tooth
-ectomy	excision	-oid	like
-emia	blood	-ole	small
-ergy	work	-oma	tumor
-esthesia	sensation	-opia	sight
-ferent	carry	-ose	sugar
-form	shape	-otomy	a cutting, opening
-fuge	flee	-ous	full of, pertains to
-gen, -genesis	origin, production	-pathy	disease
-glossal	tongue	-penia	deficiency
-gogue	to make flow	-pexy	to fix
-gram	picture, tracing	-phage	eating
-graph	write	-phasia	speech

Suffixes

-phil	liking for
-phobia	fear
-phone	voice
-phylaxis	protection
-phyma	swelling, growth
-phyte	plant
-plast	formation
-plegia	paralysis
-pnea	breathing
-poesis	producing
-pod	foot
-ptosis	displacement
-rhythmia	rhythm
-rragia	abnormal
-rrhaphy	saturing
-rrhea	flow
-sclerosis	hardening

Suffixes

-scope	to view
-section	cutting
-soma	body
-stalsis	constriction
-stasis	standing still
-stat	stopping
-stoma	mouth
-taxia	arrangement
-thanasia	death
-tome	to cut
-tripsy	crush
-trophy	nourishment
-trope	a turning
-uria	urine
-ule	small
-vorous	eat

Prefixes

a-, an-	without
ab-	away from
acro-	extremities
actino-	ray
ad-	to
adeno-	gland
adipo-	fat
aero-	air
algio-	pain
allo-	different
alveo-	hollow
ambi-	both
ambly-	dull, faint
ambul-	walk
amphi-	both
amylo-	starch
ana-	on, back, up
andro-	man

Prefixes

angio-	blood vessel
aniso-	dissimilar
anklyo-	crooked, joining
ano-	anus
ante-	before
antero-	front
anti-, ant-	against
antro-	cavity
apo-	away from
arch-	first
argyro-	silver
arterio-	artery
arthro-	joint
astro-	star
audio-	hearing
auri-	ear, fold
auto-	self
auxo-	increase

Prefixes		Prefixes	
axo-	axis	colo-	colon
baro-	weight	colpo-	vagina
basi-	base	con-	with
bi-	two	condylo-	knuckle, joint
bili-	bile	contra-	against
bio-	life	copro-	feces
blast-	bud	core-	pupil
blephar-	eyelid	corpus-	body
brachio-	arm	cortico-	cortex
brachy-	short	costo-	rib
brady-	slow	counter-	against
broncho-	bronchus	cranio-	skull
bucco-	cheek	crypto-	hidden
caco-	ill, bad	cuti-	skin
calor-	heat	cyano-	blue
carcino-	cancer	cyclo-	cycle
cardio-	heart	cyrto-	curved
cata-	down, destroy	cysto-	bladder, cyst
caudo-	tail	cyto-	cell
celio-	abdomen	dacryo-	tear
centro-	center	dactylo-	finger or toe
cephalo-	head	de-	from
cerebro-	brain	dent-	tooth
cero-	wax	dermo-	skin
cervi-	neck	desmo-	ligament
chiel-	lip	dextro-	right
chemo-	chemistry	di-	two
chiro-	hand	dia-	across
chloro-	green	diplo-	double
chole-	bile	dipso-	thirst
chondro-	cartilage	dis-	separate
chroma-	color	dolor-	pain
chron-	time	dorso-	back
chylo-	emulsion	dys-	painful
cilio-	eyelid, cilia	e-	out from
circum-	around	ecto-	outside
cleido-	clavicle	emeto-	vomiting
co-	together	en-	into
coleo-	sheath	endo-	within

Prefixes	
entero-	intestine
ento-	within
epi-	on, upper
equi-	equal
ergo-	work
ero-	love
eryth-	red
eso-	within
eu-	well
ex-	out of
extra-	outside of
febri-	fever
fibro-	fiber
flav-	yellow
fore-	before
fronto-	anterior
galacto-	milk
gastro-	stomach
genito-	genital
genu-	knee
gero-	old
glosso-	tongue
gluco-	glucose
glyco-	sweet
gono-	seed
gyno-	woman
hemi-	half
hemo-	blood
hepato-	liver
hetero-	different, other
hidro-	sweat
histo-	tissue
holo-	whole
homo-	same, alike
hydro-	water
hyper-	excessive
hypno-	sleep
hypo-	lack, under
hystero-	uterus

Prefixes	
ictero-	jaundice
idio-	self-generated
ileo-	ileum
ilio-	flank, iliac
in-	not
infra-	below
inter-	between
intra-	within
irido-	iris
ischo-	supression
iso-	equal
juxta-	near
karyo-	cell nucleus
kera-	horn
labio-	lip
lacri-	tear
lacto-	milk
laparo-	abdomen
latero-	side
lepido-	scale
lepto-	small, thin, weak
leuco-	white
levo-	left
linguo-	tongue
lipo-	fat
litho-	stone
lobo-	lobe
luteo-	yellow
lyso-	dissolve
macro-	large
maculo-	spot
mal-	ill, bad
mammo-	breast
mammillo-	nipple
mani-	hand
masto-	breast
medio-	middle
mega-	large
melano-	dark

Prefixes		Prefixes	
meningo-	membrane	ovi-	egg
meno-	month	pachy-	thick
mero-	part	palp-	feel
meso-	middle	pan-	all
meta-	after, change, beyond	para-	beside
		patho-	disease
metro-	uterus	pedo-	child
micro-	small	per-	through
miso-	dislike	peri-	around
mito-	thread	phago-	eat
mono-	one	phlebo-	vein
myco-	fungus	phreno-	diaphragm
myelo-	bone marrow	phyto-	plant
myo-	muscle	pilo-	hair
myxo-	slime	plano-	flat
narco-	stupor	platy-	broad, flat
naso-	nose	pleo-	more
necro-	dead	pneumo-	air
neo-	new	poly-	many
nephro-	kidney	post-	after, behind
neuro-	nerve	pre-	before
neutro-	neither	presby-	old
nevo-	birthmark	pro-	before
noct-	night	procto-	rectum
non-	not	proto-	first
noso-	disease	pseudo-	false
nycto-	night	psycho-	mind
oculo-	eye	pulmo-	lung
odont-	tooth	pyo-	pus
oligo-	few	pyro-	fever
onco-	bulk, tumor	quadri-	four
onycho-	nail, claw	rachio-	spine
oo-	egg	re-	back
opistho-	behind	reno-	kidney
orchio-	testis	retro-	backward
oro-	oral	rhino-	nose
oss-	bone	sapro-	rotten
osteo-	bone	sarco-	flesh
oto-	ear	scapulo-	shoulder

Prefixes

schizo-	cleft, split
sclero-	hard
semi-	half
sero-	serum
sialo-	saliva
sidero-	iron
sino-	sinus
somno-	sleep
spheno-	wedge
splanchno-	viscera
spleno-	spleen
spondylo-	vertebra
steat-	fat
stereo-	dimensional, solid
sterno-	breast, chest
stetho-	breast, chest
stoma-	mouth
sub-	under
sudo-	sweat
super-	above
syn-	together, union
syringo-	pipe, tube
tacho-	swift
tacto-	touch
tele-	distant
teno-	tendon
tetra-	four

Prefixes

thanato-	death
thermo-	heat
thoraco-	chest
thrombo-	clot
topo-	local, place
toxi-	poison
trans-	through
tri-	three
tricho-	hair
tropho-	nutrition
tuber-	swell
tympano-	drum
ultra-	beyond
uni-	one
vago-	vagus (wander)
varico-	twisted, swollen
vas-	vessel
ventro-	anterior
vesico-	bladder
vita-	life
vivi-	living
vermi-	worm
xantho-	yellow
xeno-	foreign, strange
xero-	dry
zoo-	animal
zymo-	ferment

APPENDIX D

Below are the questions used by David W. Schack in his questionnaire to determine professional attitudes among pharmacists.

PERSONAL QUESTIONNAIRE

A. POSITION TITLE:

_____ 1. Hospital Pharmacist (please also check one below):

_____ (a) Director _____ (d) Staff Pharmacist

_____ (b) Assistant Director _____ (e) Resident

_____ (c) Supervisor _____ (f) Other-please specify ________

_____ 2. Pharmacy Educator—please identify specialty and academic title:

____

_____ 3. Other—please specify: __________________

B. DEGREE PRESENTLY HELD: _____ 1. B.S. _____ 2. PharmD _____ 3. M.S. _____ 4. PhD _____ 5. Other-specify ________

C. AGE: _____ Years

D. SEX: _____ 1. M _____ 2. F

E. FIRST YEAR OF LICENSURE: 19_____

F. PLEASE SPECIFY HOW MANY YEARS YOU HAVE BEEN PRACTICING *IN ABOVE POSITION TITLE:* _____ Years

G. ZIP CODE OF YOUR WORK LOCATION: __ __ __ __ __

H. PLEASE INDICATE THE SINGLE PROFESSIONAL ORGANIZATION YOU MOST CLOSELY IDENTIFY WITH:

____

I. TYPE OF HOSPITAL: _____ 1. Urban _____ 2. Rural

J. HOSPITAL SIZE: _____Number of Beds

K. HAVE YOU COMPLETED A RESIDENCY IN HOSPITAL PHARMACY? _____ 1. Yes _____ 2. No

L. DO YOU ACTIVELY PARTICIPATE IN THE TEACHING OF PHARMACY STUDENT INTERNS AND/OR HOSPITAL PHARMACY RESIDENTS? _____ 1. Yes _____ 2. No

---

PHARMACIST QUESTIONNAIRE

The following statements refer to various aspects of your practice. I am most interested in obtaining your *candid* opinions to these statements. Please choose one of five possible responses for each statement:

SA = strongly agree ? = uncertain or no opinion D = disagree

A = agree SD = strongly disagree

PLEASE NOTE: Any reference to professional organization refers to the single organization you most closely identify with.

1. My professional organization competently represents my views on pharmacy issues.
2. If I do not monitor patient drug therapy, an unfavorable therapeutic outcome is probable.
3. My pharmacy colleagues and I should be the only ones who determine and set standards for our practice.
4. I often wish that I had chosen another occupation.
5. My employer should establish specific guidelines for making professional decisions in my work.
6. I can maintain an acceptable standard of practice without attending continuing education programs.
7. My professional organization fails to promote advancement of the profession of pharmacy.
8. Patients probably would not be harmed if I failed to instruct them concerning the proper use of their medications.
9. The only professional standards I will accept are those established by my pharmacy colleagues.
10. There is no occupation I could be happier in than pharmacy.
11. The opportunity to exercise professional judgment in my work should be determined by my employer.
12. Continuing education such as self-study or seminars is essential for my work.
13. My professional organization does not help to ensure quality practice.
14. Optimum drug therapy for the patient is impossible to achieve without my services.
15. I would be willing to modify the basic standards which guide my practice in order to conform to the wishes of the public.
16. The practice of pharmacy is gratifying and satisfying to me.
17. My employer has the right to review and change the professional decisions I make.
18. My daily practice is all the continuing education I need.
19. My professional organization provides me with a better understanding of the values and beliefs of my profession.
20. The health care of the patient would suffer without my services.
21. Only another pharmacist is qualified to judge the competence of my work.
22. If I had the opportunity to begin over again, I would choose to practice pharmacy.
23. I would depart from my employer's policies whenever I judged it professionally necessary.
24. I would attend continuing education seminars only if they were required for relicensure.

25. The official statements and standards of my professional organization are important guides to my practice.
26. Patient care would suffer very little if I failed to provide drug information to the physician.
27. Pharmacists who violate professional standards should be judged only by their pharmacy colleagues.
28. I feel dedicated to pharmacy because I believe in my work.
29. My employer has the right to influence my professional decisions because my employer is the one who pays my salary.
30. My involvement with drug therapy has little consequence on prevention of adverse drug reactions to the patient.
31. Standards for professional competence which guide my practice are best defined and established via government regulation.
32. Continuing education is of little importance to my practice.
33. The practice of pharmacy promoted by my professional organization is close to my personal ideal.
34. Patient care would be unsatisfactory without my services.
35. The public should be allowed input into the development of standards for professional competence which guide my practice.
36. I want others to enter pharmacy because I am proud of the unique skills and knowledge they would acquire.
37. My employer has no right to place limitations on the decisions I make concerning professional matters.
38. My practice would suffer if I did not attend continuing education programs.
39. Patient drug compliance is improved by my explanation of drug therapy to patients.
40. I would modify the professional standards which guide my practice only in response to recommendations made by my pharmacy colleagues.

Please indicate any statements which you feel are ambiguous or difficult to understand on the back of the preceding page. Please also feel free to make any comments.

THANK YOU!

INDEX